Nim in Action

Nim in Action

DOMINIK PICHETA

MANNING
SHELTER ISLAND

For online information and ordering of this and other Manning books, please visit
www.manning.com. The publisher offers discounts on this book when ordered in quantity.
For more information, please contact

> Special Sales Department
> Manning Publications Co.
> 20 Baldwin Road
> PO Box 761
> Shelter Island, NY 11964
> Email: orders@manning.com

Manning Publications Co
20 Baldwin Road
PO Box 761
Shelter Island, NY 11964

Development editors:	Cynthia Kane, Dan Seiter, Marina Michaels
Technical development editor:	Andrew West
Review editor:	Donna Clements
Project editor:	Karen Gulliver
Copyeditor:	Andy Carroll
Proofreader:	Katie Tennant
Technical proofreader:	Michiel Trimpe
Typesetter:	Dottie Marsico
Cover designer:	Marija Tudor

ISBN 9781617293436
Printed in the United States of America
1 2 3 4 5 6 7 8 9 10 – EBM – 22 21 20 19 18 17

contents

preface

Nim has been my labor of love over the years. Gradually, from the time I discovered it, I've become increasingly involved in its development. Although I sacrificed considerable time working on it, Nim gave back in the form of experience and knowledge. My work with Nim has taught me far more than any other work or studies have done. Many opportunities have also opened up for me, a shining example being this book.

I never actually thought I would end up writing a book, and until a Manning acquisitions editor got in touch with me, I didn't realize that I wanted to. While planning this book, I looked to other books and determined where they fell short. I realized that this, the first book on Nim, must be written for programmers with a bit of experience. I decided that I wanted to write a book that teaches programmers about Nim, but that also teaches other programming concepts that work well in Nim's particular programming paradigms. These concepts can also be applied to other programming languages and have been very useful in my career.

My other goal for this book was to make it fun and engaging. I decided to do this by building some chapters around small projects. The projects are designed to be practical and to teach a number of Nim features and concepts. By following along and developing these projects, you'll gain hands-on experience developing Nim applications. This should put you in a good position to write your own software, which is the ultimate goal of this book.

Nim in Action covers a lot, but it can't cover everything. It shouldn't be viewed as a complete Nim reference; instead, it should be considered a practical guide to writing software in Nim.

It's my hope that this book helps you learn Nim and that you find it a useful reference for many years to come. I and the Nim community are at your disposal and are available online to help you solve any problems you run into. Thank you for purchasing this book and taking an interest in Nim.

acknowledgments

First, I would like to thank Andreas Rumpf for creating Nim and for both his reviews and words of encouragement throughout the development of this book. Andreas created a one-of-a-kind programming language, and without his commitment to Nim, this book wouldn't exist.

This book wouldn't be what it is today without the brilliant and passionate people at Manning publications. I give my thanks to Marjan Bace, who made it possible to publish this book; my editors Cynthia Kane, Dan Seiter, and Marina Michaels, for helping me improve my writing; and the production team, including Andy Carroll, Janet Vail, Karen Gulliver, and Katie Tennant.

I thank the Nim community and everyone who participated in reviews and provided feedback on the manuscript, including technical proofreader Michiel Trimpe, and the following reviewers: Andrea Ferretti, Yuriy Glukhov, Michał Zieliński, Stefan Salewski, Konstantin Molchanov, Sébastien Ménard, Abel Brown, Alessandro Campeis, Angelo Costa, Christoffer Fink, Cosimo Attanasi, James Anaipakos, Jonathan Rioux, Marleny Nunez, Mikkel Arentoft, Mohsen Mostafa Jokar, Paulo Nuin, Peter Hampton, Robert Walsh, Samuel Bosch, Thomas Ballinger, and Vincent Keller.

Thanks also to the readers of the Manning Early Access Program (MEAP). Their corrections and comments on the manuscript as it was being written were invaluable.

Finally, I'd like to thank my family and friends, who in their own way steered my life in a positive direction, leading me to authoring this book. First, I thank my mother, Bogumiła Picheta, for her bravery and hard work, without which I wouldn't have had the means to start my programming journey, and I especially thank her for making a hard decision that turned out to be very beneficial for my future. I would also like to thank my uncle, Piotr Kossakowski-Stefański, and aunt, Marzena Kossakowska-Stefańska, for inspiring and challenging me to write software, and also for always being there to share their advice. Thanks to Ilona, Maciej Sr., and Maciej Jr. Łosinski for my first exposure to a computer and the internet. And I thank Kazimierz Ślebioda, a.k.a Kazik, for the Age of Empires 2 LAN parties and for showing me how delicious chicken with garlic can be.

Most of all, I thank my partner, Amy-Leigh Shaw, for always believing in me, and for her patience and support throughout my work on this book. I love you very much Amy, and am lucky to have you.

about this book

Nim in Action is a practical way to learn how to develop software using the open source Nim programming language. This book includes many examples, both large and small, to show and teach you how software is written in Nim.

Nim is unique. It's multi-paradigm, and unlike most other languages, it doesn't emphasize object-oriented programming. Because of this, I encourage you to consciously absorb the styles used in this book instead of applying your own. *Nim in Action* will teach you a set of best practices and idioms that you'll also find useful in other programming languages.

By learning Nim, you'll discover a language that straddles the lines between efficiency, expressiveness, and elegance. Nim will make you productive and your end users happy.

Who should read this book

This is by no means a beginner's book. It assumes that you know at least one other programming language and have experience writing software in it. For example, I expect you to be aware of basic programming language features such as functions, variables, and types. The fundamentals of programming aren't explained in this book.

This book will teach you how to develop practical software in the Nim programming language. It covers features that are present in all programming languages, such as concurrency, parallelism, user-defined types, the standard library, and more. In addition, it covers Nim features that you may not be familiar with, such as asynchronous input/output, metaprogramming, and the foreign function interface.

How the book is organized

The book is divided into three parts and includes a total of nine chapters.

Part 1 introduces the language and its basic features:

- Chapter 1 explains what Nim is, compares it to other programming languages, and discusses its strengths and weaknesses.
- Chapter 2 teaches the basics, such as the syntax and fundamental features of the language. This includes a demonstration of procedure definitions and exception handling.

Part 2 includes a wide range of examples to show how Nim is used in practice:

- Chapter 3 is where you'll develop your first nontrivial Nim application. The primary purpose of this application is communication: it allows messages to be sent through a network. You'll learn, among other things, how to create command-line interfaces, parse JSON, and transfer data over a network in Nim.
- Chapter 4 gives an overview of the standard library, particularly the parts of it that aren't covered in other chapters but are useful.
- Chapter 5 discusses package management in Nim and teaches you how to create your own packages and make them available to others.
- Chapter 6 explains what parallelism is and how it can be applied to different programming tasks. You'll see a parsing example, demonstrating different ways to parse data in Nim and how parsing can be parallelized.
- Chapter 7 is where you'll develop your second nontrivial Nim application: a web application based on Twitter. You'll learn how to store data in a SQL database and generate HTML.

Part 3 introduces some advanced Nim features:

- Chapter 8 looks at the foreign function interface and shows how it can be used to make use of C and JavaScript libraries. You'll develop a simple application that draws the letter N on the screen, first using a C library and then using JavaScript's Canvas API.
- Chapter 9 explains what metaprogramming is, discussing features such as generics, templates, and macros. At the end of this chapter, you'll use macros to create a domain-specific language.

You may wish to skip the first two chapters if you already know the basics of Nim. I recommend reading the book from beginning to end, and I especially encourage you to follow along with the examples. Each chapter teaches you something new about Nim, even if it primarily focuses on a standalone example. If you get stuck, feel free to get in touch with me or the Nim community. Appendix A contains information on how to get help, so use it to your advantage.

Code conventions and downloads

The source code examples in this book are fairly close to the samples that you'll find online, but for the sake of brevity, many of the comments were removed. The online samples include a lot of comments to make them as easy to understand as possible, so you're encouraged to take a look at them to learn more.

The source code is available for download from the publisher's website at https://manning.com/books/nim-in-action and from GitHub at https://github.com/dom96/nim-in-action-code. Nim is still evolving, so be sure to watch the repository for changes. I'll do my best to keep it up to date with the latest Nim version.

This book contains many examples of source code, both in numbered listings and inline with normal text. In both cases, source code is formatted in a `mono-spaced typeface like this`, to distinguish it from ordinary text. Sometimes code is **also in bold** to highlight code that has changed from previous steps in the chapter, such as when a new feature is added to existing code.

In many cases, the original source code has been reformatted for print; we've added line breaks and reworked the indentation to accommodate the available page space in the book. In rare cases, even this was not enough, and listings include line-continuation markers (➡). Additionally, comments in the source code have often been removed from the listings when the code is described in the text.

Book forum

The purchase of *Nim in Action* includes free access to a private web forum run by Manning Publications, where you can make comments about the book, ask technical questions, and receive help from the author and from other users. To access the forum, go to https://forums.manning.com/forums/nim-in-action. You can also learn more about Manning's forums and the rules of conduct at https://forums.manning.com/forums/about.

Manning's commitment to our readers is to provide a venue where a meaningful dialogue between individual readers and between readers and the author can take place. It is not a commitment to any specific amount of participation on the part of the author, whose contribution to the forum remains voluntary (and unpaid). We suggest you try asking him some challenging questions lest his interest stray! The forum and the archives of previous discussions will be accessible from the publisher's website as long as the book is in print.

about the author

DOMINIK PICHETA (@d0m96, picheta.me) is a Computer Science student at Queen's University Belfast. He is one of the core developers of the Nim programming language and has been using it for most of its history. He also wrote Nimble, the official Nim package manager, and many other Nim libraries and tools.

about the cover illustration

The figure on the cover of *Nim in Action* is captioned "Morlaque de l'Isle Opus," or "A Morlach from the Island of Opus." The Morlachs were a Vlach people originally centered around the eastern Adriatic port of Ragusa, or modern Dubrovnik. The illustration is taken from a collection of dress costumes from various countries by Jacques Grasset de Saint-Sauveur (1757–1810), titled *Costumes de Différents Pays*, published in France in 1797. Each illustration is finely drawn and colored by hand. The rich variety of Grasset de Saint-Sauveur's collection reminds us vividly of how culturally apart the world's towns and regions were just 200 years ago. Isolated from each other, people spoke different dialects and languages. In the streets or in the countryside, it was easy to identify where they lived and what their trade or station in life was just by their dress.

The way we dress has changed since then and the diversity by region, so rich at the time, has faded away. It is now hard to tell apart the inhabitants of different continents, let alone different towns, regions, or countries. Perhaps we have traded cultural diversity for a more varied personal life—certainly, for a more varied and fast-paced technological life.

At a time when it is hard to tell one computer book from another, Manning celebrates the inventiveness and initiative of the computer business with book covers based on the rich diversity of regional life of two centuries ago, brought back to life by Grasset de Saint-Sauveur's pictures.

Part 1

The basics of Nim

This part of the book begins your study of the Nim programming language. It doesn't assume you know much about Nim, so chapter 1 begins by looking at the characteristics of the language, what makes it different from other languages, and how it's used in the real world. Chapter 2 looks at some of the most commonly used elements of any programming language—the syntax, semantics, and type system—and in doing so teaches you the necessary foundations for writing simple applications in Nim.

Why Nim?

This chapter covers

- What Nim is
- Why you should learn about it
- Comparing Nim to other programming languages
- Use cases
- Strengths and weaknesses

Nim is still a relatively new programming language. In fact, you're holding one of the very first books about it. The language is still not fully complete, but core aspects, like its syntax, the semantics of procedures, methods, iterators, generics, templates, and more, are all set in stone. Despite its newness, there has been significant interest in Nim from the programming community because of the unique set of features that it implements and offers its users.

This chapter answers questions that you may ask before learning Nim, such as why you might want to use it. In this chapter, I outline some of the common practical uses of Nim, compare it to other programming languages, and discuss some of its strengths and weaknesses.

1.1   *What is Nim?*

Nim is a general-purpose programming language designed to be efficient, expressive, and elegant. These three goals are difficult to achieve at the same time, so Nim's designers gave each of them different priorities, with efficiency being the most important and elegance being the least.

But despite the fact that elegance is relatively unimportant to Nim's design, it's still considered during the design process. Because of this, the language remains elegant in its own right. It's only when trade-offs between efficiency and elegance need to be made that efficiency wins.

On the surface, Nim shares many of Python's characteristics. In particular, many aspects of Nim's syntax are similar to Python's, including the use of indentation to delimit scope as well as the tendency to use words instead of symbols for certain operators. Nim also shares other aspects with Python that aren't related to syntax, such as the highly user-friendly exception tracebacks, shown here:

```
Traceback (most recent call last)
request.nim(74)          request
request.nim(25)          getUsers
json.nim(837)            []
tables.nim(147)          []
Error: unhandled exception: key not found: totalsForAllResults [KeyError]
```

You'll also see many differences, especially when it comes to the semantics of the language. The major differences lie within the type system and execution model, which you'll learn about in the next sections.

A little bit about Nim's history

Andreas Rumpf started developing Nim in 2005. The project soon gained support and many contributions from the open source community, with many volunteers around the world contributing code via pull requests on GitHub. You can see the current open Nim pull requests at https://github.com/nim-lang/Nim/pulls.

CONTRIBUTING TO NIM   The compiler, standard library, and related tools are all open source and written in Nim. The project is available on GitHub, and everyone is encouraged to contribute. Contributing to Nim is a good way to learn how it works and to help with its development. See Nim's GitHub page for more information: https://github.com/nim-lang/Nim#contributing.

1.1.1   *Use cases*

Nim was designed to be a general-purpose programming language from the outset. As such, it consists of a wide range of features that make it usable for just about any software project. This makes it a good candidate for writing software in a wide variety of application domains, ranging from web applications to kernels. In this section, I'll discuss how Nim's features and programming support apply in several use cases.

Although Nim may support practically any application domain, this doesn't make it the right choice for everything. Certain aspects of the language make it more suitable for some categories of applications than others. This doesn't mean that some applications can't be written using Nim; it just means that Nim may not support the code styles that are best suited for writing some kinds of applications.

Nim is a compiled language, but the way in which it's compiled is special. When the Nim compiler compiles source code, it first translates the code into C code. C is an old but well supported systems programming language that allows easier and more direct access to the physical hardware of the machine. This makes Nim well suited to systems programming, allowing projects such as operating systems (OSs), compilers, device drivers, and embedded system software to be written.

Internet of Things (IoT) devices, which are physical devices with embedded electronics that are connected to the internet, are good targets for Nim, primarily thanks to the power offered by Nim's ease of use and its systems programming capabilities.

A good example of a project making use of Nim's systems programming features is a very simple OS called NimKernel available on GitHub: https://github.com/dom96/nimkernel.

HOW DOES NIM COMPILE SOURCE CODE? I describe Nim's unusual compilation model and its benefits in detail in section 1.1.3.

Applications written in Nim are very fast; in many cases, just as fast as applications written in C, and more than thirteen times faster than applications written in Python. Efficiency is the highest priority, and some features make optimizing code easy. This goes hand in hand with a soft real-time garbage collector, which allows you to specify the amount of time that should be spent collecting memory. This feature becomes important during game development, where an ordinary garbage collector may slow down the rendering of frames on the screen if it uses too much time collecting memory. It's also useful in real-time systems that need to run in very strict time frames.

Nim can be used alongside other much slower languages to speed up certain performance-critical components. For example, an application written in Ruby that requires certain CPU-intensive calculations can be partially written in Nim to gain a considerable speed advantage. Such speed-ups are important in areas such as scientific computing and high-speed trading.

Applications that perform I/O operations, such as reading files or sending data over a network, are also well supported by Nim. Web applications, for example, can be written easily using a number of web frameworks like Jester (https://github.com/dom96/jester). Nim's script-like syntax, together with its powerful, asynchronous I/O support, makes it easy to develop these applications rapidly.

Command-line applications can benefit greatly from Nim's efficiency. Also, because Nim applications are compiled, they're standalone and so don't require any bulky runtime dependencies. This makes their distribution incredibly easy. One such application written in Nim is Nimble; it's a package manager for Nim that allows users to install Nim libraries and applications.

These are just a few use cases that Nim fits well; it's certainly not an exhaustive list.

Another thing to keep in mind is that, at the time of writing, Nim is still in development, not having yet reached version 1.0. Certain features haven't been implemented yet, making Nim less suited for some applications. For example, Nim includes a backend that allows you to write JavaScript applications for your web pages in Nim. This backend works, but it's not yet as mature as the rest of the language. This will improve with time.

Of course, Nim's ability to compile to JavaScript makes it suitable for full-stack applications that need components that run on a server and in a browser. This is a huge advantage, because code can easily be reused for both the browser and server components of the application.

Now that you know a little bit about what Nim is, its history, and some of the applications that it's particularly well suited for, let's look at some of Nim's features and talk about how it works.

1.1.2 Core features

In many ways, Nim is very innovative. Many of Nim's features can't be found in any other programming language. If you enjoy learning new programming languages, especially those with interesting and unique features, then Nim is definitely the language for you.

In this section, we'll look at some of the core features of Nim—in particular, the features that make Nim stand out from other programming languages:

- A facility called *metaprogramming*, used for, among many things, molding the language to your needs.
- Style-insensitive variable, function, and type names. By using this feature, which is slightly controversial, you can treat identifiers in whatever style you wish, no matter if they were defined using `camelCase` or `snake_case`.
- A type system that's rich in features such as generics, which make code easier to write and maintain.
- Compilation to C, which allows Nim programs to be efficient and portable. The compilation itself is also very fast.
- A number of different types of garbage collectors that can be freely selected or removed altogether.

METAPROGRAMMING

The most practical, and in some senses unique, feature of Nim is its extensive metaprogramming support. Metaprogramming allows you to read, generate, analyze, and transform source code. It was by no means a Nim invention, but there's no other programming language with metaprogramming that's so extensive and at the same time easy to pick up as Nim's. If you're familiar with Lisp, then you might have some experience with metaprogramming already.

With metaprogramming, you treat code as data in the form of an *abstract syntax tree*. This allows you to manipulate existing code as well as generate brand new code while your application is being compiled.

Metaprogramming in Nim is special because languages with good metaprogramming features typically belong to the Lisp family of languages. If you're already familiar with the likes of Java or Python, you'll find it easier to start using Nim than Lisp. You'll also find it more natural to learn how to use Nim's metaprogramming features than Lisp's.

Although it's generally an advanced topic, metaprogramming is a very powerful feature that you'll get to know in far more detail in chapter 9 of this book. One of the main benefits that metaprogramming offers is the ability to remove boilerplate code. Metaprogramming also allows the creation of domain-specific languages (DSLs); for example,

```
html:
  body:
    p: "Hello World"
```

This DSL specifies a bit of HTML code. Depending on how it's implemented, the DSL will likely be translated into Nim code resembling the following:

```
echo("<html>")
echo("  <body>")
echo("    <p>Hello World</p>")
echo("  </body>")
echo("</html>")
```

That Nim code will result in the following output:

```
<html>
  <body>
    <p>Hello World</p>
  </body>
</html>
```

With Nim's metaprogramming, you can define DSLs and mix them freely with your ordinary Nim code. Such languages have many use cases; for example, the preceding one can be used to create HTML templates for your web apps.

Metaprogramming is at the center of Nim's design. Nim's designer wants to encourage users to use metaprogramming in order to accommodate their style of programming. For example, although Nim does offer some object-oriented programming (OOP) features, it doesn't have a class definition construct. Instead, anyone wishing to use OOP in Nim in a style similar to that of other languages should use metaprogramming to create such a construct.

STYLE INSENSITIVITY

Another of Nim's interesting and likely unique features is style insensitivity. One of the hardest things a programmer has to do is come up with names for all sorts of identifiers like variables, functions, and modules. In many programming languages, these names can't contain whitespace, so programmers have been forced to adopt other ways of separating multiple words in a single name. Multiple differing methods were devised, the most popular being snake_case and camelCase. With Nim, you can use snake_case even if the identifier has been defined using camelCase, and vice versa. So you can write code in your preferred style even if the library you're using adopted a different style for its identifiers.

Listing 1.1   Style insensitivity

```
import strutils            ◁── The strutils module defines a procedure called toUpper.
echo("hello".to_upper())   ◁── You can call it using snake_case.
echo("world".toUpper())    ◁── As it was originally defined, you can call it using camelCase.
```

This works because Nim considers the identifiers to_upper and toUpper to be equal.

When comparing identifiers, Nim considers the case of the *first character*, but it doesn't bother with the case of the rest of the identifier's characters, ignoring the underscores as well. As a result, the identifiers toUpper and ToUpper aren't equal because the case of the first character differs. This allows type names to be distinguished from variable names, because, by convention, type names should start with an uppercase letter and variable names should start with a lowercase letter.

The following listing shows one scenario where this convention is useful.

Listing 1.2   Style insensitivity and type identifiers

```
type
  Dog = object      ◁──┐ The Dog type is defined with
    age: int           ┘ an uppercase first letter.
                   ◁──────── Only primitive types such as int
let dog = Dog(age: 3)  ◁──    start with a lowercase letter.

                       A dog variable can be safely defined because
                       it won't clash with the Dog type.
```

POWERFUL TYPE SYSTEM

One of the many characteristics that differentiate programming languages from one another is their type system. The main purpose of a type system is to reduce the opportunities for bugs in your programs. Other benefits that a good type system provides are certain compiler optimizations and better documentation of code.

The main categories used to classify type systems are *static* and *dynamic*. Most programming languages fall somewhere between the two extremes and incorporate ideas from both. This is because both static and dynamic type systems require certain trade-offs. Static typing finds more errors at compile time, but it also decreases the speed at which programs can be written. Dynamic typing is the opposite.

Nim is statically typed, but unlike some statically typed programming languages, it also incorporates many features that make development fast. Type inference is a good example of that: types can be resolved by the compiler without the need for you to write the types out yourself (though you can choose to). Because of that, your program can be bug-free and yet your development speed isn't hindered. Nim also incorporates some dynamic type-checking features, such as runtime type information, which allows for the dynamic dispatch of functions.

One way that a type system ensures that your program is free of bugs is by verifying memory safety. Some programming languages, like C, aren't memory safe because they allow programs to access memory that hasn't been assigned for their use. Other programming languages are memory safe at the expense of not allowing programs to access low-level details of memory, which in some cases is necessary. Nim combines both: it's memory safe as long as you don't use any of the unsafe types, such as `ptr`, in your program, but the `ptr` type is necessary when interfacing with C libraries. Supporting these unsafe features makes Nim a powerful systems programming language.

By default, Nim protects you against every type of memory error:

- Arrays are bounds-checked at compile time, or at runtime when compile-time checks aren't possible, preventing both buffer overflows and buffer overreads.
- Pointer arithmetic isn't possible for reference types as they're entirely managed by Nim's garbage collector; this prevents issues such as dangling pointers and other memory issues related to managing memory manually.
- Variables are always initialized by Nim to their default values, which prevents variables containing unexpected and corrupt data.

Finally, one of the most important features of Nim's type system is the ability to use generic programming. Generics in Nim allow for a great deal of code reuse without sacrificing type safety. Among other things, they allow you to specify that a single function can accept multiple different types. For example, you may have a `showNumber` procedure that displays both integers and floats on the screen:

```
proc showNumber(num: int | float) =
  echo(num)

showNumber(3.14)
showNumber(42)
```

Here, the `showNumber` procedure accepts either an `int` type or a `float` type. The `|` operator specifies that both `int` and `float` can be passed to the procedure.

This is a simple demonstration of Nim's generics. You'll learn a lot more about Nim's type system, as well as its generics, in later chapters.

COMPILATION

I mentioned in the previous section that the Nim compiler compiles source code into C first, and then feeds that source code into a C compiler. You'll learn a lot more about how this works in section 1.1.3, but right now I'll talk about some of the many practical advantages of this compilation model.

The C programming language is very well established as a systems programming language and has been in use for over 40 years. C is one of the most portable programming languages, with multiple implementations for Windows, Linux, Mac OS, x86, AMD64, ARM, and many other, more obscure OSs and platforms. C compilers support everything from supercomputers to microcontrollers. They're also very mature and implement many powerful optimizations, which makes C very efficient.

Nim takes advantage of these aspects of C, including its portability, widespread use, and efficiency.

Compiling to C also makes it easy to use existing C and C++ libraries—all you need to do is write some simple wrapper code. You can write this code much faster by using a tool called c2nim. This tool converts C and C++ header files to Nim code, which wraps those files. This is of great benefit because many popular libraries are written in C and C++.

Nim also offers you the ability to build libraries that are compatible with C and C++. This is handy if you want your library to be used from other programming languages. You'll learn all about wrapping C and C++ libraries in chapter 8.

Nim source code can also be compiled into Objective C and JavaScript. The Objective C language is mainly used for iOS software development; by compiling to it, you can write iOS applications natively in Nim. You can also use Nim to develop Android applications by using the C++ compilation backend. JavaScript is the client-side language used by billions of websites; it's sometimes called the "assembly language of the web" because it's the only programming language that's supported by all the major web browsers. By compiling to JavaScript, you can write client-side applications for web browsers in Nim. Figure 1.1 shows the available Nim backends.

You may now be wondering just how fast Nim is at compiling software. Perhaps you're thinking that it's very slow; after all, Nim needs to translate source code to an intermediate language first. But in fact it's fairly fast. As an example, the Nim compiler, which consists of around 100,000 lines of Nim code, takes about 12 seconds to

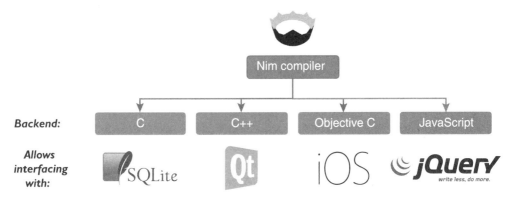

Figure 1.1 Compilation backends

compile on a MacBook Pro with a 2.7 GHz Intel Core i5 CPU. Each compilation is cached, so the time drops to 5 seconds after the initial compilation.

MEMORY MANAGEMENT

C and C++ both require you to manually manage memory, carefully ensuring that what you allocate is deallocated once it's no longer needed. Nim, on the other hand, manages memory for you using a garbage collector. But there are situations when you may want to avoid garbage collectors; they're considered by many to be inadequate for certain application domains, like embedded systems and games. For this reason, Nim supports a number of different garbage collectors with different applications in mind. The garbage collector can also be removed completely, giving you the ability to manage memory yourself.

> **GARBAGE COLLECTORS** Switching between garbage collectors is easy. You just need to specify the `--gc:<gc_name>` flag during compilation and replace `<gc_name>` with `markandsweep`, `boehm`, or `none`.

This was just a small taste of Nim's most prominent features. There's a lot more to it: not just the unique and innovative features, but also the unique composition of features from existing programming languages that makes Nim as a whole very unique indeed.

1.1.3 How does Nim work?

One of the things that makes Nim unique is its implementation. Every programming language has an implementation in the form of an application, which either interprets the source code or compiles the source code into an executable. These implementations are called an *interpreter* and a *compiler*, respectively. Some languages may have multiple implementations, but Nim's only implementation is a compiler. The compiler compiles Nim source code by first translating the code to another programming language, C, and then passing that C source code to a C compiler, which then compiles it into a binary executable. The executable file contains instructions that indicate the specific tasks that the computer should perform, including the ones specified in the original Nim source code. Figure 1.2 shows how a piece of Nim code is compiled into an executable.

The compilers for most programming languages don't have this extra step; they compile the source code into a binary executable themselves. There are also others that don't compile code at all. Figure 1.3 shows how different programming languages transform source code into something that can be executed.

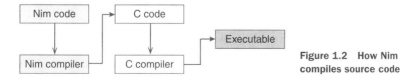

Figure 1.2 How Nim compiles source code

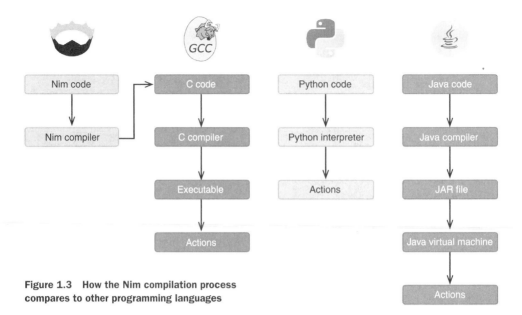

Figure 1.3   How the Nim compilation process compares to other programming languages

Nim connects to the C compilation process in order to compile the C source code that was generated by it. This means that the Nim compiler depends on an external C compiler, such as GCC or Clang. The result of the compilation is an executable that's specific to the CPU architecture and OS it was compiled on.

This should give you a good idea of how Nim source code is transformed into a working application, and how this process is different from the one used in other programming languages. Every time you make a change to your Nim source code, you'll need to recompile it.

Now let's look at Nim's positive and negative aspects.

1.2   *Nim's benefits and shortcomings*

It's important to understand why you might want to use a language, but it's just as important to learn why that language may not be correct for your particular use case.

In this section, I'll compare Nim to a number of other programming languages, focusing on a variety of characteristics and factors that are typically used in such comparisons. After that, I'll discuss some of the areas where Nim still needs to catch up with other languages.

1.2.1   *Benefits*

As you read this book, you may wonder how Nim compares to the programming languages that you're familiar with. There are many ways to draw a comparison and multiple factors that can be considered, including the language's execution speed, expressiveness, development speed, readability, ecosystem, and more. This section looks at some of these factors to give you a better idea of the benefits of Nim.

NIM IS EFFICIENT

The speed at which applications written in a programming language execute is often used in comparisons. One of Nim's goals is efficiency, so it should be no surprise that it's a very efficient programming language.

C is one of the most efficient programming languages, so you may be wondering how Nim compares. In the previous section, you learned that the Nim compiler first translates Nim code into an intermediate language. By default, the intermediate language is C, which suggests that Nim's performance is similar to C's, and that's true.

Because of this feature, you can use Nim as a complete replacement for C, with a few bonuses:

- Nim has performance similar to C.
- Nim results in software that's more reliable than software written in C.
- Nim features an improved type system.
- Nim supports generics.
- Nim implements an advanced form of metaprogramming.

In comparison to C, metaprogramming in Nim is unique, as it doesn't use a preprocessor but is instead a part of the main compilation process. In general, you can expect to find many modern features in Nim that you won't find in C, so picking Nim as a C replacement makes a lot of sense.

Table 1.1 shows the results of a small benchmark test.[1] Nim matches C's speed and is significantly faster than Python.

Table 1.1   Time taken to find which numbers from 0 to 100 million are prime

Programming language	Time (seconds)
C	2.6
Nim	2.6
Python (CPython)	35.1

In this benchmark, the Nim application's runtime matches the speed of the C app and is significantly faster than the app implemented in Python. Micro benchmarks such as this are often unreliable, but there aren't many alternatives. Nim's performance matches that of C, which is already one of the most efficient programming languages out there.

NIM IS READABLE

Nim is a very expressive language, which means that it's easy to write Nim code that's clear to both the compiler and the human reader. Nim code isn't cluttered with the curly brackets and semicolons of C-like programming languages, such as JavaScript

---

[1] You can read more about this benchmark test on Dennis Felsing's HookRace blog: http://hookrace.net/blog/what-is-special-about-nim/#good-performance.

and C++, nor does it require the do and end keywords that are present in languages such as Ruby.

Compare this expressive Nim code with the less-expressive C++ code

Listing 1.3   Iterating from 0 to 9 in Nim

```
for i in 0 .. <10:
  echo(i)
```

Listing 1.4   Iterating from 0 to 9 in C++

```cpp
#include <iostream>
using namespace std;

int main()
{
    for (int i = 0; i < 10; i++)
    {
        cout << i << endl;
    }

    return 0;
}
```

The Nim code is more readable and far more compact. The C++ code contains many elements that are optional in Nim, such as the main function declaration, which is entirely implicit in Nim.

Nim is easy to write but, more importantly, it's also easy to read. Good code readability goes a long way. For example, it makes debugging easier, allowing you to spend more time writing beautiful Nim code, cutting down your development time.

NIM STANDS ON ITS OWN

This has been mentioned already, but it's worth revisiting to describe how other languages compare, and in particular why some require a runtime.

Compiled programming languages such as Nim, C, Go, D, and Rust produce an executable that's native to the OS on which the compiler is running. Compiling a Nim application on Windows results in an executable that can only be executed on Windows. Similarly, compiling it on Mac OS results in an executable that can only be executed on Mac OS. The CPU architecture also comes into play: compilation on ARM results in an executable that's only compatible with ARM CPUs. This is how things work by default, but it's possible to instruct Nim to compile an executable for a different OS and CPU combination through a process known as *cross-compilation*.

Cross-compilation is usually used when a computer with the desired architecture or OS is unavailable, or the compilation takes too long. One common use case would be compiling for ARM devices such as the Raspberry Pi, where the CPU is typically slow. More information about cross-compilation can be found in the Nim Compiler User Guide: http://nim-lang.org/docs/nimc.html#cross-compilation.

Among other things, the JVM was created to remove the need for cross-compilation. You may have heard the phrase "write once, run anywhere." Sun Microsystems created this slogan to illustrate Java's cross-platform benefits. A Java application only needs to be compiled once, and the result of this compilation is a JAR file that holds all the compiled Java classes. The JAR file can then be executed by the JVM to perform the programmed actions on any platform and architecture. This makes the JAR file a platform- and architecture-agnostic executable. The downside to this is that in order to run these JAR files, the JVM must be installed on the user's system. The JVM is a very big dependency that may contain bugs and security issues. But on the other hand, it does allow the Java application to be compiled only once.

Python, Ruby, and Perl are similar. They also use a virtual machine (VM) to execute code. In Python's case, a VM is used to optimize the execution of Python code, but it's mostly hidden away as an implementation detail of the Python interpreter. The Python interpreter parses the code, determines what actions that code is describing, and immediately executes those actions. There's no compilation step like with Java, C, or Nim. But the advantages and disadvantages are mostly the same as the JVM's; there's no need for cross-compilation, but in order to execute a Python application, the system needs to have a Python interpreter installed.

Write once, run anywhere

Similar to the "write once, run anywhere" slogan, other programming languages adopted the "write once, compile anywhere" philosophy, giving a computer program the ability to be compiled on all platforms without the need to modify its source code. This applies to languages such as C, Pascal, and Ada. But these languages still require platform-specific code when dealing with more-specialized features of the OS, such as when creating new threads or downloading the contents of a web page. Nim goes a step further; its standard library abstracts away the differences between OSs so you can use a lot of the features that modern OSs offer.

Unfortunately, in many cases, virtual machines and interpreters cause more problems than they solve. The number of common CPU architectures and the most popular OSs is not that large, so compiling for each of them isn't that difficult. In contrast, the source code for applications written in interpreted languages is often distributed to the user, and they're expected to install the correct version of the interpreter or virtual machine. This can result in a lot of problems.

One example of the difficulty associated with distributing such applications is the recent introduction of Python 3. Because it's not backward compatible with the previous version, it has caused many issues for software written originally in Python 2. Python 3 was released in 2008, and as of this writing, there are still libraries written for Python 2 that don't work with the Python 3 interpreter.[2] This wouldn't be a problem with a compiled language because the binaries would still continue to work.

The lightweight nature of Nim should make it particularly appealing, especially in contrast to some of the languages mentioned in this section.

---

[2] See the Python 3 Readiness page for a list of Python 3–ready packages: http://py3readiness.org/.

NIM IS FLEXIBLE

There are many different styles that software can be written in. A programming para-digm is a fundamental style of writing software, and each programming language sup-ports a different set of paradigms. You're probably already familiar with one or more of them, and at the very least you know what object-oriented programming (OOP) is because it's taught as part of many computer science courses.

Nim is a multi-paradigm programming language. Unlike some popular program-ming languages, Nim doesn't focus on the OOP paradigm. It's mainly a procedural programming language, with varying support for OOP, functional, declarative, concur-rent, and other programming styles.

That's not to say that OOP isn't well supported. OOP as a programming style is sim-ply not forced on you. Nim supports common OOP features, including inheritance, polymorphism, and dynamic dispatch.

To give you a better idea of what Nim's primary paradigm looks like, let's look at the one big difference between the OOP paradigm and the procedural paradigm. In the OOP paradigm, methods and attributes are bound to objects, and the methods operate on their own data structure. In the procedural paradigm, procedures are standalone entities that operate on data structures. This may be hard for you to visual-ize, so let's look at some code examples to illustrate it.

> **SUBROUTINE TERMINOLOGY**   In this subsection I mention *methods* and *proce-dures*. These are simply different names for *subroutines* or *functions*. *Method* is the term used in the context of OOP, *procedure* is used in procedural program-ming, and *function* is used in functional programming.

The following code listings show the same application. The first is written in Python using the OOP style. The second is written in Nim using the procedural style.

Listing 1.5   Barking dog modeled using OOP in Python

```python
class Dog:
  def bark(self):          The bark method is associated with the
    print("Woof!")         Dog class by being defined within it.

dog = Dog()
                           The bark method can be directly invoked on the
dog.bark()                 dog object by accessing the method via the dot.
```

Listing 1.6   Barking dog modeled using procedural programming in Nim

```nim
type                       The bark procedure isn't directly associated with the
  Dog = object             Dog type by being defined within it. This procedure
                           could also easily be defined outside this module.
proc bark(self: Dog) =
  echo("Woof!")
                           The bark procedure can still be directly invoked on the
let dog = Dog()            dog object, despite the fact that the procedure isn't
dog.bark()                 associated with the Dog type as it is in the Python version.
```

In the Python code, the `bark` method is placed under the `class` definition. In the Nim code, the `bark` method (called a *procedure* in Nim) isn't bound to the `Dog` type in the same way as it is in the Python code; it's independent of the definition of the `Dog` type. Instead, its first argument specifies the type it's associated with.

You could also implement something similar in Python, but it wouldn't allow you to call the `bark` method in the same manner. You'd be forced to call it like so: `bark(dog)`, explicitly passing the `dog` variable to the method as its first argument. The reason this is not the case with Nim is because Nim rewrites `dog.bark()` to `bark(dog)`, making it possible for you to call methods using the traditional OOP style without having to explicitly bind them to a class.

This ability, which is referred to as Uniform Function Call Syntax (UFCS), has multiple advantages. It allows you to create new procedures on existing objects externally and allows procedure calls to be chained.

> **CLASSES IN NIM**   Defining classes and methods in Nim in a manner similar to Python is also possible. Metaprogramming can be used to do this, and the community has already created numerous libraries that emulate the syntax. See, for example, the Nim OOP macro: https://nim-by-example.github .io/oop_macro/.

Another paradigm that Nim supports is the functional programming (FP) paradigm. FP is not as popular as OOP, though in recent years it has seen a surge in popularity. FP is a style of programming that primarily avoids the changing of state and the use of mutable data. It uses certain features such as first-class functions, anonymous functions, and closures, all of which Nim supports.

Let's look at an example to see the differences between programming in a procedural style and a functional one. The following code listings show code that separates people's full names into first and last names. Listing 1.7 shows this done in a functional style and listing 1.8 in a procedural style.

Listing 1.7   Iterating over a sequence using functional programming in Nim

Imports the sequtils, future, and strutils modules. These modules define the map, ->, and split procedures respectively.

Defines new list variable containing a list of names

```
import sequtils, future, strutils
let list = @["Dominik Picheta", "Andreas Rumpf", "Desmond Hume"]
list.map(
  (x: string) -> (string, string) => (x.split[0], x.split[1])
).echo
```

The map procedure is used to iterate over the list.

The modified list is then displayed on the screen.

The map procedure takes a closure that specifies how to modify each item in the list.

Listing 1.8   Iterating over a sequence using a procedural style in Nim

Imports the strutils module,   **A for loop is used to iterate**
which defines the split procedure   **over each item in the list.**

```
import strutils
let list = @["Dominik Picheta", "Andreas Rumpf", "Desmond Hume"]
for name in list:
  echo((name.split[0], name.split[1]))
```

The code inside the for loop is executed during each iteration; in this case, each name is split into two and displayed as a tuple.

The functional version uses the map procedure to iterate over the list variable, which contains a list of names. The procedural version uses a for loop. Both versions split the name into a first and last name. They then display the result in a tuple. (I'm throwing a lot of new terms at you here. Don't worry if you aren't familiar with them; I'll introduce you to them in chapter 2.) The output of the code listings will look similar to this:

```
(Field0: Dominik, Field1: Picheta)
(Field0: Andreas, Field1: Rumpf)
(Field0: Desmond, Field1: Hume)
```

> **THE MEANING OF FIELD0 AND FIELD1**   Field0 and Field1 are just default field names given to tuples when a field name isn't specified.

Nim is incredibly flexible and allows you to write software in many different styles. This was just a small taste of the most popular paradigms supported by Nim and of how they compare to Nim's main paradigm. Nim also supports more-obscure paradigms, and support for others can be introduced easily using metaprogramming.

NIM CATCHES ERRORS AHEAD OF TIME

Throughout this chapter, I've been comparing Python to Nim. While Nim does take a lot of inspiration from Python, the two languages differ in one important way: Python is dynamically typed and Nim is statically typed. As a statically typed language, Nim provides a certain level of type safety that dynamically typed programming languages don't provide.

Although Nim is statically typed, it feels very dynamic because it supports type inference and generics. You'll learn more about these features later in the book. For now, think of it as a way to retain the high development speed that dynamically typed programming languages allow, while also providing extra type safety at compile time.

In addition to being statically typed, Nim implements an exception-tracking mechanism that is entirely opt-in. With exception tracking, you can ensure that a procedure won't raise any exceptions, or that it will only raise exceptions from a predefined list. This prevents unexpected crashes by ensuring that you handle exceptions.

COMPARING DIFFERENT PROGRAMMING LANGUAGE FEATURES

Throughout this section, I've compared Nim to various other programming languages. I've discussed efficiency, the dependencies of the resulting software, the flexibility of the language, and the language's ability to catch errors before the software is deployed. Based on these characteristics alone, Nim is an excellent candidate for replacing some of the most popular programming languages out there, including Python, Java, C, and more.

For reference, table 1.2 lists different programming languages and shows some of the features that they do and don't support.

Table 1.2   Common programming language features

Programming language	Type system	Generics	Modules	GC	Syntax	Metaprogramming	Execution
Nim	Static and strong	Yes	Yes	Yes, multiple and optional[a]	Python-like	Yes	Compiled binary
C	Static and weak	No	No	No	C	Very limited[b]	Compiled binary
C++	Static and weak	Yes	No	No	C-like	Limited[c]	Compiled binary
D	Static and strong	Yes	Yes	Yes, optional	C-like	Yes	Compiled binary
Go	Static and strong	No	Yes	Yes	C-like	No	Compiled binary
Rust	Static and strong	Yes	Yes	No	C-like	Limited[d]	Compiled binary
Java	Static and strong	Yes	Yes	Yes, multiple[e]	C-like	No	Executed via the JVM
Python	Dynamic and strong	N/A	Yes	Yes	Python	Yes[f]	Executed via the Python interpreter
Lua	Dynamic and weak	N/A	Yes	Yes	Modula-like[g]	Yes via Metalua	Executed via the Lua interpreter or Lua JIT compiler

[a] Nim supports ref counting, a custom GC, and Boehm. Nim also allows the GC to be switched off altogether.

[b] Some very limited metaprogramming can be achieved via C's preprocessor.

[c] C++ only offers metaprogramming through templates, limited CTFE (compile-time function execution), and no AST macros.

[d] Rust has some support for declarative macros through its `macro_rules!` directive, but no built-in procedural macros that allow you to transform the AST except for compiler plugins, and no CTFE.

[e] See the "Oracle JVM Garbage Collectors Available From JDK 1.7.0_04 And After" article on Fasterj: www.fasterj.com/articles/oraclecollectors1.shtml.

[f] You can modify the behavior of functions, including manipulating their AST, using the `ast` module, but only at runtime.

[g] Lua uses `do` and `end` keywords to delimit scope.

1.2.2   *Areas where Nim still needs to improve*

Nothing in this world is perfect, and programming languages are no exception. There's no programming language that can solve every problem in the most reliable and rapid manner. Each programming language has its own strengths and weaknesses, and Nim is no exception.

So far, I've been focusing on Nim's strengths. Nim has many more fine aspects that I haven't yet mentioned, and you'll discover them throughout this book. But it would be unfair to only talk about Nim's strengths. Nim is still a young programming language, so of course it can still improve.

NIM IS STILL YOUNG AND IMMATURE

All programming languages go through a period of immaturity. Some of Nim's newer and more-advanced features are still unstable. Using them can result in buggy behavior in the compiler, such as crashes, though crashes don't happen very often. Importantly, Nim's unstable features are opt-in, which means that you can't accidentally use them.

Nim has a package manager called Nimble. Where other programming languages may have thousands of packages available, Nim only has about 500. This means that you may need to write libraries for certain tasks yourself. This situation is, of course, improving, with new packages being created by the Nim community every day. In chapter 5, I'll show you how to create your own Nimble packages.

NIM'S USER BASE AND COMMUNITY IS STILL QUITE SMALL

Nim has a small number of users compared to the mainstream programming languages. The result is that few Nim jobs exist. Finding a company that uses Nim in production is rare, but when it does happen, the demand for good Nim programmers can make the salaries quite high.

On the other hand, one of the most unique things about Nim is that its development is exceptionally open. Andreas Rumpf (Nim's creator) and many other Nim developers (including me) openly discuss Nim's future development plans on GitHub and on IRC. Anyone is free to challenge these plans and, because the community is still quite small, it's easy to do so. IRC is also a great place for newcomers to ask questions about Nim and to meet fellow Nim programmers.

> **IRC**   Take a look at appendix A for details on how to connect to Nim's IRC channel.

These problems are temporary. Nim has a bright future ahead of it, and you can help shape it. This book teaches you how.

1.3   *Summary*

- Created by Andreas Rumpf in 2005, Nim is still a very new programming language; it hasn't yet reached version 1.0. Because Nim is so new, it's a bit immature and its user base is relatively small.

- Nim is efficient, expressive, and elegant (in that order).
- Nim is an open source project that's developed entirely by the Nim community of volunteers.
- Nim is general-purpose programming language and can be used to develop anything from web applications to kernels.
- Nim is a compiled programming language that compiles to C and takes advantage of C's speed and portability.
- Nim supports multiple programming paradigms, including OOP, procedural programming, and functional programming.

Getting started

This chapter covers

- Understanding Nim basics
- Mastering control flow
- Using collection types
- Handling exceptions
- Defining data types

In this chapter, you'll learn about Nim's syntax, procedures, `for` loops, and other basic aspects of the language. Throughout this chapter, we'll cover a lot of information to give you a broad taste of the language.

Before you begin, make sure you have Nim installed and that it works on your computer. You'll also need a text editor to edit Nim code. Take a look at appendix B for instructions on how to install Nim and other related tools.

2.1 Nim syntax

The syntax of a programming language is a set of rules that govern the way programs are written in that language. You've already had a small taste of Nim's syntax in the previous chapter.

Most languages share many similarities in terms of syntax. This is especially true for the C family of languages, which happens to also be the most popular—so much so that four of the most popular programming languages are syntactically heavily inspired by C.[1] Nim aims to be highly readable, so it often uses keywords instead of punctuation. Because of this, the syntax of Nim differs significantly from the C language family; instead, much of it is inspired by Python and Pascal.

In this section, I'll teach you the basics of Nim's syntax. Learning the syntax is a very important first step, as it teaches you the specific ways in which Nim code should be written.

2.1.1 Keywords

Most programming languages have the notion of a *keyword*, and Nim is no exception. A keyword is a word with a special meaning associated with it when it's used in a specific context. Because of this, you may not use keywords as identifiers in your source code.

> **STROPPING** You can get around this limitation by using *stropping*. See section 1.2 to learn more.

As of version 0.12.0, Nim has 70 keywords. This may sound like a lot, but you must remember that you won't be using most of them. Some of them don't yet have a meaning and are reserved for future versions of the language; others have minor use cases.

The most commonly used keywords allow you to do the following:

- Specify conditional branches: `if`, `case`, `of`, and `when`
- Define variables, procedures, and types: `var`, `let`, `proc`, `type`, and `object`
- Handle runtime errors in your code: `try`, `except`, and `finally`

You'll learn exactly what these keywords mean and how to use them in the next sections of this chapter. For a full list of keywords, consult the Nim manual, available at http://nim-lang.org/docs/manual.html#lexical-analysis-identifiers-keywords.

2.1.2 Indentation

Many programmers indent their code to make the program's structure more apparent. In most programming languages, this isn't a requirement and serves only as an aid to human readers of the code. In those languages, keywords and punctuation are often used to delimit code blocks. In Nim, just like in Python, the indentation itself is used.

Let's look at a simple example to demonstrate the difference. The following three code samples written in C, Ruby, and Nim all do the same thing. But note the different ways in which code blocks are delimited.

---

[1] According to the TIOBE Index for December 2016, www.tiobe.com/index.php/content/paperinfo/tpci/index.html.

Listing 2.1   C

```c
if (42 >= 0) {
  printf("42 is greater than 0");
}
```

Listing 2.2   Ruby

```ruby
if 42 >= 0
  puts "42 is greater than 0"
end
```

Listing 2.3   Nim

```nim
if 42 >= 0:
  echo "42 is greater than 0"
```

As you can see, C uses curly brackets to delimit a block of code, Ruby uses the keyword end, and Nim uses indentation. Nim also uses the colon character on the line that precedes the start of the indentation. This is required for the if statement and for many others. But as you continue learning about Nim, you'll see that the colon isn't required for all statements that start an indented code block.

Note also the use of the semicolon in listing 2.1. This is required at the end of each line in some programming languages (mostly the C family). It tells the compiler where a line of code ends. This means that a single statement can span multiple lines, or multiple statements can be on the same line. In C, you'd achieve both like this:

```c
printf("The output is: %d",
  0);
printf("Hello"); printf("World");
```

In Nim, the semicolon is optional and can be used to write two statements on a single line. Spanning a single statement over multiple lines is a bit more complex—you can only split up a statement after punctuation, and the next line must be indented. Here's an example:

```nim
echo("Output: ",
  5)
echo(5 +
  5)
```
Both of these statements are correct because they've been split after the punctuation and the next line has been indented.

```nim
echo(5
  + 5)
```
This statement has been incorrectly split before the punctuation.

```nim
echo(5 +
5)
```
This statement has not been correctly indented after the split.

Because indentation is important in Nim, you need to be consistent in its style. The convention states that all Nim code should be indented by two spaces. The Nim compiler currently disallows tabs because the inevitable mixing of spaces and tabs can have detrimental effects, especially in a whitespace-significant programming language.

2.1.3 Comments

Comments in code are important because they allow you to add additional meaning to pieces of code. Comments in Nim are written using the hash character (#). Anything following it will be a comment until the start of a new line. A multiline comment can be created with #[and]#, and code can also be disabled by using when false:. Here's an example:

```
# Single-line comment
#[
Multiline comment
]#
when false:
  echo("Commented-out code")
```

The first of the two types of multiline comment can be used to comment out both text and code, whereas the latter should only be used to comment out code. The compiler will still parse the code and ensure that it's syntactically valid, but it won't be included in the resulting program. This is because the compiler checks when statements at compile time.

2.2 Nim basics

Now that you have a basic understanding of Nim's syntax, you have a good foundation for learning some of the semantics of Nim. In this section, you'll learn some of the essentials that every Nim programmer uses on a daily basis. You'll learn about the most commonly used static types, the details of mutable and immutable variables, and how to separate commonly used code into standalone units by defining procedures.

2.2.1 Basic types

Nim is a statically typed programming language. This means that each identifier in Nim has a type associated with it at compile time. When you compile your Nim program, the compiler ensures that your code is type safe. If it isn't, compilation terminates and the compiler outputs an error. This is in contrast to dynamically typed programming languages, such as Ruby, that will only ensure that your code is type safe at runtime.

By convention, type names start with an uppercase letter. Built-in types don't follow this convention, so it's easy for you to distinguish between built-in types and user-defined types by checking the first letter of the name. Nim supports many built-in types, including ones for dealing with the C foreign function interface (FFI). I don't cover all of them here, but they will be covered later in this book.

FOREIGN FUNCTION INTERFACE The foreign function interface (FFI) is what allows you to use libraries written in other programming languages. Nim includes types that are native to C and C++, allowing libraries written in those languages to be used.

Most of the built-in types are defined in the `system` module, which is imported automatically into your source code. When referring to these types in your code, you can qualify them with the module name (for example, `system.int`), but doing so isn't necessary. See table 2.1 for a list of the basic types defined in the `system` module.

MODULES   Modules are imported using the `import` keyword. You'll learn more about modules later in this book.

Table 2.1   Basic types

Type	Description and uses
int	The integer type is the type used for whole numbers; for example, `52`.
float	The `float` is the type used for numbers with a decimal point; for example, `2.5`.
string	The `string` type is used to store multiple characters. String literals are created by placing multiple characters inside double quotes: `"Nim is awesome"`.
bool	The Boolean type stores one of two values, either `true` or `false`.
char	The character type stores a single ASCII character. Character literals are created by placing a character inside single quotes; for example, `'A'`.

INTEGER

The integer type represents numerical data without a fractional component; that is, whole numbers. The amount of data this type can store is finite, so there are multiple versions of it in Nim, each suited to different size requirements. The main integer type in Nim is `int`. It's the integer type you should be using most in your Nim programs. See table 2.2 for a list of integer types.

Table 2.2   Integer types

Type	Size	Range	Description
int	Architecture-dependent. 32-bit on 32-bit systems, 64-bit on 64-bit systems.	**32-bit:** `-2,147,483,648` to `2,147,483,647` **64-bit:** `-9,223,372,036,854,775,808` to `9,223,372,036,854,775,807`	Generic *signed* two's complement integer. Generally, you should be using this integer type in most programs.

int8
 int16
 int32
 int64
	8-bit
	 16-bit
	 32-bit
	 64-bit
		`-128` to `127`
		 `-32,768` to `32,767`
		 `-2,147,483,648` to `2,147,483,647`
		 `-9,223,372,036,854,775,808` to `9,223,372,036,854,775,807`
			Signed two's complement integer. These types can be used if you want to be explicit about the size requirements of your data.

uint	Architecture-dependent. 32-bit on 32-bit systems, 64-bit on 64-bit systems.	**32-bit:** `0` to `4,294,967,295` **64-bit:** `0` to `18,446,744,073,709,551,615`	Generic *unsigned* integer.

Table 2.2 Integer types *(continued)*

Type	Size	Range	Description
uint8 uint16 uint32 uint64	8-bit 16-bit 32-bit 64-bit	0 to 2550 0 to 65,5350 0 to 4,294,967,2950 0 to 18,446,744,073,709,551,615	*Unsigned* integer. These types can be used if you want to be explicit about the size requirements of your data.

An integer literal in Nim can be represented using decimal, octal, hexadecimal, or binary notation.

Listing 2.4   Integer literals

```
let decimal = 42
let hex = 0x42
let octal = 0o42
let binary = 0b101010
```

Listing 2.4 defines four integer variables and assigns a different integer literal to each of them, using the four different integer-literal formats.

You'll note that the type isn't specified for any of the defined variables. The Nim compiler will infer the correct type based on the integer literal that's specified. In this case, all variables will have the type `int`.

The compiler determines which integer type to use by looking at the size of the integer literal. The type is `int64` if the integer literal exceeds the 32-bit range; otherwise, it's `int`. But what if you want to use a specific integer type for your variable? There are multiple ways to accomplish this:

```
let a: int16 = 42      ◁──── int16
let b = 42'i8          ◁──── Uses a type suffix to specify the type of the integer literal
```

> **INTEGER SIZE**   Explicitly using a small integer type such as `int8` may result in a compile-time or, in some cases, a runtime error. Take a look at the ranges in table 2.2 to see what size of integer can fit into which integer type. You should be careful not to attempt to assign an integer that's bigger or smaller than the type can hold.

Nim supports type suffixes for all integer types, both signed and unsigned. The format is `'iX`, where X is the size of the signed integer, and `'uX`, where X is the size of the unsigned integer.[2]

---

[2] See the Nim manual for more on numerical constants: http://nim-lang.org/docs/manual.html#lexical-analysis-numerical-constants.

FLOATING-POINT

The floating-point type represents an approximation of numerical data with a fractional component. The main floating-point type in Nim is `float`, and its size depends on the platform.

Listing 2.5   Float literals

```
let a = 1'f32
let b = 1.0e19
```

The compiler will implicitly use the `float` type for floating-point literals.

You can specify the type of the literal using a type suffix. There are two type suffixes for floats that correspond to the available floating-point types: `'f32` for `float32` and `'f64` for `float64`.

Exponents can also be specified after the number. Variable b in the preceding listing will be equal to $1x10^{19}$ (1 times 10 to the power of 19).

BOOLEAN

The Boolean type represents one of two values: usually a true or false value. In Nim, the Boolean type is called `bool`.

Listing 2.6   Boolean literals

```
let a = false
let b = true
```

The `false` and `true` values of a Boolean must begin with a lowercase letter.

CHARACTER

The character type represents a single character. In Nim, the character type is called `char`. It can't represent UTF-8 characters but instead encodes ASCII characters. Because of this, `char` is really just a number.

A character literal in Nim is a single character enclosed in quotes. The character may also be an escape sequence introduced by a backward slash (\). Some common character-escape sequences are listed in table 2.3.

Listing 2.7   Character literals

```
let a = 'A'
let b = '\109'
let c = '\x79'
```

UNICODE   The `unicode` module contains a `Rune` type that can hold any unicode character.

NEWLINE ESCAPE SEQUENCE   The newline escape sequence \n isn't allowed in a character literal as it may be composed of multiple characters on some platforms. On Windows, it's \r\l (carriage return followed by line feed),whereas on Linux it's just \l (line feed). Specify the character you want explicitly, such as '\r' to get a carriage return, or use a string.

Escape sequence	Result
\r, \c	Carriage return
\l	Line feed
\t	Tab
\\	Backslash
\'	Apostrophe
\"	Quotation mark

Table 2.3 Common character-escape sequences

STRING

The string type represents a sequence of characters. In Nim, the string type is called string. It's a list of characters terminated by '\0'.

The string type also stores its length. A string in Nim can store UTF-8 text, but the unicode module should be used for processing it, such as when you want to change the case of UTF-8 characters in a string.

There are multiple ways to define string literals, such as this:

```
let text = "The book title is \"Nim in Action\""
```

When defining string literals this way, certain characters must be escaped in them. For instance, the double-quote character (") should be escaped as \" and the backward-slash character (\) as \\. String literals support the same character-escape sequences that character literals support; see table 2.3 for a good list of the common ones. One major additional escape sequence that string literals support is \n, which produces a newline; the actual characters that are produced depend on the platform.

The need to escape some characters makes some things tedious to write. One example is Windows file paths:

```
let filepath = "C:\\Program Files\\Nim"
```

Nim supports raw string literals that don't require escape sequences. Apart from the double-quote character ("), which still needs to be escaped as "", any character placed in a raw string literal will be stored verbatim in the string. A raw string literal is a string literal preceded by an r:

```
let filepath = r"C:\Program Files\Nim"
```

It's also possible to specify multiline strings using triple-quoted string literals:

```
let multiLine = """foo
  bar
  baz
"""
echo multiLine
```

The output for the preceding code looks like this:

```
foo
  bar
  baz
```

Triple-quoted string literals are enclosed between three double-quote characters, and these string literals may contain any characters, including the double-quote character, without any escape sequences. The only exception is that your string literal may not repeat the double-quote character three times. There's no way to include three double-quote characters in a triple-quoted string literal.

The indentation added to the string literal defining the `multiLine` variable causes leading whitespace to appear at the start of each line. This can be easily fixed by the use of the unindent procedure. It lives in the `strutils` module, so you must first import it:

```
import strutils
let multiLine = """foo
  bar
  baz
"""
echo multiLine.unindent
```

This will produce the following output:

```
foo
bar
baz
```

2.2.2   *Defining variables and other storage*

Storage in Nim is defined using three different keywords. In addition to the `let` keyword, which you saw in the previous section, you can also define storage using `const` and `var`.

```
let number = 10
```

By using the `let` keyword, you'll be creating what's known as an *immutable variable*—a variable that can only be assigned to once. In this case, a new immutable variable named `number` is created, and the identifier `number` is bound to the value `10`. If you attempt to assign a different value to this variable, your program won't compile, as in the following numbers.nim example:

```
let number = 10
number = 4000
```

The preceding code will produce the following output when compiled:

```
numbers.nim(2, 1) Error: 'number' cannot be assigned to
```

Nim also supports mutable variables using the keyword `var`. Use these if you intend on changing the value of a variable. The previous example can be fixed by replacing the `let` keyword with the `var` keyword:

```
var number = 10
number = 4000
```

In both examples, the compiler will infer the type of the `number` variable based on the value assigned to it. In this case, `number` will be an `int`. You can specify the type explicitly by writing the type after the variable name and separating it with a colon character (`:`). By doing this, you can omit the assignment, which is useful when you don't want to assign a value to the variable when defining it.

```
var number: int       ◁—— This will be initialized to 0.
```

> **IMMUTABLE VARIABLES** Immutable variables must be assigned a value when they're defined because their values can't change. This includes both `const` and `let` defined storage.

A variable's initial value will always be binary zero. This will manifest in different ways, depending on the type. For example, by default, integers will be `0` and strings will be `nil`. `nil` is a special value that signifies the lack of a value for any reference type. You'll learn more about this later.

The type of a variable can't change. For example, assigning a `string` to an `int` variable will result in a compile-time error, as in this typeMismatch.nim example:

```
var number = 10
number = "error"
```

Here's the error output:

```
typeMismatch.nim(2, 10) Error: type mismatch: got (string) but expected 'int'
```

Nim also supports constants. Because the value of a constant is also immutable, constants are similar to immutable variables defined using `let`. But a Nim constant differs in one important way: its value must be computable at compile time.

Listing 2.8 Constant example

```
proc fillString(): string =
  result = ""
  echo("Generating string")       The $ is a commonly used
  for i in 0 .. 4:                 operator in Nim that converts
    result.add($i)          ◁——   its input to a string.

const count = fillString()
```

> **PROCEDURES** Don't worry about not understanding the details of procedures in Nim yet. You'll be introduced to them shortly.

The `fillString` procedure in listing 2.8 will generate a new string, equal to `"01234"`. The constant `count` will then be assigned this string.

I added the `echo` at the top of `fillString`'s body, in order to show you that it's executed at compile time. Try compiling the example using Aporia or in a terminal by executing `nim c file.nim`. You'll see `"Generating string"` amongst the output. Running the binary will never display that message because the result of the `fillString` procedure is embedded in it.

In order to generate the value of the constant, the `fillString` procedure must be executed at compile time by the Nim compiler. You have to be aware, though, that not all code can be executed at compile time. For example, if a compile-time procedure uses the FFI, you'll find that the compiler will output an error similar to "Error: cannot 'importc' variable at compile time."

The main benefit of using constants is efficiency. The compiler can compute a value for you at compile time, saving time that would be otherwise spent during runtime. The obvious downside is longer compilation time, but it could also produce a larger executable size. As with many things, you must find the right balance for your use case. Nim gives you the tools, but you must use them responsibly.[3]

You can also specify multiple variable definitions under the same `var`, `let`, or `const` keyword. To do this, add a new line after the keyword and indent the identifier on the next line:

```
var
  text = "hello"
  number: int = 10
  isTrue = false
```

The identifier of a variable is its name. It can contain any characters, as long as the name doesn't begin with a number and doesn't contain two consecutive underscores. This applies to all identifiers, including procedure and type names. Identifiers can even make use of Unicode characters:

```
var 火 = "Fire"
let ogień = true
```

Unlike in many other programming languages, identifiers in Nim are case insensitive with the exception of the first letter of the identifier. This is to help distinguish variable names, which must begin with lowercase letters, from type names, which must begin with uppercase letters.

Identifiers in Nim are also *style insensitive*. This allows identifiers written in `camelCase` to be equivalent to identifiers written in `snake_case`. The way this is accomplished is by ignoring the underscore character in identifiers, so `fooBar` is equivalent to `foo_bar`. You're free to write identifiers in whichever style you prefer,

---

[3] With great power comes great responsibility.

Stropping

As you may recall from section 2.1, there are identifiers in Nim that are reserved. Such identifiers are called *keyword*s, and because they have a special meaning, they can't be used as names for variables, types, or procedures.

In order to get around this limitation, you can either pick a different name or explicitly mark the identifier using backticks (`` ` ``). The latter approach is called *stropping*, and here's how it can be used:

```
var `var` = "Hello"
echo(`var`)
```

The `var` keyword is enclosed in backticks, allowing a variable with that name to be defined.

---

even when they're defined in a different style. But you're encouraged to follow Nim's style conventions, which specify that variables should use `camelCase` and types should use `PascalCase`. For more information about Nim's conventions, take a look at the "Style Guide for Nim Code" on GitHub: https://github.com/nim-lang/Nim/wiki/Style-Guide-for-Nim-Code.

2.2.3 *Procedure definitions*

Procedures allow you to separate your program into different units of code. These units generally perform a single task, after being given some input data, usually in the form of one or more parameters.

In this section, we'll explore procedures in Nim. In other programming languages a procedure may be known as a *function, method,* or *subroutine*. Each programming language attaches different meanings to these terms, and Nim is no exception. A *procedure* in Nim can be defined using the `proc` keyword, followed by the procedure's name, parameters, optional return type, =, and the procedure body. Figure 2.1 shows the syntax of a Nim procedure definition.

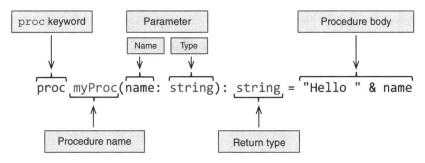

Figure 2.1   The syntax of a Nim procedure definition

The procedure in figure 2.1 is named `myProc` and it takes one parameter (`name`) of type `string`, and returns a value of type `string`. The procedure body implicitly returns a concatenation of the string literal `"Hello "` and the parameter `name`.

You can call a procedure by writing the name of the procedure followed by parentheses: `myProc("Dominik")`. Any parameters can be specified inside the parentheses. Calling the `myProc` procedure with a `"Dominik"` parameter, as in the preceding example, will cause the string `"Hello Dominik"` to be returned.

Whenever procedures with a return value are called, their results must be used in some way.

```
proc myProc(name: string): string = "Hello " & name
myProc("Dominik")
```

Compiling this example will result in an error: "file.nim(2, 7) Error: value of type 'string' has to be discarded." This error occurs as a result of the value returned by the `myProc` procedure being implicitly discarded. In most cases, ignoring the result of a procedure is a bug in your code, because the result could describe an error that occurred or give you a piece of vital information. You'll likely want to do something with the result, such as store it in a variable or pass it to another procedure via a call. In cases where you really don't want to do anything with the result of a procedure, you can use the `discard` keyword to tell the compiler to be quiet:

```
proc myProc(name: string): string = "Hello " & name
discard myProc("Dominik")
```

The `discard` keyword simply lets the compiler know that you're happy to ignore the value that the procedure returns.

Order of procedures

Procedures must be defined above the call site. For example, the following code will fail to compile:

```
myProc()
proc myProc() = echo("Hello World")
```

For procedures that have a circular dependency, a forward declaration must be used:

```
proc bar(): int                          ◄────      A forward declaration contains no
                                                     procedure body, just the procedure's
proc foo(): float = bar().float                      name, parameters, and return type.
proc bar(): int = foo().int
```

A future version of Nim will likely remove the need for forward declarations and allow procedures to be defined in any order.

When a procedure returns no values, the return type can be omitted. In that case, the procedure is said to return `void`. The following two examples return no value:

```
proc noReturn() = echo("Hello")
proc noReturn2(): void = echo("Hello")
```

It's idiomatic to avoid writing the redundant void in procedure definitions. The special void type is useful in other contexts, such as generics, which you'll learn about in chapter 9.

Nim allows you to cut down on unnecessary syntax even further. If your procedure takes no parameters, you can omit the parentheses:

```
proc noReturn = echo("Hello")
```

RETURNING VALUES FROM PROCEDURES

A procedure body can contain multiple statements, separated either by a semicolon or a newline character. In the case where the last expression of a procedure has a non-void value associated with it, that expression will be implicitly returned from that procedure. You can always use the return keyword as the last statement of your procedure if you wish, but doing so is not idiomatic nor necessary. The return keyword is still necessary for early returns from a procedure.

The following code block shows different examples of returning values from procedures:

```
proc implicit: string =
  "I will be returned"

proc discarded: string =
  discard "I will not be returned"

proc explicit: string =
  return "I will be returned"

proc resultVar: string =
  result = "I will be returned"

proc resultVar2: string =
  result = ""
  result.add("I will be ")
  result.add("returned")

proc resultVar3: string =
  result = "I am the result"
  "I will cause an error"

assert implicit() == "I will be returned"
assert discarded() == nil
assert explicit() == "I will be returned"
assert resultVar() == "I will be returned"
assert resultVar2() == "I will be returned"
# resultVar3 does not compile!
```

> **ASSERT** The code block showing examples of returning values from procedures uses assert to show the output that you should expect when calling each of the defined procedures. You'll learn more about assert when it comes time to test your code in chapter 3.

Just like a variable's default value, a procedure's return value will be binary zero by default. Nim supports a lot of different methods of setting the return value, and you're free to combine them.

Every procedure with a return type has a `result` variable declared inside its body implicitly. This `result` variable is mutable and is of the same type as the procedure's return type. It can be used just like any other variable; the `resultVar` and `resultVar2` procedures are two examples. You should make use of it whenever you can, instead of defining your own variable and returning it explicitly.

The `result` variable comes with some restrictions when it's combined with implicit returns. These restrictions prevent ambiguities. For example, in the `resultVar3` procedure, what do you think should be returned: the last expression, or the value that `result` was assigned? The compiler doesn't choose for you; it simply shows an error so you can correct the ambiguity.

So far, I've been explicitly specifying the return types of procedures. You may recall that this isn't necessary for variable definition. It's also possible to ask the compiler to infer the return type of your procedure for you. In order to do this, you need to use the `auto` type:

```
proc message(recipient: string): auto =
  "Hello " & recipient

assert message("Dom") == "Hello Dom"
```

Although this is handy, you should specify the type explicitly whenever possible. Doing so makes it easier for you and others to determine the return type of a procedure, without needing to understand the procedure's body.

> **WARNING: TYPE INFERENCE**   Type inference for procedures is still a bit experimental in Nim. You may find that it's limited in some circumstances, especially if you're used to more advanced forms of type inference, such as those found in Haskell or OCaml.

PROCEDURE PARAMETERS

A procedure with multiple parameters can be defined by listing the parameters and separating them with the comma character:

```
proc max(a: int, b: int): int =
  if a > b: a else: b

assert max(5, 10) == 10
```

You don't need to repeat the types of parameters if they're specified consecutively:

```
proc max(a, b: int): int =
  if a > b: a else: b
```

Default parameters can be used to ask for arguments that can be optionally specified at the call site. You can introduce default parameters by assigning a value to a parameter using the equals character; the type can also be omitted in that case:

```
proc genHello(name: string, surname = "Doe"): string =
  "Hello " & name & " " & surname

assert genHello("Peter") == "Hello Peter Doe"
assert genHello("Peter", "Smith") == "Hello Peter Smith"
```

In this case, the default value for the surname argument is used.

In this case, the default value is overridden with the string literal "Smith".

A procedure taking a variable number of parameters can be specified using the varargs type:

```
proc genHello(names: varargs[string]): string =
  result = ""
  for name in names:
    result.add("Hello " & name & "\n")

assert genHello("John", "Bob") == "Hello John\nHello Bob\n"
```

Initializes the result variable with a new string

Iterates through each of the arguments. You'll learn more about for loops in section 2.4.

Adds the string "Hello" concatenated with the current argument and a newline character to the result variable

PROCEDURE OVERLOADING

Overloading a procedure is a feature that you may not have come across yet, but it's one that's commonly used in Nim. Procedure overloading is the ability to define different implementations of procedures with the same name. Each of these procedures shares the same name but accept different parameters. Depending on the arguments passed to the procedure, the appropriate implementation is picked by the compiler.

As an example, consider a getUserCity procedure. It may take two parameters: firstName and lastName.

```
proc getUserCity(firstName, lastName: string): string =
  case firstName
  of "Damien": return "Tokyo"
  of "Alex": return "New York"
  else: return "Unknown"
```

CASE STATEMENTS Case statements might still be new to you. They'll be explained later in section 2.4.

This kind of procedure may be used to retrieve a person's city of residence from a database, based on the name specified. You may also wish to offer alternative search criteria—something more unique, such as an ID number. To do this, you can overload the getUserCity procedure like so:

```
proc getUserCity(userID: int): string =
  case userID
  of 1: return "Tokyo"
  of 2: return "New York"
  else: return "Unknown"
```

This way, you can reuse the name, but you're still able to use the different implementations, as shown here:

```
doAssert getUserCity("Damien", "Lundi") == "Tokyo"
doAssert getUserCity(2) == "New York"
```

ANONYMOUS PROCEDURES

Sometimes you may wish to pass procedures as parameters to other procedures. The following listing shows the definition of a new procedure, and how a reference to it can be passed to the filter procedure.

> **Listing 2.9   Using anonymous procedures**

Definition of an immutable
variable holding a list of numbers

```
import sequtils
let numbers = @[1, 2, 3, 4, 5, 6]          ◁┘
let odd = filter(numbers, proc (x: int): bool = x mod 2 != 0)
assert odd == @[1, 3, 5]    ◁─────┐
```

The filter procedure used to
filter out even numbers

Assertion to show
the output

These procedures are called *anonymous procedures* because there's no name associated with them. In listing 2.9, the anonymous procedure is highlighted in bold.

> **THE @ SYMBOL**   The @ symbol creates a new sequence. You'll learn more about it in the next section.

The anonymous procedure gets a single parameter, x, of type int. This parameter is one of the items in the numbers sequence. The job of this anonymous procedure is to determine whether that item should be filtered out or whether it should remain. When the procedure returns true, the item isn't filtered out.

The filter procedure is the one doing the actual filtering. It takes two parameters: a sequence and an anonymous procedure. It then iterates through each item and uses the anonymous procedure it got to see whether it should filter the item out or keep it. The filter procedure then returns a new sequence that includes only the items that the anonymous procedure determined should be kept and not filtered out.

In listing 2.9, the resulting sequence will only contain odd numbers. This is reflected in the anonymous procedure, which checks whether dividing each item by 2 results in a remainder. If a remainder is produced, true is returned because that means the number is odd.

The syntax for anonymous procedures is a bit cumbersome. Thankfully, Nim supports some syntactic sugar for defining anonymous procedures and procedure types. The syntactic sugar isn't part of the language but is instead defined in the standard library, so to use it you must import the future module. (The syntactic sugar is defined using macros, which you'll learn about in chapter 9.)

Compare the following code to listing 2.9, and note the differences shown in bold:

```
import sequtils, future
let numbers = @[1, 2, 3, 4, 5, 6]
let odd = filter(numbers, (x: int) -> bool => x mod 2 != 0)
assert odd == @[1, 3, 5]
```

The syntactic sugar doesn't actually make the definition that much shorter, but it does remove some of the noise. It can be shortened further using type inference: `x => x mod 2 != 0`. But keep in mind that this may not work in some cases. The compiler may not be able to infer the types for your anonymous procedure. In that case, you'll need to explicitly state the types. The `->` symbol is used to specify types.

> **DOCUMENTATION** The documentation for each module (available on Nim's website: http://nim-lang.org/) contains links under each procedure definition to the source code for that procedure. Take a look at it to learn more about the procedures mentioned in this book.

The `->` symbol can also be used on its own in place of procedure types. For example, you can use it when defining a procedure that takes another procedure as a parameter.

For example, consider the following code:

```
proc isValid(x: int, validator: proc (x: int): bool) =
  if validator(x): echo(x, " is valid")
  else: echo(x, " is NOT valid")
```

It can be rewritten as follows:

```
import future
proc isValid(x: int, validator: (x: int) -> bool) =
  if validator(x): echo(x, " is valid")
  else: echo(x, " is NOT valid")
```

The `proc` keyword can be omitted, and the `:` is replaced by the `->` symbol.

This ends the section on Nim basics. So far, this chapter has been very heavy with information, but don't worry if you don't remember everything that you've read or you don't understand some concepts. The next chapter will put these ideas into practice and solidify your knowledge. You can also go back over this section at any time.

2.3 Collection types

Collections such as lists, arrays, sets, and more are incredibly useful. In this section, I'll talk about the three most commonly used collection types in Nim: the `array`, `seq`, and `set` types.

2.3.1 Arrays

The `array` type represents a list of a static number of items. This type is similar to C arrays but offers more memory safety, as demonstrated in the following example:

```
var list: array[3, int]
list[0] = 1
list[1] = 42
assert list[0] == 1
assert list[1] == 42
assert list[2] == 0

echo list.repr

echo list[500]
```

The array contains three elements. Any elements that have not been set are given a default value.

This will output [1, 42, 0]. The repr procedure converts any variable into a string, but the resulting string sometimes contains debug information such as the memory address of the variable.

Compilation will fail with "Error: index out of bounds."

Arrays are value types, just like int, float, and many others, which means they're allocated on the stack. This is similar to C arrays, but it differs completely from Java's arrays, which are reference types and are stored on the heap.

Arrays are static in size, so an array can't change its size once it's declared. This is why the compiler can give you an error when you try to access an index outside its bounds. In C, checks for index bounds aren't made, so it's possible to access memory that's outside the bounds of the array.

Nim performs these checks at compile time and at runtime. The runtime checks are performed as long as the --boundsChecks option is not turned off.

WARNING: THE -D:RELEASE FLAG   Compiling with the -d:release flag will turn the bounds checks off. This will result in higher performance but less safety.

Custom array ranges

It's possible to define arrays with a custom range. By default, arrays range from 0 to the number specified in the array type, but you can also specify the lower bound, as in this array of two integers:

```
var list: array[-10 .. -9, int]
list[-10] = 1
list[-9] = 2
```

This is useful when your array indices don't start at 0.

An array constructor can be used to assign a list of items to the array when it's defined:

```
var list = ["Hi", "There"]
```

You can iterate over most collection types using a for loop. Iterating over a collection type will yield a single item from the collection during each iteration. If you prefer to iterate over each index rather than each item, you can access an array's bounds using the low and high fields and then iterate from the lowest index to the highest:

```
var list = ["My", "name", "is", "Dominik"]
for item in list:                           Loops through each item
  echo(item)

for i in list.low .. list.high:      Loops through each index
  echo(list[i])
```

2.3.2 Sequences

Arrays are static in size. You can't add more items to them; you can only overwrite existing items with new data. This is where Nim's sequences come in. They're dynamic in size and can grow to as many items as needed (within the limits of your memory). You've already seen a few examples of sequences in the previous section.

Sequences are defined using the `seq` type:

```
var list: seq[int] = @[]
list[0] = 1
```
Assigns 1 to the first item in the sequence. This will result in an index-out-of-bounds exception at runtime because there are currently no items in the sequence.

```
list.add(1)
```
⊲—— **Appends 1 as an item to the list sequence**

```
assert list[0] == 1
echo list[42]
```
⊲—— **Attempts to access an item that doesn't exist. An index-out-of-bounds exception will be raised.**

Sequences are stored on the heap, and as such are garbage collected. This means that they need to be initialized before they're used, just like strings.

```
var list: seq[int]
echo(list[0])
```

Accessing the items of an uninitialized sequence will result in a segmentation fault at runtime. Copy the preceding code into your favorite text editor and save it as segfault .nim. Then compile and run it. If you're using Aporia, just press F5, or open a terminal and execute `nim c -r segfault.nim`. You should see that your program crashes with the following output:

```
Traceback (most recent call last)
segfault.nim(2)          segfault
SIGSEGV: Illegal storage access. (Attempt to read from nil?)
```

As long as your program isn't compiled in release mode, any crashes will display a traceback that shows the procedure calls leading up to your program's crash. In this case, the 2 in the parentheses corresponds to line 2 in the source code, `echo(list[0])`. This hints that `list` is nil, and that it must be initialized.

A sequence can be initialized in two ways: using the sequence constructor syntax (`@[]`), as in the previous example, and using the `newSeq` procedure. Each is more or less appropriate, depending on the use case.

> **The sequence constructor**
>
> When using the sequence constructor syntax, you must be careful to specify the type of the sequence.
>
> ```
> var list = @[]
> ```
>
> This example won't work because the compiler has no way of knowing what type of sequence you want to define. This isn't a problem when you're constructing a non-empty sequence: `var list = @[4, 8, 15, 16, 23, 42]`. In this case, the compiler knows that the sequence type is `seq[int]`.

The newSeq procedure provides another way to construct a sequence. It also offers an important optimization—you should use it when you know the size of the sequence ahead of time.

```
var list = newSeq[string](3)
assert list[0] == nil        ◁——— The items will exist but will not be initialized.
list[0] = "Foo"              ◁——— You can assign new values to them easily.
list[1] = "Bar"
list[2] = "Baz"

list.add("Lorem")            ◁——— The seq can still grow in size; new items can be added.
```

The size of the sequence that you specify in the call to newSeq will correspond to the number of items that the new sequence will contain. The items themselves won't be initialized, and you can still add more items to the sequence if you wish.

Iterating over a sequence is done in the same way as iterating over an array. But although sequences do have low and high fields, it's more idiomatic to use the len field, which gives you the length of the sequence. The reason for this is that the low field for sequences is always 0.

```
let list = @[4, 8, 15, 16, 23, 42]
for i in 0 .. <list.len:
  stdout.write($list[i] & " ")
```

This outputs the following:

```
4 8 15 16 23 42
```

The range of iteration is inclusive, so you must subtract 1 from the length of the sequence in order to iterate fewer times. This is achieved by prefixing the length of the sequence with the < operator. You can also simply subtract 1, but using the < operator is more idiomatic.

You've already seen an example of manipulating sequences using the filter procedure. You can find more procedures that manipulate sequences in the system and sequtils modules.

2.3.3   Sets

The third collection type that I'll show you is the set type, which stores a collection of distinct values. A set[int16], for example, stores a distinct collection of integers. But because of the nature of sets, only unique numbers can be stored.

A Nim set's base type must be an ordinal type, which is a type with values that can be counted. The char type is ordinal because there's a clear order for its values: A is followed by B, B is followed by C, and so on. A string isn't an ordinal type because there's no clear order for a string's values.

This restriction only applies to the built-in set type. There's another set type in the sets module called HashSet that supports any type as its base type. But the built-in set type is more efficient and thus should be used whenever possible.

The set type is a value type and so doesn't need to be initialized.

```
var collection: set[int16]
assert collection == {}
```

A set is constructed using {}. A list of values is specified inside the curly brackets, and items are separated by commas.

A set pays no attention to the order of the items that it stores, so you can't access items in it via an index. Sets are useful for cases where you want to check for the presence of a certain value in a collection—this is where the in keyword comes in.

```
let collection = {'a', 'x', 'r'}
assert 'a' in collection
```

Although they're simple, sets can be used to perform some interesting checks.

```
let collection = {'a', 'T', 'z'}
let isAllLowerCase = {'A' .. 'Z'} * collection == {}
assert(not isAllLowerCase)
```

One of the operations that can be performed on sets is the intersection of two sets using the * operator. This returns a new set containing the values that the intersected sets have in common. The preceding example uses this to check whether the collection set contains any uppercase letters. A set constructor can contain ranges of items too: the range 'A' .. 'Z' is deduced by the compiler to contain all the uppercase letters.

Sets are often used in the standard library to represent a collection of unique flags. In other languages such as C, flags may be represented by an integer, which is interpreted as a sequence of Boolean bits. Compared to sets, this approach is very unsafe and often leads to errors.

I encourage you to experiment with these collection types to gain a deeper insight into how they work. You'll be using these types throughout the book and whenever you write Nim programs.

2.4 Control flow

There are many ways to control the flow of execution in Nim. The most common is the if statement, which you've already seen in action in section 2.1.

The if statement is a conditional statement: when its condition is true, its body is executed. Nim's if statement is similar to the if statement in other languages. It supports multiple "else if" blocks specified using the elif keyword and an "else" block using the else keyword.

```
if age > 0 and age <= 10:
  echo("You're still a child")
elif age > 10 and age < 18:
  echo("You're a teenager")
else:
  echo("You're an adult")
```

Switch statements are also supported, although in Nim they're known as `case` statements because they begin with the `case` keyword. They reduce repetition when you need to handle many different conditions.

```
case variable
of "Arthur", "Zaphod", "Ford":
  echo("Male")
of "Marvin":
  echo("Robot")
of "Trillian":
  echo("Female")
else:
  echo("Unknown")
```

Where the Nim `case` statement differs from the ones in other languages is in its lack of fall-through, which is the continuing execution of further case statements until a `break` keyword is used. Fall-through enables multiple values to match the same code block, but it usually requires a large number of `break` keywords to be used. Nim still allows multiple values to match the same code block, but it uses a different syntax.

An `of` branch in a `case` statement can contain a list of values to be matched, as well as a range, similar to the ranges used in set constructors. For example, matching every number from 0 to 9 can be done like this: `of 0 .. 9:`.

In Nim, every statement can be an expression. One case where this is useful is when you wish to assign a value depending on a condition:

```
let ageDesc = if age < 18: "Non-Adult" else: "Adult"
```

You can use the `case` statement as an expression in a similar way.

The flow of your program can also be controlled using loops. There are two looping statements in Nim. You've already seen examples of the `for` loop. There's also a `while` loop that you can use.

The `while` loop is the most basic of the looping statements. It consists of a condition that gets evaluated before each loop. If that condition is `true`, the loop continues.

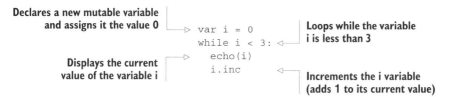

Declares a new mutable variable and assigns it the value 0

Displays the current value of the variable i

```
var i = 0
while i < 3:
  echo(i)
  i.inc
```

Loops while the variable i is less than 3

Increments the i variable (adds 1 to its current value)

This code would output the following:

```
0
1
2
```

Just like in other languages, the `continue` and `break` keywords allow you to control a loop. The `continue` keyword will skip the current iteration and restart from the top of the loop body. The `break` keyword will end the iteration.

You can also nest looping statements, and you may wonder how to break out of multiple loops at once. This can be solved by specifying a label for the break keyword. The label must be defined by the block keyword, and breaking to that label will cause the execution to break out of every loop inside that block.

```
                                   block label:
This loop will iterate forever.        var i = 0
                               └──▷  while true:                          Loops while variable i is less than 5
                                       while i < 5:    ◁─┘
Once i is greater than 3, jumps   ┌─▷    if i > 3: break label
out of the block named label │           i.inc              ◁────  Increments the variable i
                               ◁────  Execution will resume here once break label is called.
```

Another feature of the block keyword is that it introduces a new scope whenever it's used.

Nim supports the concept of iterators. These are similar to procedures, but they yield values to their caller multiple times, instead of returning just once. An iterator can be specified in a for statement, and it's then advanced after each iteration. The value that it yields is available in the body of the for statement.

```
iterator values(): int =
  var i = 0
  while i < 5:
    yield i
    i.inc

for value in values():
  echo(value)
```

The preceding example produces the following output:

```
0
1
2
3
4
```

There are many general iterators that work on sequences and other collection types, and there are also specific iterators like the walkFiles iterator, which, when given a pattern, iterates over the files in the current directory that match that pattern. For example, to find all the files ending with a .nim extension in the current directory, you'd do something like this:

```
                              Imports the os module that
                              defines the walkFiles iterator
                                                                    Iterates over each filename
import os              ◁─┘                                          with the .nim extension
for filename in walkFiles("*.nim"):                        ◁─┘
  echo(filename)            ◁────  Displays the filename during each iteration
```

The for loop in Nim is most similar to the one in Python, as shown in figure 2.2.

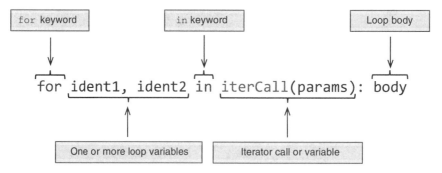

Figure 2.2   for loop syntax in Nim

In Python, you can iterate over any object that defines the __iter__ method, and this can be done implicitly without needing to call the __iter__ method in the for loop. Nim supports a similar mechanism:

```
for item in @[1, 2, 3]:
  echo(item)
```

Nim will implicitly call an iterator by the name of items. Which specific items iterator will be called depends on the type of the value specified after the in keyword; in this case it's seq[int].

   If an items iterator that matches the type can't be found, the compilation will fail with a type mismatch error, as in this example:

```
for i in 5:
  echo i
```

Here's the compilation output:

```
file.nim(1, 10) Error: type mismatch: got (int literal(5))
but expected one of:
system.items(a: array[IX, T])
system.items(E: typedesc[enum])
system.items(s: Slice[items.T])
system.items(a: seq[T])
system.items(a: openarray[T])
system.items(a: string)
system.items(a: set[T])
system.items(a: cstring)
```

The items iterator is only invoked when you specify one variable in the for loop; a pairs iterator is invoked for two variables. The values that the pairs iterator typically returns are the current iteration index and the current item at that index:

```
for i, value in @[1, 2, 3]: echo("Value at ", i, ": ", value)
```

The preceding code will produce this output:

```
Value at 0: 1
Value at 1: 2
Value at 2: 3
```

There's no default name for an iterator yielding three values or more.

2.5 Exception handling

Exceptions are yet another method for controlling flow. Raising an exception will cause the execution of a program to cease until the exception is caught or the program exits.

An exception is an object consisting of a message describing the error that occurred. A new exception is raised using the `raise` keyword. You can create new exceptions using the `newException` procedure.

Handling exceptions in Nim is very similar to Python. Exceptions are caught using a `try` statement, with one or more `except` branches specifying the exception type to be handled.

One of the most powerful features of Nim is its brilliant tracebacks. When an exception is raised and not caught, your program will display a stack traceback and quit.

Listing 2.10 Raising an exception

```
proc second() =
  raise newException(IOError, "Somebody set us up the bomb")

proc first() =
  second()

first()
```

The preceding code will produce the following output:

```
Traceback (most recent call last)
file.nim(7)              file
file.nim(5)              first
file.nim(2)              second
Error: unhandled exception: Somebody set us up the bomb [IOError]
```

A traceback gives you a list of events leading up to the crash of your program. It's a very useful debugging tool. Each line in the traceback is a call to a procedure. The number in parentheses is the line number where the call was made, and the name on the right is the procedure that was called.

These tracebacks will be your best friend throughout your time working with the Nim programming language.

In order to stop your program from crashing, you must handle the exceptions and decide what your program should do when these exceptions occur. You can handle exceptions by wrapping the affected code in a `try` statement. The top part of a `try` statement consists of the `try` keyword, followed by a colon, which is then followed by indented code. The bottom part of a `try` statement consists of one or more except branches—each except branch matches a specific exception that should be caught. If an except branch omits the exception type, then all exceptions are caught. When an exception is matched, the corresponding except branch's code is executed.

Listing 2.11 The `try` statements

```
try:
```
| Code statements that will
| be checked for exceptions

```
except ErrorType:
```
| Code statements that will be executed when the
| code under the try raises an ErrorType exception

```
except:
```
| Code statements that will be executed when the
| code under the try raises another type of exception

Let's rewrite listing 2.10 to handle the exception by using a `try` statement.

Listing 2.12 Handling an exception using a `try` statement

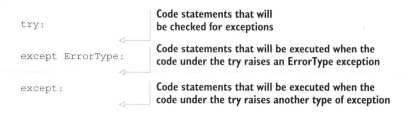

Raises a new IOError exception

```
proc second() =
  raise newException(IOError, "Somebody set us up the bomb")
```

The try statement will catch any exceptions raised in its body.

```
proc first() =
  try:
    second()
  except:
    echo("Cannot perform second action because: " &
      getCurrentExceptionMsg())

first()
```

Catches all exceptions

Returns the message of the exception that was just caught

Displays a message stating that the second action couldn't be performed and displaying the message of the exception that was caught

---

The exception is raised in the `second` procedure, but because it's called under the `try` statement, the exception is caught. The except branch is then executed, leading to the following output:

```
Cannot perform second action because: Somebody set us up the bomb
```

You should now know the basics of exception handling in Nim and be able to debug and handle simple exceptions on your own. Exceptions are a very important feature of the Nim programming language, and we'll continue to discuss them throughout this book.

2.6   *User-defined types*

The ability to define custom data structures is essential in many programming languages. Defining them in Nim is simple, and although they support some OOP features, their semantics don't unnecessarily bog you down in any OOP concepts.

Nim features three different kinds of user-defined types: objects, tuples, and enums. This section explains their main differences and use cases.

2.6.1   *Objects*

A basic object definition in Nim is equivalent to a C struct type and can be passed to C via the FFI. All types are defined under a `type` section. An object definition can be placed under the `type` keyword or alongside it. The definition starts with the name of the type, followed by =, the `object` keyword, a new line, and then an indented list of fields:

```
type
  Person = object
    name: string
    age: int
```

A `type` section can define multiple types, and you should collect related types under it. Just like procedures, types must be defined above the code in which they're used.

A variable utilizing the `Person` type can be declared just like any other variable:

```
var person: Person
```

You can initialize the `Person` type using the object construction syntax:

```
var person = Person(name: "Neo", age: 28)
```

You can specify all, some, or none of the fields. The type is an `object`, so its memory will be allocated on the stack. Data types that are stored on the stack can't be `nil` in Nim, so this extends to the `Person` type.

When you're defining a new variable, you can't change whether it's defined on the stack or on the heap. You must change the type definition itself. You can use the `ref object` keywords to define a data type that will live on the heap.

Types defined with the `ref` keyword are known as *reference types*. When an instance of a reference type is passed as a parameter to a procedure, instead of passing the underlying object by value, it's passed by reference. This allows you to modify the original data stored in the passed variable from inside your procedure. A non-`ref` type passed as a parameter to a procedure is immutable.

Listing 2.13   Mutable and immutable parameters

```
type
  PersonObj = object      ⊲──┐  When both non-ref and ref types are defined, the
    name: string               │  convention is to use an Obj suffix for the non-ref
    age: int                   │  name, and a Ref suffix for the ref name.
  PersonRef = ref PersonObj  ⊲───── In this case, you don't need to repeat the definition.
```

```
      proc setName(person: PersonObj) =
⊳       person.name = "George"

      proc setName(person: PersonRef) =
        person.name = "George"      ◁
```

This will work because
PersonRef is defined as a ref.

**This will fail. You can't modify a non-ref parameter
because it might have been copied before being passed to
the procedure. The parameter is said to be immutable.**

The preceding listing gives you a small taste of the behavior that `ref` and non-ref
types exhibit. It also introduces the syntax used to access the fields of an object and to
assign new values to these fields.

2.6.2   Tuples

Objects aren't the only way to define data types. Tuples are similar to objects, with the
key difference being that they use *structural typing*, whereas objects use *nominative typing*.

Nominative vs. structural typing

The key difference between nominative typing and structural typing is the way in which
equivalence of types is determined.

Consider the following example:

```
type
   Dog = object
      name: string

   Cat = object
      name: string

let dog: Dog = Dog(name: "Fluffy")
let cat: Cat = Cat(name: "Fluffy")

echo(dog == cat)          ◁
```

**Error: type mismatch:
got (Dog, Cat)**

The compiler gives an error because the `Dog` and `Cat` types aren't equivalent. That's
because they were defined separately with two different names.

Now let's replace the `object` with `tuple`:

```
type
   Dog = tuple
      name: string

   Cat = tuple
      name: string

let dog: Dog = (name: "Fluffy")
let cat: Cat = (name: "Fluffy")
echo(dog == cat)          ◁——— true
```

In this case, the compiler is happy to compile this code. The resulting executable displays the message "true," because the `dog` and `cat` variables contain the same data. The compiler doesn't look at the names of the type; instead, it looks at their structure to determine whether they're equivalent.

That's the fundamental difference between tuples and objects.

There are many different ways that tuples can be defined. The two most compact ways are shown here:

```
type
  Point = tuple[x, y: int]
  Point2 = (int, int)
```

You'll note that a tuple doesn't need to define the names of its fields. As long as the order and type of the values in two tuple types match, their types are considered to be the same.

```
let pos: Point = (x: 100, y: 50)
doAssert pos == (100, 50)
```

When a tuple's fields have no names, you can still access them by using the indexing operator: `[]`. When a name is defined, the fields can be accessed in the same way that object fields can be accessed.

Nim also supports *tuple unpacking*. A tuple's fields can be assigned directly to multiple identifiers. Here's an example:

```
let pos: Point = (x: 100, y: 50)
let (x, y) = pos
let (left, _) = pos
doAssert x == pos[0]
doAssert y == pos[1]
doAssert left == x
```

You can use a single underscore (_) in order to discard fields.

You can specify any name, as long as the number of fields on the left of the equals sign is the same as the number of fields in the tuple.

Tuples are useful for lightweight types with few fields. They're most commonly used as a way to return multiple values from procedures.

2.6.3 Enums

An enum or enumerated type is the third and final type that I'll introduce in this section. Nim enums are very similar to ANSI C's enums. An enum defines a collection of identifiers that have some meaning attached to them.

In Nim, enums have an order attached to them, which means they're ordinal types and can be used in `case` statements and as the base type of sets.

Listing 2.14   Enumerator type

```
type
  Color = enum
    colRed,
    colGreen,
    colBlue

let color: Color = colRed
```

Listing 2.14 defines a new `Color` enum. You'll note that when specifying the values, you don't need to prefix them with the name of the enum—I added a prefix to each value to make them a little bit more distinguishable. There's a pragma called `pure` that makes it mandatory to prefix each of the enum's values with the name of that enum, followed by a dot.

```
type
  Color {.pure.} = enum
    red, green, blue

let color = Color.red
```

Depending on your use case, you may wish to prefix the enum values manually with something that's shorter than the enum's name, or you can let Nim enforce the prefix automatically with the `pure` pragma.

Pragmas

Pragmas are language constructs that specify how a compiler should process its input. They're used in Nim fairly often, and depending on their type, they can be applied to the whole file or to a single definition.

You can also define your own pragmas using macros, which you'll learn more about in chapter 9.

For a list of pragmas, take a look at the Nim manual: http://nim-lang.org/docs/manual.html#pragmas.

Enums can be used to create a collection of meaningful identifiers; they're most commonly used to denote flags.

This section gave you a small taste of the different ways types can be defined in Nim. Nim's type system is very powerful, and this was by no means an extensive description of it all. You'll find out more about Nim's type system throughout this book. Chapter 9, in particular, will introduce you to generics, which are a very powerful feature of Nim's type system.

2.7 Summary

- Nim uses indentation to delimit scope and uses # for comments.
- The basic types include `int`, `float`, `char`, `string`, and `bool`.
- Mutable and immutable variables can be defined using the `var` and `let` keywords, respectively.
- A value assigned to a constant must be computable at compile time.
- Procedures are defined using the `proc` keyword.
- The `result` variable is implicitly defined in every procedure with a return type.
- An array stores a constant number of items.
- A sequence can grow dynamically at runtime.
- The flow of your application can be controlled via the `if` and `case` statements.
- One or more statements can be executed multiple times with the `while` statement.
- Collection types can be iterated through using the `for` statement.
- A `try` statement can be used to handle exceptions at runtime.
- Multiple different data types can be defined under a single `type` section.
- Non-reference types can't be modified from inside a procedure.
- Tuples can be used to return multiple values from a single procedure.

Part 2

Nim in practice

Now that you know the basics of Nim, you're ready to move on to writing some software.

In chapter 3, you'll be developing a simple but functional chat application. This chapter will mainly teach you about asynchronous sockets, but you'll also learn something about parsing and generating JSON, reading text from the standard input stream, and using Nim's module system.

Chapter 4 focuses on the standard library, showing you usage examples of various algorithms and data structures defined there. It also offers a more in-depth look at the module system.

Chapter 5 looks at package management, which is extremely common nowadays. Package managers are useful because they offer an easy way to install third-party libraries for use in your applications.

Chapter 6 is about parallelism. This is an important topic as it allows for some powerful optimizations, especially in today's multicore world. In this chapter we'll look at a parsing problem that's easy to parallelize. Different parsing methods are also demonstrated.

Chapter 7 leads you through the development of a significantly simplified Twitter clone. You'll learn how a web application is created using the Jester web framework, how HTML can be generated using Nim's filters, and how to store data in an SQLite database.

Writing a chat application

This chapter covers

- Asking the user for input
- Creating a command-line interface
- Parsing and generating JSON
- Transferring data over the network
- Using and creating modules

In the previous chapter, you learned the basics of the Nim programming language, including the syntax, some of the built-in types, how to define variables and procedures, how to use control-flow statements, and much more.

In this chapter, you'll build on and solidify that knowledge by developing a fully functional chat application. You'll also learn many new concepts that are essential to the development of certain applications. In particular, you'll do the following:

- Build a command-line interface, which can be used to ask the user for input.
- Learn how to use sockets to transfer data over networks, such as the internet.

- Use a JSON parser to build a simple chat protocol. The application will use this protocol to exchange messages in a standard and consistent manner.
- Learn how to use modules to separate your code into standalone units, which will make your code more reusable.

With the popularity of the internet, computer networks have become increasingly important. The most basic feature of the internet is the transfer of data, but implementing this feature isn't always easy at the programming language level. In creating this chapter's chat application, you'll learn the basics of transferring data between multiple computers.

By the end of this chapter, you'll have successfully written an application consisting of two different components: a server and a client. You'll be able to send the client to your friends and use it to chat with each other in real time over the internet.

The source code for all the examples in this book is available on GitHub at https://github.com/dom96/nim-in-action-code.

Let's begin by exploring how the application will work and what it will look like.

3.1   *The architecture of a chat application*

The main purpose of a chat application is to allow multiple people to communicate using their personal computers. One way to accomplish this is by using a network that these computers are connected to, like the internet, and sending data over it.

Unlike applications such as Facebook Messenger or WhatsApp, which are primarily used for one-to-one communication, the chat application developed in this chapter will primarily support group communication (many-to-many) similar to Internet Relay Chat (IRC) or Slack. This means that a single message will be sent to multiple users.

3.1.1   *What will the finished application look like?*

Let's say I just watched the latest *Game of Thrones* episode and am now excited to talk with my friends about it. I'll call them John and Grace, in case they don't appreciate me using their real names in this book. The conversation might go something like this (no *Game of Thrones* spoilers, I promise).

> **Listing 3.1   Conversation between me, John, and Grace about Game of Thrones**

```
Dominik said: What did you guys think about the latest Game of Thrones
episode?
Grace said: I thought Tyrion was really great in it!
John said: I agree with Grace. Tyrion deserves an Emmy for his performance.
```

At the end of this chapter, you'll have built an application that will allow this discussion to take place. Let's see what the finished application will look like in the context of the preceding conversation.

Figure 3.1   My screen after I send the message

I first asked John and Grace what they thought of the latest *Game of Thrones* episode. I did this by entering my message into the chat application and pressing the Enter key to send it (figure 3.1).

Both John and Grace will receive this message on their computers, and the client application will show it to both of them in the same way (figure 3.2). Note how my message is prefixed by "Dominik said," letting John and Grace know who sent the message.

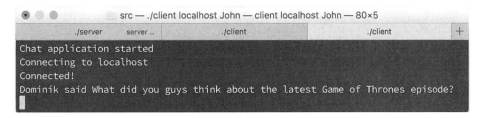

Figure 3.2   John's and Grace's screens

Grace can now answer my question by typing in her response and pressing Enter; John and I will receive her reply. This way, we can have a discussion over the internet relatively easily.

This should give you an idea of what you're aiming to achieve by the end of this chapter. Sure, it might not be as impressive as a full-blown application with a graphical user interface, but it's a start.

Now let's move on to discussing some of the basic aspects of this application, in particular, its network architecture.

NETWORK ARCHITECTURES AND MODELS

There are two primary network architectures that can be used for this application: peer-to-peer networking and the client-server model. With peer-to-peer networking, there's no server; instead, each client is connected to multiple other clients that then exchange information between each other. With the client-server model, there's a single server to which all the clients connect. The messages are all sent to the server, and the server redistributes them to the correct clients. Figure 3.3 shows how these models compare.

The client-server model is the simpler of the two, and because it works well for the kind of application that you'll be writing, we'll use it.

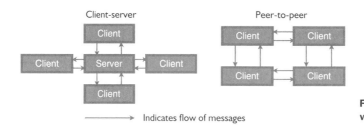

Figure 3.3   **Client-server vs. peer-to-peer**

Another thing to consider is the transport protocol, which you'll use to transfer messages in your application. The two major protocols in use today are TCP and UDP. They're used widely for many different types of applications, but they differ in two important ways.

The most important feature of TCP is that it ensures that messages are delivered to their destination. Extra information is sent along with the messages to verify that they have been delivered correctly, but this comes at the cost of some performance.

UDP doesn't do this. With UDP, data is sent rapidly, and the protocol doesn't check whether the data arrives at its destination. This makes UDP perform better than TCP, but data transmission is less reliable.

Chat applications should be efficient, but reliable delivery of messages is more important. Based on this aspect alone, TCP wins.

> **NETWORKING**   There's a vast amount of information about networking that's outside the scope of this book. I encourage you to research this topic further if it's of interest to you.

THE CLIENT AND SERVER COMPONENTS

Now that you know a bit about the networking side of things, let's look at how the software will actually work. The plan is to create two separate applications, or *components*: a server component and a client component.

When the server first starts, it will begin listening for connections from a client on a specific port. The port will be hardcoded into the server and chosen ahead of time so it won't conflict with any other application. I wouldn't want it to prevent you from enjoying a good game of Counter-Strike, would I? Once a connection on that port is detected, the server will accept it and wait for messages from it. A newly received message will be sent to any other client whose connection was previously accepted by the server.

When the client first starts, it will connect to the server address that the user specified on the command line. Once it successfully connects, the user of the client will be able to send messages to the server by inputting them through the command line. The client will also actively listen for messages from the server, and once a message is received, it will be displayed to the user.

Figure 3.4 shows how the chat application operates in a simple use case involving three clients. Dom, John, and Grace are all running clients connected to the server. In the figure, Dom sends a "Hello" message using their client. The server will accept this message and pass it on to other clients currently connected to it.

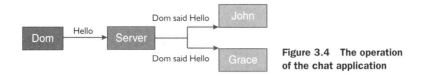

Figure 3.4 The operation of the chat application

You should now have a good idea of how the chat application will work. The next section will show you how to implement it.

3.2 *Starting the project*

The previous section outlined how the chat application will work. This section describes the first steps needed to begin the project. This chapter is an exercise, and I encourage you to follow along, developing the application as you read it.

You might find this surprising, but starting a project in Nim is very quick and easy. You can simply open your favorite text editor, create a new file, and start coding.

But before you do that, you should decide on a directory layout for your project. This is entirely optional—the compiler won't mind if you save all your code in C:\code, but doing so is bad practice. You should ideally create a new directory just for this project, such as C:\code\ChatApp (or ~/code/ChatApp). Inside the project directory, create a src directory to store all your source code. In the future you can, when necessary, create other directories such as tests, images, docs, and more. Most Nim projects are laid out this way, as illustrated in the following listing. This project is small, so it will only use the src directory for now.

Listing 3.2 Typical directory layout for a Nim project

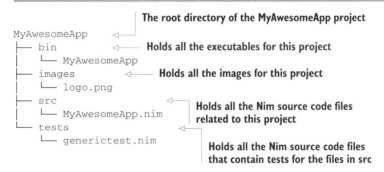

PROJECT DIRECTORY LAYOUT A good project directory layout is very beneficial, especially for large applications. It's better to set it up sooner rather than later. Separating your application source code from your tests means that you can easily write test code that doesn't conflict or otherwise affect your application. In general, this separation also makes code navigation easier.

Now create a client.nim file in the src directory. This file will compile into a `client` executable and act as the client component of the chat application. You're now ready to start writing code.

As a small test, begin by writing the following into your new client.nim file, and then save it:

```
echo("Chat application started")
```

To compile your new client.nim file, follow these steps.

1. Open a new terminal window.
2. cd into your project directory by executing `cd ~/code/ChatApp`, replacing `~/code/ChatApp` with the path to your project directory.
3. Compile the client.nim file by executing `nim c src/client.nim`.

APORIA If you're using Aporia, you can just press F4 or select Tools > Compile Current File in the menu bar to compile the currently selected tab. You can also press F5 to compile and run.

If you've done everything correctly, you should see the results shown in figure 3.5 in your terminal window.

OUTPUT DIRECTORY By default, the Nim compiler will produce the executable beside the Nim source code file that was compiled. You can use the `-o` flag to change this. For example, `nim c -o:chat src/client.nim` will place a `chat` executable in the current directory.

Assuming that the compilation was successful, the executable that was created by the compiler can now be started. To execute it, use the `./src/client` command, or `.\src\client.exe` if you're on Windows. This should display "Chat application started" on the screen and then exit.

You now have a good starting point for further development. We started out slowly, and so far your application isn't doing much. But it gives you an idea of how application development in Nim should be initiated, and it ensures that the Nim compiler works correctly on your computer.

Now that you've made a start on this project, let's move on to the first task: the command-line interface.

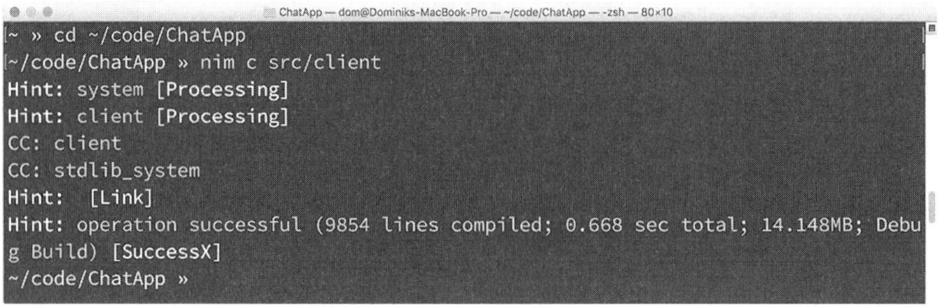
ChatApp — dom@Dominiks-MacBook-Pro — ~/code/ChatApp — -zsh — 80×10
~ » cd ~/code/ChatApp
~/code/ChatApp » nim c src/client
Hint: system [Processing]
Hint: client [Processing]
CC: client
CC: stdlib_system
Hint: [Link]
Hint: operation successful (9854 lines compiled; 0.668 sec total; 14.148MB; Debug Build) [SuccessX]
~/code/ChatApp »

Figure 3.5 Successful compilation of client.nim

3.3 Retrieving input in the client component

Applications typically expect to receive some sort of guidance from the user, such as the URL of a website to navigate to or the filename of a video to play. Applications need this guidance because, sadly, they can't (yet) read our intentions directly from our brains. They need explicit instructions in the form of commands or mouse clicks. The simplest way to guide a piece of software is to give it an explicit command.

The client component of the chat application will need the following input: the address of the server to send messages to and one or more messages to send to the server. These are the minimum inputs the user will need to provide to the chat application. You need both a way to ask the user for specific input and a way to then get the data that the user enters using their keyboard.

Let's focus on the minimum data that we need from the user. The address of the server to connect to is somewhat critical, because it's needed before the client can do anything. We should ask the user for it as soon as the client starts. Until the client connects to the server, the user won't be able to send any messages, so asking the user for a message will come after.

3.3.1 Retrieving command-line parameters supplied by the user

On the command line, there are two ways you can get data from the user:

- Through command-line parameters, which are passed to your application when it's started
- Through the standard input stream, which can be read from at any time

Typically, a piece of information such as the server address would be passed to an application through command-line parameters, because the server address needs to be known when the application starts.

In Nim, command-line parameters can be accessed via the `paramStr` procedure defined in the `os` module. But before this procedure can be used, it must be imported. Let's extend client.nim so that it reads the first command-line parameter. Code additions are shown in bold.

Listing 3.3 Reading command-line parameters

This is required in order to use the paramCount and paramStr procedures defined in the os module.

Ensures that the user has specified a parameter on the command line

Stops the application prematurely because it can't continue without that parameter

```
import os
echo("Chat application started")
if paramCount() == 0:
  quit("Please specify the server address, e.g. ./client localhost")

let serverAddr = paramStr(1)
echo("Connecting to ", serverAddr)
```

Retrieves the first parameter that the user specified and assigns it to the new serverAddr variable

Displays the message "Connecting to <serverAddr>" to the user, where <serverAddr> is the address the user specified

It's always important to check the number of parameters supplied to your executable. The `paramCount` procedure returns the number of parameters as an integer. The preceding example checks whether the number of parameters is 0, and if so, it calls the `quit` procedure with a detailed message of why the application is exiting. If supplied with a message, `quit` first displays that message and then quits with an exit code that tells the OS that the application failed.

When the user does supply the command-line parameter, the `paramStr` procedure is used to retrieve the first parameter supplied. An index of 1 is used because the executable name is stored at an index of 0. The first command-line parameter is then bound to the `serverAddr` variable.

> **WARNING: EXECUTABLE NAME** Don't retrieve the executable name via `paramStr(0)`, as it may give you OS-specific data that's not portable. The `getAppFilename` procedure defined in the `os` module should be used instead.

> **WARNING: ALWAYS USE PARAMCOUNT** When accessing a parameter with `paramStr` that doesn't exist (for example, `paramStr(56)` when `paramCount()` `== 1`), an `IndexError` exception is raised. You should always use `paramCount` ahead of time to check the number of parameters that have been supplied.

The last line in listing 3.3 uses the `echo` procedure to display the string `"Connecting to "` appended to the contents of the `serverAddr` variable on the screen. The `echo` procedure accepts a variable number of arguments and displays each of them on the same line.

> **PARSING COMMAND-LINE PARAMETERS** Applications typically implement a special syntax for command-line arguments. This syntax includes flags such as `--help`. The `parseopt` module included in Nim's standard library allows these parameters to be parsed. There are also other, more intuitive packages created by the Nim community for retrieving and parsing command-line parameters.

Recompile your new client.nim module as you did in the previous section, and execute it as you did previously. As you can see in figure 3.6, the application will exit immediately with the message "Please specify the server address, e.g. ./client localhost."

Now, execute it with a single parameter, as shown in the message: `src/client localhost`. Figure 3.7 shows that the application now displays the message "Connecting to localhost."

Now, try specifying different parameters and see what results you get. No matter how many parameters you type, as long as there's at least one, the message will always consist of `"Connecting to "` followed by the first parameter that you specified.

Figure 3.8 shows how the command-line parameters map to different `paramStr` indexes.

Now that the client successfully captures the server address, it knows which server to connect to. You now need to think about asking the user for the messagethat they want to send.

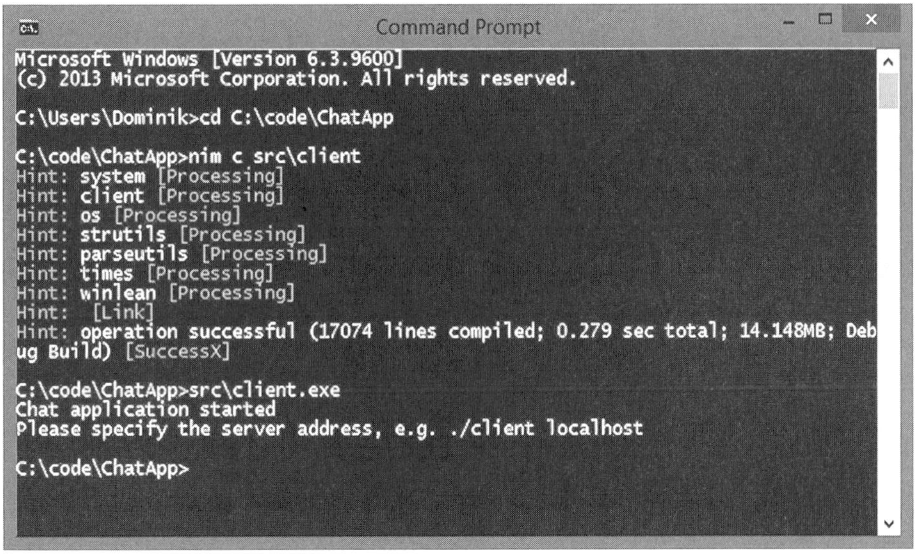

Figure 3.6   Starting the client without any parameters

Figure 3.7   Starting the client with one parameter

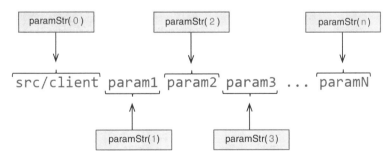

Figure 3.8   The supplied command-line parameters and how to access them

3.3.2   *Reading data from the standard input stream*

Unlike the command-line parameters, which are passed to the application before it starts, messages are provided by the user in real time, in response to messages they receive from other users. This means that the application should ideally always be ready to read data from the user.

When an application is running inside of a terminal or command line, characters can be typed in the terminal window. These characters can be retrieved by the application through the standard input stream. Just like in Python, the standard input stream can be accessed via the `stdin` variable. In Nim, this variable is defined in the implicitly imported `system` module, and it's of type `File`, so the standard input stream can be read from just like any other `File` object. Many procedures are defined for reading data from a `File` object. Typically, the most useful is `readLine`, which reads a single line of data from the specified `File`.

Add the following code to the bottom of client.nim, and then recompile and run it (you can do so quickly with the following command: `nim c -r src/client.nim localhost`).

Listing 3.4   Reading from the standard input stream

```
let message = stdin.readLine()
echo("Sending \"", message, "\"")
```

Reads a single line of text from the standard input stream and assigns it to the message variable.

Displays the message "Sending "<message>"," where <message> is the content of the message variable, which contains the line of text the user typed into their terminal window

CHARACTER ESCAPE SEQUENCES   The last line in listing 3.4 uses a character-escape sequence to show the double quote (`"`) character. This needs to be escaped because the compiler would otherwise think that the string literal has ended.

You'll see that your application no longer exits immediately. Instead, it waits for you to type something into the terminal window and press Enter. Once you do so, a message is displayed with the text that you typed into the terminal window.

Reading from the standard input stream will cause your application to stop executing—your application transitions into a *blocked* state. The execution will resume once the requested data is fully read. In the case of `stdin.readLine`, the application remains blocked until the user inputs some characters into the terminal and presses Enter. When the user performs those actions, they're essentially storing a line of text into the `stdin` buffer.

Blocking is an unfortunate side effect of most input/output (I/O) calls. It means that, sadly, your application won't be able to do any useful work while it's waiting for the user's input. This is a problem, because this application will need to actively stay connected to the chat server, something it won't be able to do if it's waiting for the user to type text into the terminal window. Figure 3.9 shows the problem that this causes.

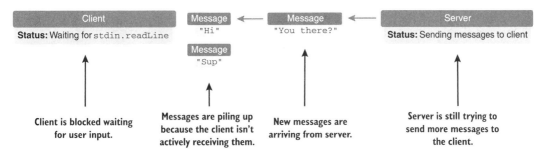

Figure 3.9 Problem caused by the client being blocked indefinitely

Before we move on to solving that problem, there's something missing from listing 3.4. The code only reads the message once, but the aim is to allow the user to send multiple messages. Fixing this is relatively simple. You just need to introduce an infinite loop using the `while` statement. Simply wrap the code in listing 3.4 in a `while` statement as follows:

```
while true:
    let message = stdin.readLine()
    echo("Sending \"", message, "\"")
```

These two lines will be repeated an infinite number of times because they're indented under the while statement.

The while statement will repeat the statements in its body as long as its condition is true. In this case, it will repeat the following two statements until the application is closed manually by the user.

Now compile and run your code again to see for yourself what the result is. You should be able to input as many lines of text as you wish into the terminal window, until you terminate your application by pressing Ctrl-C.

When you terminate your application, you should see a traceback similar to the following:

```
Traceback (most recent call last)
client.nim(9)           client
sysio.nim(115)          readLine
sysio.nim(72)           raiseEIO
system.nim(2531)        sysFatal
SIGINT: Interrupted by Ctrl-C.
```

Terminating your application is a very good way to determine which line of code is currently being executed. In the traceback, you can see that when the application was terminated, line 9 in client.nim was being executed. This corresponds to `let message = stdin.readLine()`, which is the blocking `readLine` call that waits for input from the user.

Figure 3.10 shows the current flow of execution in client.nim. The main thread is blocked as it waits for input from the user. As a result, the application will sit

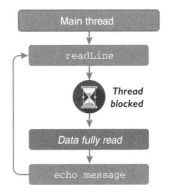

Figure 3.10 Blocking execution of client.nim

idle until the user wakes it up by typing some text into the terminal window and pressing Enter.

This is an inherent issue with blocking I/O operations. You wouldn't need to worry about it if the client only needed to react to the user's input, but, unfortunately, the client must keep a persistent connection to the server in order to receive messages from other clients.

3.3.3   *Using spawn to avoid blocking input/output*

There are a number of ways to ensure that your application doesn't block when it reads data from the standard input stream.

One is to use *asynchronous input/output*, which allows the application to continue execution even if the result isn't immediately available. Unfortunately, the standard input stream can't be read asynchronously in Nim, so asynchronous I/O can't be used here. It will be used later, when it's time to transfer data over a network.

The other solution is to create another thread that will read the standard input stream, keeping the main thread unblocked and free to perform other tasks. Every process consists of at least one thread known as the *main thread*—all of the code in client .nim is currently executed in this main thread. The main thread becomes blocked when the call to readLine is made, and it becomes unblocked when the user inputs a single line into the terminal. But a separate thread can be created to make the call to read-Line, in order to leave the main thread active. The newly created thread is the one that becomes blocked. This approach of using two threads is called *parallelism*. We won't look at the full details of parallelism and how it works in Nim in this chapter, but we'll discuss it in chapter 6.

A procedure can be executed in a new thread using the spawn procedure. Replace the while statement that you created previously with the following one, but don't compile the code just yet:

```
while true:
  let message = spawn stdin.readLine()
  echo("Sending \"", ^message, "\"")
```

The spawn keyword is used to call the readLine procedure. This will spawn a new thread and execute readLine there.

The value returned from the thread isn't immediately available, so you must read it explicitly with the ^ operator.

The readLine procedure returns a string value, but when this procedure is executed in another thread, its return value isn't immediately available. To deal with this, spawn returns a special type called FlowVar[T], which holds the value that the procedure you spawned returns.

The ^ operator can be used to retrieve the value from a FlowVar[T] object, but there's no value until the spawned procedure returns one. When the FlowVar[T] object is empty, the ^ operator will block the current thread until a value has been stored. If it's not empty in the first place, the ^ operator will return immediately with the value. That's why the preceding code will behave much like the code in listing 3.4.

You can also check whether a `FlowVar[T]` type contains a value by using the `isReady` procedure. You can use that procedure to avoid blocking behavior.

See figure 3.11 to see how the two different threads interact with each other. Compare it to figure 3.10 to see how the execution of the `client` changed after the introduction of `spawn`.

There's now a secondary `readLine` thread, but the result is the same. Both the main thread and the `readLine` thread become blocked, creating the same results.

Generics

Generics are a feature of Nim that you'll be introduced to in full detail in chapter 9. For now, all you need to know is that `FlowVar[T]` is a generic type that can store values of any type. The type of the value that's stored is specified in the square brackets.

For example, the `spawn stdin.readLine()` expression returns a `FlowVar[string]` type because the return type of `readLine` is a `string`, and `FlowVar` wraps the return value of the spawned procedure.

Applying the `spawn` call to any procedure that returns a `string` will return a `FlowVar[string]` value:

```
import threadpool
proc foo: string = "Dog"
var x: FlowVar[string] = spawn foo()
assert(^x == "Dog")
```

To successfully compile the preceding example, make sure you use the `--threads:on` flag.

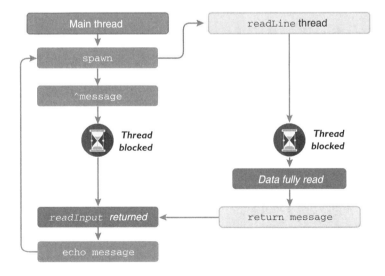

Figure 3.11 Blocking execution of client.nim with **spawn**

Listing 3.5 shows how you can modify client.nim to use `spawn`, with the changed lines in bold. One key point to note is that the `spawn` procedure is defined in the `threadpool` module, so you must remember to import it via `import threadpool`.

Listing 3.5 Spawning `readLine` in a new thread

```
import os, threadpool

echo("Chat application started")
if paramCount() == 0:
  quit("Please specify the server address, e.g. ./client localhost")
let serverAddr = paramStr(1)
echo("Connecting to ", serverAddr)
while true:
  let message = spawn stdin.readLine()
  echo("Sending \"", ^message, "\"")
```

Compilation now requires the `--threads:on` flag to enable Nim's threading support. Without it, `spawn` can't function. To compile and run the client.nim file, you should now be executing `nim c -r --threads:on src/client.nim localhost`.

> **NIM CONFIG FILES** Flags such as `--threads:on` can accumulate quickly, but the Nim compiler supports config files, which save you from having to retype all these flags on the command line. Simply create a client.nims file (beside the client.nim file) and add `--threads:on` there. Each flag needs to be on its own line, so you can add extra flags by separating them with newlines. To learn more about this configuration system, see the NimScript page: https://nim-lang.org/docs/nims.html.

The `client` application still functions the same way as before, but the changes to the code that reads the standard input stream will be useful later on in this chapter.

In the next section, I'll show you how to add asynchronous networking code, allowing the client application to connect to the server. The server itself will use the same asynchronous I/O approach to communicate with more than one client at a time.

You've now seen how to read input from the user in two different ways: from command-line parameters and from the standard input stream while your application is running. You also learned about the problem of blocking I/O, and I showed you one way to solve it. Now let's move on to writing the protocol for your chat application.

3.4   *Implementing the protocol*

Every application that communicates over a network with another application needs to define a protocol for that communication to ensure that the two applications can understand each other. A protocol is similar to a language—it's a standard that's mostly consistent and that can be understood by both of the communicating parties. Imagine trying to communicate in English with somebody who can speak only Chinese. As in figure 3.12, you won't understand them, and they won't understand you. Similarly, the

Figure 3.12 Good and bad protocols

different components in your application must use the same language to understand each other.

It's important to remember that even if protocols are well defined, there's still plenty of room for error, such as if the message isn't transmitted correctly. This is why it's vital that the code that parses messages can handle incorrectly formatted messages, or messages that don't contain the necessary data. The code that I'll show you in this section won't go to great lengths to verify the validity of the messages it receives. But I will encourage you later on to add exception-handling code to verify the validity of messages and to provide the users of your code with better exception messages.

Code that parses and generates a message is easy to test, so in this section, I'll also show you some basic ways to test your code.

The chat application's protocol will be a simple one. The information that it will transfer between clients consists of two parts: the message that the user wants to send to the other clients, and the user's name. There are many ways that this information could be encoded, but one of the simplest is to encode it as a JSON object. That's what I'll show you how to do.

3.4.1 Modules

You've already seen many examples of modules, but I haven't yet explained precisely what a module is. Your client.nim file is itself a module, and you've also imported modules from Nim's standard library into your code using the `import` keyword. The upcoming message parser should ideally be written in a separate module, so it's a good practical example to use as I teach you about modules.

Many programming languages today utilize a module system. Nim's module system is rather simple: every file ending with a .nim extension is a module. As long as the compiler can find the file, then it can be successfully imported.

A module system allows you to separate the functionality of your application into independent modules. One advantage of this is that modules are interchangeable. As long as the interface of the module remains the same, the underlying implementation can be changed. Later on, you can easily use something other than JSON to encode the messages.

By default, everything you define in a module is private, which means that it can only be accessed inside that module. Private definitions ensure that the implementation details of modules are hidden, whereas public definitions are exposed to other modules. In some languages, the `public` and `private` keywords are used to specify the visibility of a definition.[1]

In Nim, each definition is private by default. You can make a definition public by using the `*` operator. The `*` can be placed at the end of procedure names, variable names, method names, and field names.

The basics of the module system should be easy to grasp. There are some extra things to be aware of, but this should be enough to get you started writing simple modules. Chapter 4 looks at modules in more depth.

To create a module for your new message parser, simply create a new file named protocol.nim in the src directory beside the client.nim file.

Listing 3.6 shows the definition of the `Message` type, which will store the two pieces of information that a message from the server contains: the username of the client and the actual message. Both of these definitions are exported using the `*` marker.

At the end, the `parseMessage` procedure is defined. It takes in a `data` parameter that contains the raw string received from a server. The `parseMessage` procedure then returns a new `Message` object containing the parsed data. This procedure is also exported, and together with the `Message` type it forms the public interface of the `protocol` module.

Listing 3.6   Message type definition and proc stub

```
type
  Message* = object              Defines a new Message type. The * export
    username*: string            marker is placed after the name of the type.
    message*: string
                                 Field definitions follow the type definition
                                 and are exported in a similar way.

proc parseMessage*(data: string): Message =
  discard

Defines a new parseMessage           The discard is necessary
procedure. The export marker is      because the body of a procedure
also used to export it.              can't be empty.
```

Add the code in listing 3.6 to the `protocol` module you created, and make sure it compiles with `nim c src/protocol`.

Now, let's move on to implementing the `parseMessage` procedure.

3.4.2   Parsing JSON

JSON is a very simple data format. It's widely used, and Nim's standard library has support for both parsing and generating it. This makes JSON a good candidate for storing the two message fields.

A typical JSON object contains multiple fields. The field names are simple quoted strings, and the values can be integers, floats, strings, arrays, or other objects.

---

[1] In particular, C++ and Java use the `public` and `private` keywords to denote the visibility of identifiers.

Let's look back to the conversation about *Game of Thrones* in listing 3.1. One of the first messages that I sent was, "What did you guys think about the latest *Game of Thrones* episode?" This can be represented using JSON like so.

Listing 3.7 A representation of a message in JSON

The curly brackets define an object.

The username field with the corresponding value

```
{
  "username": "Dominik",
  "message": "What did you guys think about the latest Game of Thrones
     episode?"
}
```

The message field with the corresponding value

Parsing JSON is very easy in Nim. First, import the `json` module by adding `import json` to the top of your file. Then, replace the `discard` statement in the `parseMessage` proc with `let dataJson = parseJson(data)`. The next listing shows the `protocol` module with the additions in bold.

Listing 3.8 Parsing JSON in protocol.nim

```
import json
type
  Message* = object
    username*: string
    message*: string

proc parseMessage*(data: string): Message =
  let dataJson = parseJson(data)
```

The `parseJson` procedure defined in the `json` module accepts a string and returns a value of the `JsonNode` type.

`JsonNode` is a variant type. This means that which fields in the object can be accessed is determined by the value of one or more other fields that are always defined in that type. In the case of `JsonNode`, the `kind` field determines the kind of JSON node that was parsed.

There are seven different kinds of JSON values. The `JsonNodeKind` type is an enum with a value for each kind of JSON value. The following listing shows a list of various JSON values together with the `JsonNodeKind` types that they map to.

Listing 3.9 The mapping between JSON values and the `JsonNodeKind` type

```
import json
assert parseJson("null").kind == JNull
assert parseJson("true").kind == JBool
assert parseJson("42").kind == JInt
assert parseJson("3.14").kind == JFloat
assert parseJson("\"Hi\"").kind == JString
assert parseJson("""{ "key": "value" }""").kind == JObject
assert parseJson("[1, 2, 3, 4]").kind == JArray
```

A little information about variant types

A *variant type* is an object type whose fields change depending on the value of one or more fields. An example will make this clearer:

A variant type is defined much like other object types.

```
type
  Box = object
    case empty: bool
    of false:
      contents: string
    else:
      discard
```

The difference is the case statement under the definition of the object. This defines an empty field in this type.

If the empty field is false, the fields defined under this branch will be accessible.

The contents field will be accessible if empty == false.

No additional fields are defined if empty == true.

```
var obj = Box(empty: false, contents: "Hello")
assert obj.contents == "Hello"

var obj2 = Box(empty: true)
echo(obj2.contents)
```

When the empty field is set to false in the constructor, the contents field can also be specified.

This will result in an error because the contents field can't be accessed, because empty is true.

Because obj.empty is false, the contents field can be accessed.

The preceding code shows how an ordinary box that may be empty can be modeled. The end of the listing shows an erroneous case where the contents of an empty box are accessed. It should be no surprise that compiling and running that code will result in an error:

```
Traceback (most recent call last)
variant.nim(13)         variant
system.nim(2533)        sysFatal
Error: unhandled exception: contents is not accessible [FieldError]
```

This is a very simple variant type with only two states. You can also use enum types in the case statement of a variant type. This is common and is used in the Json-Node type.

When you're parsing arbitrary JSON data, a variant type is required because the compiler has no way of knowing at compile time what the resulting JSON type should be. The type is only known at runtime. This is why the parseJson procedure returns a JsonNode type whose contents differ depending on the kind of JSON value that was passed into it.

The last two JSON values shown in listing 3.9 are collections. The JObject kind represents a mapping between a string and a JsonNode. The JArray kind stores a list of JsonNodes.

You can access the fields of a JObject by using the [] operator. It's similar to the array and sequence [] operator but takes a string as its argument. The string determines the field whose value you want to retrieve from the JObject. The [] operator returns a JsonNode value.

```
import json
let data = """
  {"username": "Dominik"}
"""

let obj = parseJson(data)
assert obj.kind == JObject
assert obj["username"].kind == JString
assert obj["username"].str == "Dominik"
```

Parses the data string and returns a JsonNode type, which is then assigned to the obj variable

The returned JsonNode has a JObject kind because that's the kind of the JSON contained in the data string.

Because the [] operator returns a JsonNode, the value that it contains must be accessed explicitly via the field that contains it. In JString's case, this is str. Generally you're better off using the getStr proc.

Fields are accessed using the [] operator. It returns another JsonNode, and in this case its kind is a JString.

> **WARNING: THE KIND MATTERS** Calling the [] operator with a string on a Json-Node whose kind field isn't JObject will result in an exception being raised.

So, how can you retrieve the username field from the parsed JsonNode? Simply using dataJson["username"] will return another JsonNode, unless the username field doesn't exist in the parsed JObject, in which case a KeyError exception will be raised. In the preceding code, the JsonNode kind that dataJson["username"] returns is JString because that field holds a string value, so you can retrieve the string value using the getStr procedure. There's a get procedure for each of the JsonNode kinds, and each get procedure will return a default value if the type of the value it's meant to be returning doesn't match the JsonNode kind.

> **THE DEFAULT VALUE FOR GET PROCEDURES** The default value returned by the get procedures can be overridden. To override, pass the value you want to be returned by default as the second argument to the procedure; for example, node.getStr("Bad kind").

Once you have the username, you can assign it to a new instance of the Message type. The next listing shows the full protocol module with the newly added assignments in bold.

Listing 3.10 Assigning parsed data to the `result` variable

```
import json
type
  Message* = object
    username*: string
    message*: string

proc parseMessage*(data: string): Message =
  let dataJson = parseJson(data)
  result.username = dataJson["username"].getStr()
  result.message = dataJson["message"].getStr()
```

Gets the value under the "username" key and assigns its string value to the username field of the resulting Message

Does the same here, but instead gets the value under the "message" key

Just add two lines of code, and you're done.

> ### The magical result variable
>
> You may be wondering where the `result` variable comes from in listing 3.10. The answer is that Nim implicitly defines it for you. This `result` variable is defined in all procedures that are defined with a return type:
>
> ```
> proc count10(): int =
>   for i in 0 .. <10:
>     result.inc
> assert count10() == 10
> ```
>
> **The < operator subtracts 1 from its input, so it returns 9 here.**
>
> This means that you don't need to repeatedly define a `result` variable, nor do you need to return it. The `result` variable is automatically returned for you. Take a look back at section 2.2.3 for more info.

You should test your code as quickly and as often as you can. You could do so now by starting to integrate your new module with the client module, but it's much better to test code as separate units. The protocol module is a good unit of code to test in isolation.

When testing a module, it's always good to test each of the exported procedures to ensure that they work as expected. The protocol module currently exports only one procedure—the `parseMessage` procedure—so you only need to write tests for it.

There are multiple ways to test code in Nim, but the simplest is to use the `doAssert` procedure, which is defined in the `system` module. It's similar to the `assert` procedure: it takes one argument of type `boolean` and raises an `AssertionFailed` exception if the value of that `boolean` is `false`. It differs from `assert` in one simple way: `assert` statements are optimized out when you compile your application in release mode (via the `-d:release` flag), whereas `doAssert` statements are not.

RELEASE MODE By default, the Nim compiler compiles your application in debug mode. In this mode, your application runs a bit slower but performs checks that give you more information about bugs that you may have accidentally introduced into your program. When deploying your application, you should compile it with the `-d:release` flag, which puts it in release mode and provides optimal performance.

Let's define an input and then use `doAssert` to test `parseMessage`'s output.

Listing 3.11   Testing your new functionality

The when statement is a compile-time if statement that only includes the code under it if its condition is true. The isMainModule constant is true when the current module hasn't been imported. The result is that the test code is hidden if this module is imported.

Begins a new scope (useful for isolating your tests)

```
when isMainModule:
  block:
```

```
let data = """{"username": "John", "message": "Hi!"}"""
let parsed = parseMessage(data)
  doAssert parsed.username == "John"
  doAssert parsed.message == "Hi!"
```

**Calls the parseMessage procedure
on the data defined previously**

**Checks that the username that
parseMessage parsed is correct**

**Checks that the message that
parseMessage parsed is correct**

**Uses the triple-quoted string literal syntax to define the data
to be parsed. The triple-quoted string literal means that the
single quote in the JSON doesn't need to be escaped.**

Add the code in listing 3.11 to the bottom of your file, and then compile and run your code. Your program should execute successfully with no output.

This is all well and good, but it would be nice to get some sort of message letting you know that the tests succeeded, so you can just add echo("All tests passed!") to the bottom of the when isMainModule block. Your program should now output that message as long as all the tests pass.

Try changing one of the asserts to check for a different output, and observe what happens. For example, removing the exclamation mark from the doAssert parsed.message == "Hi!" statement will result in the following error:

```
Traceback (most recent call last)
protocol.nim(17) protocol
system.nim(3335) raiseAssert
system.nim(2531) sysFatal
Error: unhandled exception: parsed.message == "Hi"  [AssertionError]
```

If you modify the protocol module and break your test, you may find that suddenly you'll get such an error.

You now have a test for the correct input, but what about incorrect input? Create another test to see what happens when the input is incorrect:

```
block:
  let data = """foobar"""
  let parsed = parseMessage(data)
```

Compile and run protocol.nim, and you should get the following output:

```
Traceback (most recent call last)
protocol.nim(21) protocol_progress
protocol.nim(8)  parseMessage
json.nim(1086)   parseJson
json.nim(1082)   parseJson
json.nim(1072)   parseJson
json.nim(561)    raiseParseErr
Error: unhandled exception: input(1, 5) Error: { expected [JsonParsingError]
```

An exception is raised by `parseJson` because the specified data isn't valid JSON. But this is what should happen, so define that in the test by catching the exception and making sure that an exception has been raised.

```
block:
  let data = """foobar"""
  try:
    let parsed = parseMessage(data)
    doAssert false
  except JsonParsingError:
    doAssert true
  except:
    doAssert false
```

This line should never be executed because parseMessage will raise an exception.

Make sure that the exception that's thrown is the expected one.

An ideal way for the `parseMessage` proc to report errors would be by raising a custom exception. But this is beyond the scope of this chapter. I encourage you to come back and implement it once you've learned how to do so. For now, let's move on to generating JSON.

3.4.3   *Generating JSON*

You successfully parsed the JSON, so let's move on to generating JSON. The protocol module needs to be capable of both parsing and generating messages. Generating JSON is even simpler than parsing it.

In Nim, JSON can be generated in multiple ways. One way is to simply create a string containing the correct JSON concatenated with values, as you did in your first test. This works, but it's error prone because it's easy to miss certain syntactical elements of JSON.

Another way is to construct a new `JsonNode` and convert it to a string using the `$` operator. Let's do that now. Start by defining a new `createMessage` procedure, and then use the `%` operator to create a new `JsonNode` object. The following listing shows how the `createMessage` procedure can be defined.

Listing 3.12   Creating a new message

```
proc createMessage*(username, message: string): string =
  result = $(%{
    "username": %username,
    "message": %message
  }) & "\c\l"
```

The $ converts the JsonNode returned by the % operator into a string.

The % converts strings, integers, floats, and more into the appropriate JsonNodes.

A carriage return and the line feed characters are added to the end of the message. They act as separators for the messages.

TABLE CONSTRUCTOR SYNTAX   The `{:}` syntax used in listing 3.12 is called a *table constructor*. It's simply syntactic sugar for an array constructor. For example, `{"key1": "value1", "key2": "value2"}` is the same as `[("key1", "value1"), ("key2, "value2")]`.

The % operator is very powerful because it can convert a variety of different value types into appropriate JsonNode types. This allows you to create JSON using a very intuitive syntax.

The $ operator is, by convention, the operator used to convert any type to a string value. In the case of a JsonNode, the $ operator defined for it will produce a valid JSON string literal representation of the JsonNode object that was built.

The addition of the carriage return and line feed, which some OSs use to signify newlines, will be useful later on when the client and server components need to receive messages. They'll need a way to determine when a new message stops and another begins. In essence, these characters will be the message separators. In practice, any separator could be used, but the \c\l sequence is used in many other protocols already and it's supported by Nim's networking modules.

Just like with the parseMessage procedure, you should add tests for the create-Message procedure. Simply use doAssert again to ensure that the output is as expected. Remember to include \c\l in your expected output. The following code shows one test that could be performed—add it to the bottom of protocol.nim:

> Note that triple-quoted string literals don't support any character-escape sequences at all. As a workaround, I simply concatenate them.

```
block:
  let expected = """{"username":"dom","message":"hello"}""" & "\c\l"   ◁─┘
  doAssert createMessage("dom", "hello") == expected
```

Recompile your module and run it to ensure that the tests pass. You can also extend the tests further by checking different inputs, such as ones containing characters that have a special meaning in JSON (for example, the " character).

If all the tests pass, you've successfully completed the protocol module. You're now ready to move on to the final stage of developing this application!

3.5 *Transferring data using sockets*

You're now well on your way to completing this chat application. The protocol module is complete and the client module has mostly been completed. Before you finish the client module, let's look at the so-far-completely neglected server.

The server module is one of the most important modules. It will be compiled separately to produce a server binary. The server will act as a central hub to which all the clients connect.

The server will need to perform two primary tasks:

- Listen for new connections from potential clients
- Listen for new messages from clients that have already connected to the server

Any messages that the server receives will need to be sent to every other client that is currently connected to it.

Figure 3.4, from earlier in the chapter, showed the basic operation of the server and the clients. It was a simplified diagram, without any protocol details. Now that you're familiar with the protocol the chat application will be using, I can show you the exact messages that will be sent in figure 3.4.

First, assume that the server has successfully accepted connections from Dom, John, and Grace. The following events occur:

1 Dom sends a message to the server.

```
{"username": "Dom", "message": "Hello"}\c\l
```

2 The server passes this message on to the other clients: John and Grace.

```
{"username": "Dom", "message": "Hello"}\c\l
```

The server simply passes any messages that it receives to the other clients. For simplicity, the identity of the clients is not verified, so it's possible for them to impersonate other users. At the end of this chapter, we'll consider ways to improve this application, and security will be one aspect that you'll be encouraged to reinforce.

For now, though, let's create the server module. You can begin by defining the types that will be used by it. First, create a new server.nim file in the src directory. Then, create the types shown in the following listing.

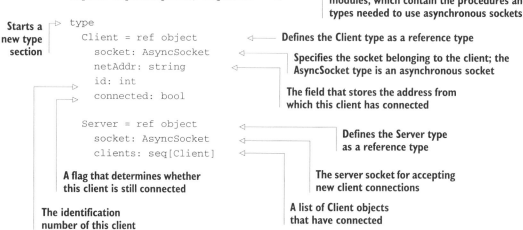

Listing 3.13 Standard library imports and type definitions

```
import asyncdispatch, asyncnet          Imports the asyncdispatch and asyncnet
                                        modules, which contain the procedures and
                                        types needed to use asynchronous sockets

type                                    Starts a new type section
   Client = ref object                  Defines the Client type as a reference type
      socket: AsyncSocket               Specifies the socket belonging to the client; the
      netAddr: string                   AsyncSocket type is an asynchronous socket
      id: int                           The field that stores the address from
      connected: bool                   which this client has connected

   Server = ref object                  Defines the Server type
      socket: AsyncSocket               as a reference type
      clients: seq[Client]              The server socket for accepting
                                        new client connections
```

A flag that determines whether this client is still connected

The identification number of this client

A list of Client objects that have connected

The `Server` and `Client` types are both defined as reference types, which you might recall from chapter 2. Being defined this way allows procedures that take these types as arguments to modify them. This will be essential, because new elements will need to be added to the `clients` field when new clients connect.

The `Server` type holds information that's directly related to the server, such as the server socket and the clients that have connected to it. Similarly, the `Client` type represents a single client that connected to the server, and it includes fields that provide useful information about each client. For example, the `netAddr` field will contain the IP address of the client, and the `id` field will hold a generated identity for each client, allowing you to distinguish between them. The `connected` flag is important because it tracks whether the client is still connected. The server needs to know this, because it shouldn't attempt to send messages to a disconnected client.

All that's left now is to create a constructor for the newly defined `Server` type.

Constructors in Nim

Constructors in Nim are simply procedures with a specific naming convention. Nim doesn't include any special syntax for defining constructors, but it does include some simple syntax for constructing your custom types, which you may recall from chapter 2.

Tuples can be constructed by placing values in parentheses:

```
type
  Point = tuple[x, y: int]

var point = (5, 10)
var point2 = (x: 5, y: 10)
```

Objects, including `ref` objects, can be constructed by calling the type—as if it were a procedure—and then specifying each field name and value separated by a colon:

```
type
  Human = object
    name: string
    age: int

var jeff = Human(name: "Jeff", age: 23)
var alex = Human(name: "Alex", age: 20)
```

There's no way to override these, so if you need more-complex constructors, you'll need to define a procedure. There's a convention in Nim for naming these constructor procedures; this table shows these conventions and how they apply to different type definitions.

Constructor naming conventions

Type definition	Name
MyType = object	initMyType
MyTypeRef = ref object	newMyTypeRef
MyTuple = tuple[x, y: int]	initMyTuple

For a ref type, such as the `Server` type, the procedure should be named `newServer`:

```
proc newServer(): Server = Server(socket: newAsyncSocket(), clients: @[])
```

This will create a new instance of the `Server` type and initialize its socket and `clients` sequence. You can now call this procedure and assign it to a new `server` variable.

```
var server = newServer()
```

Add the `newServer` procedure and `server` variable definitions below the types created in listing 3.13. The resulting code gives you a good base to begin adding the networking code to.

But before we get into that, let's look at how networking, particularly asynchronous networking, works in Nim. We'll begin by looking at the basic tool used to transfer data over a network: a *socket*.

3.5.1 What is a socket?

In almost every programming language, transferring data over a network is done using network sockets. In Nim, a network socket is represented using the `Socket` type. This type is defined in the `net` module, and a new instance of it can be created using the `newSocket` procedure.

Sockets share some similarities with file descriptors in that they support operations such as `write`, `read`, `open`, and `close`. But in practice, sockets differ enough to expose a different interface. Table 3.1 shows some of the common socket procedures and their file descriptor equivalents.

Table 3.1 Common socket procedures

Procedure	File equivalent	Description
recv	read	Allows incoming data to be read from the remote side. For TCP sockets, `recv` is used, and for UDP sockets, `recvFrom` is used.
send	write	Sends data to a socket, allowing data to be sent to the remote side. For TCP sockets, `send` is used, and for UDP sockets, `sendTo` is used.
connect	open	Connects a socket to a remote server. This is typically only used for TCP sockets.
bindAddr	None	Binds a socket to the specified address and port. When called, the socket becomes a server socket, and other sockets can connect to it. This is typically only used for TCP sockets.

Sockets can be customized a great deal by specifying different options in the `newSocket` constructor. By default, the `newSocket` constructor will create a TCP socket, which is handy because TCP is the protocol that the chat application will use.

TCP is a connection-oriented transport protocol that allows the socket to be used as a server or as a client. A newly created TCP socket is neither until the `bindAddr` or `connect` procedure is called. The former transforms it into a server socket, and the latter a client socket. We'll create a server socket first, as that's what is needed for the `server` component of this application.

A server socket's main purpose is to listen for new connections and accept them with as little delay as possible. But before this can be done, the socket must first be bound to an address and port. Figure 3.13 shows the procedures that need to be called to successfully create and bind a server socket.

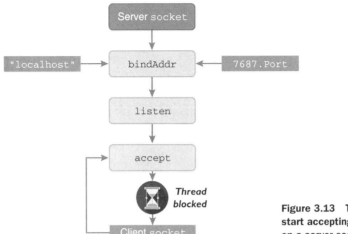

Figure 3.13 The steps needed to start accepting new connections on a server socket

First, every server socket needs to be explicitly bound to a specific port and address. This can be done using the `bindAddr` procedure, which takes a port as the first argument and an address as the second. By default, the address is simply `localhost`, but the port must always be specified. You can specify whatever port you wish, but there are some ports that are often used by other applications, such as port 80, which is used by HTTP servers. Also, binding to a port less than or equal to 1024 requires administrator privileges.

Second, before the socket can start accepting connections, you must call the `listen` procedure on it. The `listen` procedure tells the socket to start listening for incoming connections.

New connections can then be accepted by using the `accept` procedure. This procedure returns a new client socket, which corresponds to the socket that just connected to the address and port specified in the call to `bindAddr`.

> **DETAILS ABOUT SOCKETS** Don't worry about remembering all the details in this section. Use it as a reference together with the next sections, which will show you how to put this knowledge into practice.

Much like reading data from the standard input, the `accept` procedure blocks your application until a new connection is made. This is a problem, but one that's easy to solve thanks to Nim's support for asynchronous sockets. Asynchronous sockets don't block and can be used instead of synchronous sockets without much trouble. They're defined in the `asyncnet` module, and I'll explain how they work in the next section.

3.5.2 *Asynchronous input/output*

Nim supports many abstractions that make working with asynchronous I/O simple. This is achieved in part by making asynchronous I/O very similar to synchronous I/O, so your I/O code doesn't need to be particularly complex.

Let's first look at the `accept` procedure in more detail. This procedure takes one parameter, a server socket, which is used to retrieve new clients that have connected to the specified server socket.

The fundamental difference between the synchronous and asynchronous versions of the `accept` procedure is that the synchronous `accept` procedure blocks the thread it's called in until a new socket has connected to the server socket, whereas the asynchronous `accept` procedure returns immediately after it's called.

But what does the asynchronous version return? It certainly can't return the accepted socket immediately, because a new client may not have connected yet. Instead, it returns a `Future[AsyncSocket]` object. To understand asynchronous I/O, you'll need to understand what a *future* is, so let's look at it in more detail.

THE FUTURE TYPE

A `Future` is a special type that goes by many names in other languages, including *promise*, *delay*, and *deferred*. This type acts as a proxy for a result that's initially unknown, usually because the computation of its value is not yet complete.

You can think of a future as a container; initially it's empty, and while it remains empty you can't retrieve its value. At some unknown point in time, something is placed in the container and it's no longer empty. That's where the name *future* comes from.

Every asynchronous operation in Nim returns a `Future[T]` object, where the `T` corresponds to the type of value that the `Future` promises to store in the future.

The `Future[T]` type is defined in the `asyncdispatch` module, and you can easily experiment with it without involving any asynchronous I/O operations. The next listing shows the behavior of a simple `Future[int]` object.

Listing 3.14 Simple `Future[int]` example

```
import asyncdispatch

var future = newFuture[int]()
doAssert(not future.finished)
future.callback =
  proc (future: Future[int]) =
    echo("Future is no longer empty, ", future.read)

future.complete(42)
```

The `asyncdispatch` module needs to be imported because it defines the Future[T] type.

A new future can be initialized with the newFuture constructor.

A future starts out empty; when a future isn't empty, the finished procedure will return true.

The read procedure is used to retrieve the value of the future.

The callback is given the future whose value was set as a parameter.

A callback can be set, and it will be called when the future's value is set.

A future's value can be set by calling the complete procedure.

Futures can also store an exception in case the computation of the value fails. Calling read on a Future that contains an exception will result in an error.

To demonstrate the effects of this, modify the last line of listing 3.14 to future.fail(newException(ValueError, "The future failed")). Then compile and run it.

The application should crash with the following output:

```
Traceback (most recent call last)
system.nim(2510)          ch3_futures
asyncdispatch.nim(242)    fail
asyncdispatch.nim(267)    :anonymous
ch3_futures.nim(8)        :anonymous
asyncdispatch.nim(289)    read
Error: unhandled exception: The future failed
  unspecified's lead up to read of failed Future:
    Traceback (most recent call last)
    system.nim(2510)          ch3_futures
    asyncdispatch.nim(240)    fail [Exception]
```

unspecified is the name of the Future. It's called unspecified because the future is created with no name. You can name futures for better debugging by specifying a string in the newFuture constructor.

As you can see, the error message attempts to include as much information as possible. But the way it's presented isn't ideal. The error messages produced by futures are still being worked on and should improve with time. It's a good idea to get to know what they look like currently, as you'll undoubtedly see them when writing asynchronous applications in Nim.

The preceding exception is caused by calling read on a future that had an exception stored inside it. To prevent that from occurring, you can use the failed procedure, which returns a Boolean that indicates whether the future completed with an exception.

One important thing to keep in mind when working with futures is that unless they're explicitly read, any exceptions that they store may silently disappear when the future is deallocated. As such, it's important not to discard futures but to instead use the asyncCheck procedure to ensure that any exceptions are reraised in your program.

THE DIFFERENCE BETWEEN SYNCHRONOUS AND ASYNCHRONOUS EXECUTION

Hopefully, by now you understand how futures work. Let's go back to learning a little bit more about asynchronous execution in the context of the accept procedure. Figure 3.14 shows the difference between calling the synchronous version of accept and the asynchronous version.

As mentioned earlier, the asynchronous accept returns a Future object immediately, whereas the synchronous accept blocks the current thread. While the thread is blocked in the synchronous version, it's idle and performs no useful computational work. The asynchronous version, on the other hand, can perform computational work as long as this work doesn't require the client socket. It may involve client sockets that have connected previously, or it may involve calculating the 1025th decimal digit of π. In figure 3.14, this work is masked beneath a doWork procedure, which could be doing any of the tasks mentioned.

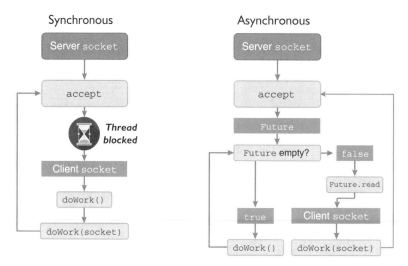

Figure 3.14   The difference between synchronous and asynchronous `accept`

The asynchronous version performs many more calls to `doWork()` than the synchronous version. It also retains the call to `doWork(socket)`, leading to the same code logic but very different performance characteristics.

It's important to note that the asynchronous execution described in figure 3.14 has a problem. It demonstrates what's known as *busy waiting*, which is repeatedly checking whether the `Future` is empty or not. This technique is very inefficient because CPU time is wasted on a useless activity.

To solve this, each `Future` stores a callback that can be overridden with a custom procedure. Whenever a `Future` is completed with a value or an exception, its callback is called. Using a callback in this case would prevent the busy waiting.

EXAMPLE OF ASYNCHRONOUS I/O USING CALLBACKS

The term *callback* provokes a feeling of horror in some people. But not to worry. You won't be forced to use callbacks in Nim. Although the most basic notification mechanism `Futures` expose is a callback, Nim provides what's known as *async await*, which hides these callbacks from you. You'll learn more about async await later.

But although you're not forced to use callbacks in Nim, I'll first explain asynchronous I/O by showing you how it works with callbacks. That's because you're likely more familiar with callbacks than with async await. Let's start with a comparison between Node and Nim, and not a comparison involving sockets but something much simpler: the reading of a file asynchronously.

Listing 3.15   Reading files asynchronously in Node

```
var fs = require('fs');
fs.readFile('/etc/passwd', function (err, data) {
  if (err) throw err;
  console.log(data);
});
```

The code in the preceding listing is taken straight from Node's documentation.[2] It simply reads the contents of the /etc/passwd file asynchronously. When this script is executed, the readFile function tells the Node runtime to read the file specified by the path in the first argument, and once it's finished doing so, to call the function specified in the second argument. The readFile function itself returns immediately, and control is given back implicitly to the Node runtime.

Now compare it to the Nim version.

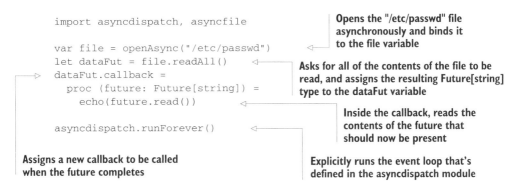

Listing 3.16 Reading files asynchronously in Nim

```
import asyncdispatch, asyncfile                    Opens the "/etc/passwd" file
                                                   asynchronously and binds it
var file = openAsync("/etc/passwd")                to the file variable
let dataFut = file.readAll()
dataFut.callback =                                 Asks for all of the contents of the file to be
  proc (future: Future[string]) =                  read, and assigns the resulting Future[string]
    echo(future.read())                            type to the dataFut variable

                                                   Inside the callback, reads the
asyncdispatch.runForever()                         contents of the future that
                                                   should now be present
Assigns a new callback to be called                Explicitly runs the event loop that's
when the future completes                          defined in the asyncdispatch module
```

The Nim version may seem more complex at first, but that's because Nim's standard library doesn't define a single readFile procedure, whereas Node's standard library does. Instead, you must first open the file using the openAsync procedure to get an AsyncFile object, and then you can read data from that object.[3]

Other than that difference in standard library APIs, the Nim version also differs in one more important way: the readAll procedure doesn't accept a callback. Instead, it returns a new instance of the Future type. The callback is then stored in the Future and is called once the future completes.

THE EVENT LOOP

In a Node application, the runtime is a form of event loop—it uses native operating system APIs to check for various events. One of these might be a file being successfully read or a socket receiving data from the server that it's connected to. The runtime dispatches these events to the appropriate callbacks.

Nim's event loop is defined in the asyncdispatch module. It's similar to Node's runtime in many ways, except that it needs to be explicitly executed. One way to do this is to call the runForever procedure. Figure 3.15 shows the behavior of the runForever procedure.

---

[2] See the Node.js fs.readFile documentation: https://nodejs.org/api/fs.html#fs_fs_readfile_file_options_ callback.

[3] Creating a single readFile procedure would be a fairly trivial undertaking. I leave the challenge of creating such a procedure to you.

asyncdispatch **event loop**

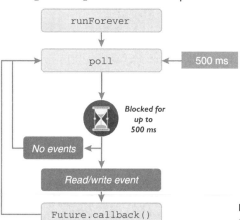

Figure 3.15   Nim's asyncdispatch event loop

The Nim event loop puts you in control. The runForever procedure is simply a wrapper around the poll procedure, which the runForever procedure calls in an infinite loop. You can call the poll procedure yourself, which will give you greater control over the event loop. The poll procedure waits for events for a specified number of milliseconds (500 ms by default), but it doesn't always take 500 ms to finish because events can occur much earlier than that. Once an event is created, the poll procedure processes it and checks each of the currently pending Future objects to see if the Future is waiting on that event. If it is, the Future's callback is called, and any appropriate values that are stored inside the future are populated.

In contrast to synchronous I/O, which can block for an unlimited amount of time, the poll procedure also blocks, but only for a finite amount of time, which can be freely specified. This allows you to commit a certain amount of time to I/O processing and the rest to other tasks, such as drawing a GUI or performing a CPU-intensive calculation. I'll show you how to utilize this procedure later in the client module, so that async sockets can be mixed with the readLine procedure that reads the standard input stream in another thread.

ASYNC AWAIT

There's a big problem with using callbacks for asynchronous I/O: for complex application logic, they're not flexible, leading to what's aptly named *callback hell.* For example, suppose you want to read another file after a first one has been read. To do so, you're forced to nest callbacks, and you end up with code that becomes ugly and unmaintainable.

Nim has a solution to this problem: the await keyword. It eliminates callback hell completely and makes asynchronous code almost identical to synchronous code.

The await keyword can only be used inside procedures marked with the {.async.} pragma. The next listing shows how to read and write files using an async procedure.

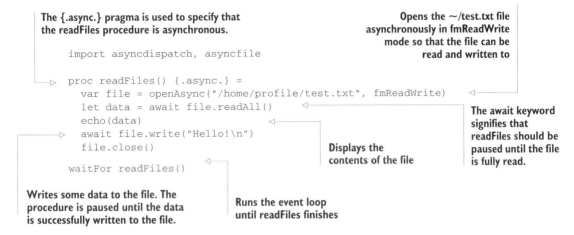

Listing 3.17 Reading files and writing to them in sequence using await

The {.async.} pragma is used to specify that the readFiles procedure is asynchronous.

Opens the ~/test.txt file asynchronously in fmReadWrite mode so that the file can be read and written to

```
import asyncdispatch, asyncfile

proc readFiles() {.async.} =
    var file = openAsync("/home/profile/test.txt", fmReadWrite)
    let data = await file.readAll()
    echo(data)
    await file.write("Hello!\n")
    file.close()

waitFor readFiles()
```

The await keyword signifies that readFiles should be paused until the file is fully read.

Displays the contents of the file

Writes some data to the file. The procedure is paused until the data is successfully written to the file.

Runs the event loop until readFiles finishes

Listing 3.17 performs the same actions and more than the code in listing 3.16. Every time the await keyword is used, the execution of the readFiles procedure is paused until the Future that's awaited is completed. Then the procedure resumes its execution, and the value of the Future is read automatically. While the procedure is paused, the application continues running, so the thread is never blocked. This is all done in a single thread. Multiple async procedures can be paused at any point, waiting for an event to resume them, and callbacks are used in the background to resume these procedures.

Every procedure marked with the {.async.} pragma must return a Future[T] object. In listing 3.17, the procedure might seem like it returns nothing, but it returns a Future[void]; this is done implicitly to avoid the pain of writing Future[void] all the time. Any procedure that returns a Future[T] can be awaited. Figure 3.16 shows what the execution of listing 3.17 looks like.

The waitFor procedure that's used instead of runForever runs the event loop until the readFiles procedure finishes its execution. Table 3.2 compares all the different async keywords you've seen so far.

Table 3.2 Comparison of common async keywords

Procedure	Controls event loop directly	Use case	Description
runForever	Yes	Usually used for server applications that need to stay alive indefinitely.	Runs the event loop forever.
waitFor	Yes	Usually used for applications that need to quit after a specific asynchronous procedure finishes its execution.	Runs the event loop until the specified future completes.

Table 3.2   Comparison of common async keywords *(continued)*

Procedure	Controls event loop directly	Use case	Description
poll	Yes	For applications that need precise control of the event loop. The runForever and waitFor procedures call this.	Listens for events for the specified amount of time.
asyncCheck	No	Used for discarding futures safely, typically to execute an async proc without worrying about its result.	Sets the specified future's callback property to a procedure that will handle exceptions appropriately.
await	No	Used to execute another async proc whose result is needed in the line of code after the await.	Pauses the execution of an async proc until the specified future completes.

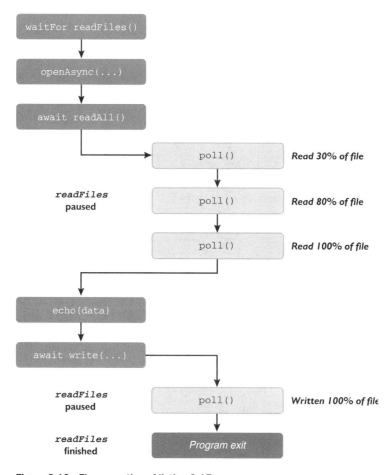

Figure 3.16   The execution of listing 3.17

WARNING: PROCEDURES THAT CONTROL THE EVENT LOOP   Typically, `runForever`, `waitFor`, and `poll` shouldn't be used within async procedures, because they control the event loop directly.

Now, I'll show you how to use `await` and asynchronous sockets to finish the implementation of the server.

3.5.3 Transferring data asynchronously

You've already initialized an asynchronous socket and stored it in the `server` variable. The next steps are as follows:

1 Bind the socket to a port such as 7687.[4]

2 Call `listen` on the socket to begin listening for new connections.

3 Start accepting connections via the `accept` procedure.

You'll need to use `await`, so you'll need to introduce a new async procedure. The following code shows a `loop` procedure that performs these steps.

Listing 3.18 Creating a server socket and accepting connections from clients

```
proc loop(server: Server, port = 7687) {.async.} =
  server.socket.bindAddr(port.Port)          ◁─────  Sets up the server socket by
  server.socket.listen()                             binding it to a port and
                                                     calling listen. The integer
  while true:                                        port param needs to be cast
    let clientSocket = await server.socket.accept()  ◁──  to a Port type that the
    echo("Accepted connection!")                         bindAddr procedure expects.
                                             Calls accept on the server
─┈▷  waitFor loop(server)                    socket to accept a new client.
                                             The await keyword ensures that
   Executes the loop procedure and           the procedure is paused until a
   then runs the event loop until the        new client has connected.
   loop procedure returns.
```

The `loop` procedure will continuously wait for new client connections to be made. Currently, nothing is done with those connections, but you can still test that this works. Add the preceding code to the end of server.nim. Then, compile and run the server by running `nim c -r src/server`.

TESTING A SERVER WITHOUT A CLIENT

Your client hasn't yet been completed, so you can't use it to test the server. But it's fairly easy to use a command-line application called `telnet` to connect to your new server.

On Windows, you may need to enable Telnet in the Windows Features menu—you can find more information at this link: http://mng.bz/eSor. After enabling the `telnet` feature, you should be able to open a new command window, type `telnet` at the

---

[4] Most of the easy-to-remember ports are used by other applications: https://en.wikipedia.org/wiki/List_of_TCP_and_UDP_port_numbers.

prompt, and then connect to your server by executing the `open localhost 7687` command. The server should then output "Accepted connection!"

On UNIX-like operating systems such as Linux and Mac OS, the `telnet` application should be available by default. You can simply open a new terminal window and execute `telnet localhost 7687`. The server should then output "Accepted connection!"

CREATING A NEW CLIENT INSTANCE TO HOLD DATA ABOUT THE CLIENT

Now, let's extend the `loop` procedure to create a new `Client` instance and add it to the `clients` field. Replace the `while` loop with the following.

Listing 3.19   Creating a new `Client` instance for each connection

acceptAddr returns a tuple[string, AsyncSocket] type. The tuple is unpacked into two variables.

A message is displayed, indicating that a client has connected and providing its network address.

```
while true:
  let (netAddr, clientSocket) = await server.socket.acceptAddr()
  echo("Accepted connection from ", netAddr)
  let client = Client(
    socket: clientSocket,
    netAddr: netAddr,
    id: server.clients.len,
    connected: true
  )
  server.clients.add(client)
```

Initializes a new instance of the Client object and sets its fields

Adds the new instance of the client to the clients sequence

The `acceptAddr` variant of the `accept` procedure has been changed to return the IP address of the client that has connected. It returns a tuple, the first value of which is the IP address of the client, and the second being the client socket. The preceding code uses *tuple unpacking*, which allows for these two values to be assigned immediately to two different variables.

When a client successfully connects, the next line writes a message to the terminal that includes the IP address of the client that just connected. After this, a new instance of the `Client` object is created, with each field assigned a new value using a constructor. Finally, the new instance is added to the server's `clients` sequence.

Recompiling this code and repeating the testing steps described in the section titled "Testing a server without a client" should display "Accepted connection from 127.0.0.1." But sending messages won't yet work.

PROCESSING THE CLIENT'S MESSAGES

Messages typed into the prompt won't be received by the server yet, even after connecting with Telnet, because the messages still aren't being read from the connected clients. Let's implement the server code to do that now.

Listing 3.20   Receiving messages from a client

```
proc processMessages(server: Server, client: Client) {.async.} =
  while true:
    let line = await client.socket.recvLine()
```

Waits for a single line to be read from the client

```
             if line.len == 0:                ◁──────────┐    Most procedures that read data from
                 echo(client, " disconnected!")          │    a socket may return an empty string,
                 client.connected = false                │    which signifies that the socket has
Stops any        client.socket.close()   ◁───────────────┤    disconnected from the server.
 further   ┌▷   return                                   │
processing │                                             │
of messages│   echo(client, " sent: ", line)             │    Closes the client's socket
                                                              because it has disconnected
```

Make sure you place this `processMessages` procedure above the `loop` procedure. Later, you'll need to call this procedure from the `loop` procedure, and this procedure must be above the call site in order for that to work.

You may find it strange to see another infinite loop, denoted by the `while true` statement, at the top of the procedure body. Surely once this procedure is called, its execution will never stop. There is truth to that, but note this is an *async* procedure, so it can be paused. This procedure will never *stop* executing, but it will *pause* its execution when `await client.socket.recvLine()` is called. Other pieces of code will be executing while this procedure waits for the result of `client.socket.recvLine()`.

The result will contain a single message sent by the client. A single message is guaranteed because the message protocol created in the previous section uses newline characters as delimiters.

There's one case that will prevent a full message from being received: the client disconnecting from the server. In that case, `recvLine` returns an empty string, which is why the next line checks the length of the resulting string. If the string is empty, a message is displayed on the terminal stating that the client disconnected. The client's `connected` flag is set to `false`, and the `close` procedure is called on the socket to free its resources.

Finally, assuming that the client hasn't disconnected, the message that the client sent is displayed in the terminal.

If you try to recompile the code now, you'll find that it doesn't compile. The error will be similar to the following:

```
server.nim(16, 54) template/generic instantiation from here
server.nim(20, 12) Error: type mismatch: got (Client)
but expected one of:
system.$(x: int)
system.$(x: seq[T])
system.$(x: cstring)
system.$(x: bool)
...
```

This is because of the `echo(client, " disconnected!")` line, which attempts to display the `Client` type in the terminal. The problem is that the `echo` procedure attempts to use the `$` operator to display all of the procedure's arguments. If a `$` operator isn't defined for the type that you pass to `echo`, you'll get an error message of this sort. The fix is to define it.

The full code listing for server.nim should now look something like this.

Listing 3.21   The full server implementation so far

```nim
import asyncdispatch, asyncnet

type
  Client = ref object
    socket: AsyncSocket
    netAddr: string
    id: int
    connected: bool

  Server = ref object
    socket: AsyncSocket
    clients: seq[Client]

proc newServer(): Server = Server(socket: newAsyncSocket(), clients: @[])
proc `$`(client: Client): string =
  $client.id & "(" & client.netAddr & ")"

proc processMessages(server: Server, client: Client) {.async.} =
  while true:
    let line = await client.socket.recvLine()
    if line.len == 0:
      echo(client, " disconnected!")
      client.connected = false
      client.socket.close()
      return

    echo(client, " sent: ", line)

proc loop(server: Server, port = 7687) {.async.} =
  server.socket.bindAddr(port.Port)
  server.socket.listen()

  while true:
    let (netAddr, clientSocket) = await server.socket.acceptAddr()
    echo("Accepted connection from ", netAddr)
    let client = Client(
      socket: clientSocket,
      netAddr: netAddr,
      id: server.clients.len,
      connected: true
    )
    server.clients.add(client)
    asyncCheck processMessages(server, client)

var server = newServer()
waitFor loop(server)
```

The code now includes the definition of $ for the Client type, as well as an async-Check command that runs the processMessages procedure in the background. These are both shown in bold. The asyncCheck command can be used to run asynchronous procedures without waiting on their result.

This code will call the processMessages procedure for each client that connects to the server, which is precisely what needs to be done. Each client needs to be continuously read from to ensure that any messages it sends are processed. Because of the nature of async procedures, all of this will be done in the background, with the execution of `loop` continuing and thus being ready to accept more connections.

Recompile the server module again, and then run it and connect to it using `telnet`. Type some text into the Telnet window and press Enter; you should see your server output messages showing the text you entered.

SENDING THE MESSAGES TO OTHER CLIENTS

Lastly, you need to send the messages received from a client to all other clients that are currently connected to the server. Add the following code to the bottom of the `processMessages` procedure, making sure you indent this code so it's within the `while` loop.

Listing 3.22 Sending messages on to other clients

Loops through each of the clients
in the clients sequence

Checks that the client isn't
the client that sent this
message and that the client
is still connected

```
for c in server.clients:
    if c.id != client.id and c.connected:
        await c.socket.send(line & "\c\l")
```

Sends the message to the client,
followed by the message separator: \c\l

For completeness, the following listing shows what your `processMessages` procedure should now look like. The addition is shown in bold.

Listing 3.23 The `processMessages` procedure after listing 3.22 is inserted

```
proc processMessages(server: Server, client: Client) {.async.} =
  while true:
    let line = await client.socket.recvLine()
    if line.len == 0:
      echo(client, " disconnected!")
      client.connected = false
      client.socket.close()
      return

    echo(client, " sent: ", line)
    for c in server.clients:
      if c.id != client.id and c.connected:
        await c.socket.send(line & "\c\l")
```

That's all there is to the server! It can now receive messages and send them on to other clients. The problem now is that the client still has no code to connect to the server or to send messages to it. Let's fix that.

ADDING NETWORK FUNCTIONALITY TO THE CLIENT

The first network functionality that should be implemented in the client is the ability for it to connect to the server. Before implementing a procedure to do that, though, you must import the `asyncdispatch` and `asyncnet` modules. You'll need to also import the `protocol` module you created earlier. You can then create a new async procedure called `connect`, as shown here.

Listing 3.24   The client's connect procedure

> **Connects to the server address supplied, on the default 7687 port.**

```
proc connect(socket: AsyncSocket, serverAddr: string) {.async.} =
  echo("Connecting to ", serverAddr)
  await socket.connect(serverAddr, 7687.Port)        ◁
  echo("Connected!")

  while true:                                         **Continuously attempts to read a
    let line = await socket.recvLine()    ◁           message from the server.**
    let parsed = parseMessage(line)
    echo(parsed.username, " said ", parsed.message) ◁  **Displays the message
                                                        together with the username
**Uses the parseMessage procedure defined in the        of the message sender.**
protocol module to parse the received message.**
```

You should place this procedure just below the `import` statement at the top of the file. It's fairly simple: it connects to the server and starts waiting for messages from it. The `recvLine` procedure is used to read a single line at a time. This line is then passed to the `parseMessage` procedure, which parses it and returns an object that allows for specific parts of the message to be accessed. The message is then displayed, together with the username of the messenger.

Before the `connect` procedure can be called, you must first define a new `socket` variable. This variable should be initialized using the `newAsyncSocket` procedure. Define it after the `serverAddr` command-line argument is read, so, after the `let serverAddr = paramStr(1)` line. The following code should do the trick: `var socket = newAsyncSocket()`.

You can then replace `echo("Connecting to ", serverAddr)` with a call to `connect`, using the `asyncCheck` procedure to discard the future safely: `asyncCheck connect(socket, serverAddr)`. This code will run in the background because neither `await` nor `waitFor` is used.

It's now time to make the reading of standard input in client.nim nonblocking. Currently, the `while` loop that reads the standard input blocks, but for the `connect` async procedure to work, the async event loop needs to be executed. This won't happen if the thread is blocked, so the `while` loop needs to be modified to integrate the standard input reading with the event loop. The following code shows how this can be done—replace the `while` loop in client.nim with it.

Listing 3.25   Reading from standard input asynchronously

```
var messageFlowVar = spawn stdin.readLine()   ◁     **The initial readLine call has been
while true:                                          moved out of the while loop.**
  if messageFlowVar.isReady():   ◁
                                  **The isReady procedure determines whether
                                  reading the value from messageFlowVar will block.**
```

```
let message = createMessage("Anonymous", ^messageFlowVar)
asyncCheck socket.send(message)
messageFlowVar = spawn stdin.readLine()

asyncdispatch.poll()
```

Spawns readLine in another thread, as the last one has returned with data

Calls the event loop manually using the poll procedure

Sends the message to the server. In this case, createMessage adds the separator for you.

Uses the createMessage procedure defined in the protocol module to create a new message. Getting the user's name is left as an exercise for you.

The `readLine` spawn call has been modified to prevent the `readLine` procedure from being executed multiple times in hundreds of threads. This would happen if the `spawn` call was placed inside the `while` statement because the `messageFlowVar` would no longer be read synchronously. Now, there is only ever one `readLine` running in a separate thread at one time.

The `while` loop uses the `isReady` procedure to check whether the `readLine` procedure returned a newly read value from the standard input stream. If so, the message is sent to the server, and the `readLine` procedure is spawned again. See figure 3.17, which shows the execution of both the main thread and the `readLine` thread. Compare it to figure 3.10, which you saw earlier.

Waiting on the standard input no longer blocks the main thread, allowing the event loop the time to check for events by calling the `poll` procedure.

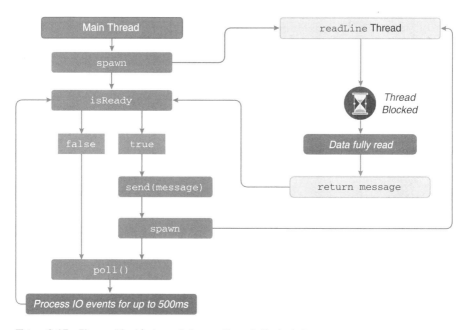

Figure 3.17   The nonblocking parallel execution of client.nim)

For completeness, here's the full code listing for client.nim. The changes made in this section are shown in bold.

Listing 3.26   The final client implementation

```nim
import os, threadpool, asyncdispatch, asyncnet
import protocol

proc connect(socket: AsyncSocket, serverAddr: string) {.async.} =
  echo("Connecting to ", serverAddr)
  await socket.connect(serverAddr, 7687.Port)
  echo("Connected!")

  while true:
    let line = await socket.recvLine()
    let parsed = parseMessage(line)
    echo(parsed.username, " said ", parsed.message)

echo("Chat application started")
if paramCount() == 0:
  quit("Please specify the server address, e.g. ./client localhost")
let serverAddr = paramStr(1)
var socket = newAsyncSocket()
asyncCheck connect(socket, serverAddr)
var messageFlowVar = spawn stdin.readLine()
while true:
  if messageFlowVar.isReady():
    let message = createMessage("Anonymous", ^messageFlowVar)
    asyncCheck socket.send(message)
    messageFlowVar = spawn stdin.readLine()

  asyncdispatch.poll()
```

THE FINAL RESULTS

That's all there is to it! You can now compile both the server and the client, and then run the server and multiple clients. If you send a message from one client, it should display in the server window but also in the other clients that are connected to the server.

There's one small feature missing, and that's the user names. Currently, the user name for each client is hardcoded as `"Anonymous"`. Changing this shouldn't take too much work, so I'll leave it as an optional challenge for you.

Let's look back at the original use case: asking John and Grace about *Game of Thrones*. The discussion looks like this.

Listing 3.27   Conversation between John, Grace, and me about *Game of Thrones*

```
Dominik said:  What did you guys think about the latest Game of Thrones
episode?
Grace said: I thought Tyrion was really great in it!
John said:  I agree with Grace. Tyrion deserves an Emmy for his performance.
```

After this discussion takes place, each person's screen should show the same output, except that each person's own messages won't be prefixed by <name> said where <name> is their name.

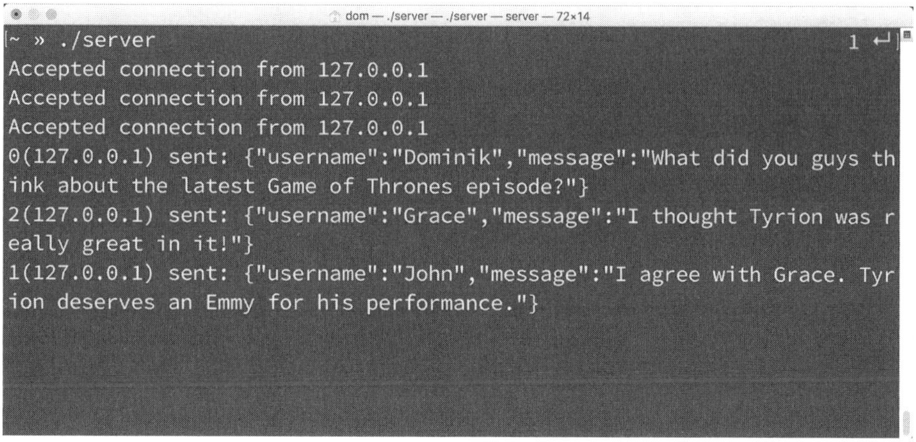

Figure 3.18 The server's output

To see it in action, try this scenario out for yourself. Set up three clients and send the messages. The server should display the information in figure 3.18 after this exchange.

Each client should show a screen similar to the one in figure 3.19.

If you got lost somewhere along the way, or if you just couldn't get the code to compile for some reason, take a look at the book's code examples on GitHub: https://github.com/dom96/nim-in-action-code.
You can now even send the client binary to one of your friends and have them chat with you. You may need to do it over your LAN or forward ports on your router for it to work, though.

There's a lot of room for improvement, such as making sure that the clients are still connected by sending special "ping" messages, or adding the ability to kick users off the server. I'm sure you'll come up with other ideas, too.

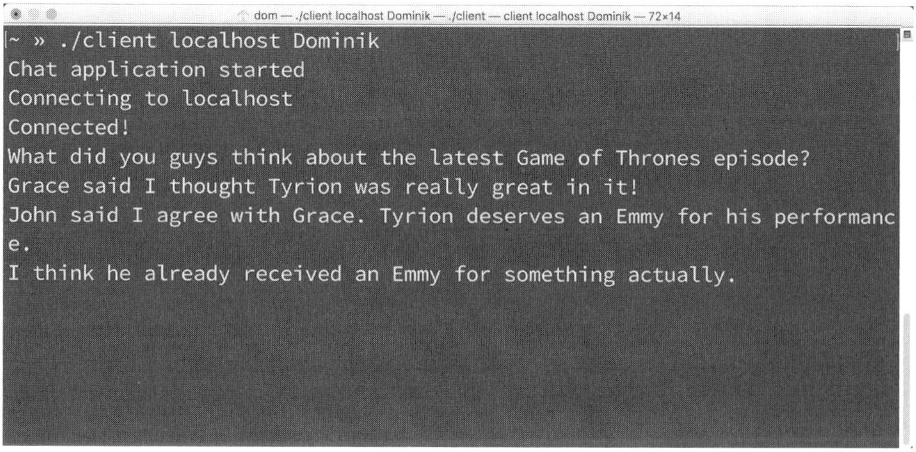

Figure 3.19 The client's output

3.6   *Summary*

- The recommended Nim project directory consists of the src, bin, and tests directories, storing the source code, the executables, and the tests, respectively.
- Command-line arguments can be retrieved using the `paramStr` procedure and counted using the `paramCount` procedure.
- Standard input, accessed via the `stdin` global variable, can be read using the `readLine` procedure.
- Reading from the standard input stream is a blocking operation, which means the application can't do any work while it waits for the data to be read.
- A new thread can be used to perform work while another thread is blocked.
- New threads can be created by using `spawn`.
- JSON can be generated and parsed using the `json` module.
- The `doAssert` procedure is a simple and easy way to create tests.
- A socket allows data to be transferred over the internet, with asynchronous sockets ensuring that the application doesn't become blocked.
- Asynchronous procedures can be created using an `async` pragma.
- A future is an object that holds a value that will be available at some point in the future.
- The `await` keyword can be used to wait for the completion of a future without blocking.

A tour through
the standard library

This chapter covers

- Understanding the standard library
- Examining modules in depth
- Getting to know the modules in Nim's standard library
- Using Nim's standard library modules

Every programming language supports the notion of a *library*. A library is a collection of prewritten software that implements a set of behaviors. These behaviors can be accessed by other libraries or applications via a library-defined interface.

For example, a music-playback library such as libogg might define `play` and `stop` procedures that start music playing and stop it. The libogg library's interface can be said to consist of those two procedures.

A library such as libogg can be reused by multiple applications, so that the behaviors the library implements don't have to be reimplemented for each application.

A *standard* library is one that's always available as part of a programming language. A standard library typically includes definitions of common algorithms, data structures, and mechanisms for interacting with the OS.

The design of a standard library differs between languages. Python's standard library rather famously follows the "batteries included" philosophy, embracing an inclusive design. C's standard library, on the other hand, takes a more conservative approach. As such, in Python you'll find packages that allow you to process XML, send email messages, and make use of the SQLite library, whereas in C, you won't.

The Nim standard library also follows the "batteries included" philosophy. It's similar to Python in that regard, because it also contains packages for processing XML, sending email messages, and making use of the SQLite library, amongst a wide range of other modules. This chapter is dedicated to Nim's standard library and will show you some of its most useful parts. In addition to describing what each part of the standard library does, this chapter presents examples of how each module in the standard library can be used.

Figures 4.1 and 4.2 show some of the most useful modules in Nim's standard library. The difference between pure and impure modules is explained in section 4.2.

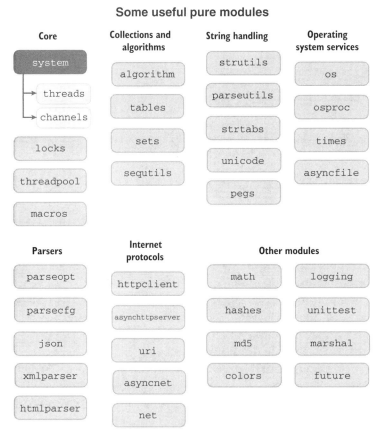

Figure 4.1   The most useful pure modules

Some useful impure modules

Figure 4.2   The most useful impure modules

Let's begin by looking in more detail at what a module is and how modules can be imported.

4.1   A closer look at modules

The Nim standard library is made up of modules. A *module* in Nim is a file containing Nim code, and by default the code inside a module is isolated from all other code. This isolation restricts which types, procedures, variables, and other definitions are accessible to code defined in a different module.

When a new definition is made inside a module, it's not visible to any other modules by default. It's *private*. But a definition can be made *public*, which means that it's visible to other modules, using the * character. The following example.nim module defines a moduleVersion variable that's made public by the * character.

Listing 4.1   Module example.nim

```
var moduleVersion* = "0.12.0"
var randomNumber* = 42
```

You might remember the * character from the previous chapter, where I introduced the * access modifier and used it to export identifiers from the protocol module. Let's now take a look at the different ways that modules can be imported.

You should remember the basic import keyword, which can be used to import the example.nim module like so.

Listing 4.2   Module main.nim

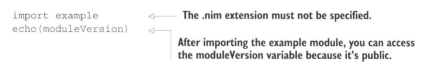

```
import example          ⊲——— The .nim extension must not be specified.
echo(moduleVersion)     ⊲—┐
                          │ After importing the example module, you can access
                          │ the moduleVersion variable because it's public.
```

The import keyword does something very straightforward—it imports all the public definitions from a specified module. But what might not be immediately obvious is how it finds the specified module.

The Nim compiler has a configurable list of directories that it searches for modules. This list is configured in a configuration file normally named nim.cfg. The compiler may use multiple configuration files, but there's one defined by the compiler that's always used. It usually resides in $nimDir/config, where *$nimDir* is the path to the Nim compiler. Listing 4.3 shows what a small part of the default Nim configuration looks like. In the listing, each line specifies a directory that the Nim compiler will look at when searching for modules.

Listing 4.3　Some of the directories in Nim's configuration file

```
path="$lib/pure"
path="$lib/impure"
path="$lib/arch"
path="$lib/core"
...
```

$lib is expanded by the Nim compiler to a full path that leads to the location where Nim's standard library has been installed.

The configuration file contains many more options. You may wish to take a look at it to see which bits of the compiler can be configured.

PROJECT CONFIG FILES　You can create a configuration file that's specific to your project and use it to customize the behavior of the compiler when compiling your project. Create a main.nims file, where main.nim is the name of the file you're compiling. The config file must be placed beside your Nim source code file. You can then place any flags you'd pass on the command line verbatim in that file, such as `--threads:on`.

When a module is imported using the `import` statement, the Nim compiler searches for files alongside the module that's doing the importing. If the module isn't found there, it searches each of the directories defined in the configuration file. This means that for the main.nim module in listing 4.2 to compile, the example.nim module in listing 4.1 should be placed alongside the main.nim module. Figure 4.3 shows how the compiler searches for modules.

Figure 4.3　The compiler searches for modules starting in the project's directory.

When compiling main.nim, the local `example` module and the standard library `system` module need to be compiled first, so the compiler will search for those modules first and compile them automatically.

Modules can also be placed in subdirectories. For example, consider the directory structure shown in figure 4.4.

With the `example` module in the misc directory, the `main` module needs to be modified as follows.

Figure 4.4　The example.nim file has been moved into the misc directory.

Listing 4.4 Importing from a subdirectory

```
import misc/example
echo(moduleVersion)
```

The misc directory simply needs to be added to the `import` statement.

4.1.1 Namespacing

Namespaces are common in many programming languages. They act as a context for identifiers, allowing the same identifier to be used in two different contexts. Language support for namespaces varies widely. C doesn't support them, C++ contains an explicit keyword for defining them, and Python uses the module name as the namespace. Just like in Python, namespaces in Nim are defined by individual modules.

To get a better idea of what namespacing is used for, let's look at an example use case. Assume that you wish to load images of two separate formats: PNG and BMP. Also assume that there are two libraries for reading the two types of files: one called libpng and the other called libbmp. Both libraries define a `load` procedure that loads the image for you, so if you want to use both libraries at the same time, how do you distinguish between the two `load` procedures?

If those libraries are written in C, they would need to emulate namespaces. They'd do this by prefixing the procedure names with the name of the library, so the procedures would be named `png_load` and `bmp_load` to avoid conflicts. C++ versions of those libraries might define namespaces such as `png` and `bmp`, and the `load` procedures could then be invoked via `png::load` and `bmp::load`. Python versions of those libraries don't need to explicitly define a namespace—the module name is the namespace. In Python, if the PNG and BMP libraries define their `load` procedures in `png` and `bmp` modules, respectively, the `load` procedures can be invoked via `png.load` and `bmp.load`.

In Nim, when a module is imported, all of its public definitions are placed in the namespace of the importing module. You can still specify the fully qualified name, but doing so isn't required. This is in contrast to how the Python module system works.

```
import example
echo(example.moduleVersion)   ◁──  Specify the module namespace explicitly by writing
                                    the module name followed by a dot character.
```

The module namespace only needs to be specified when the same definition has been imported from two different modules. Let's say a new module called `example2.nim` was imported, and `example2.nim` also defines a public `moduleVersion` variable. In that case, the code will need to explicitly specify the module name.

Listing 4.5 Module `example2.nim`

```
var moduleVersion* = "10.23"
```

Listing 4.6   Disambiguating identifiers

```
import example, example2
echo("Example's version: ", example.moduleVersion)
echo("Example 2's version: ", example2.moduleVersion)
```

An import statement can import multiple modules. You just need to separate them with a comma.

Compiling and running the code in listing 4.6 will result in the following output:

```
Example's version: 0.12.0
Example 2's version: 10.23
```

But suppose you attempt to display the value of `moduleVersion` without qualifying it.

```
import example, example2
echo(moduleVersion)
```

In that case, you'll receive an error:

```
main.nim(2,6) Error: ambiguous identifier: 'moduleVersion' -- use a qualifier
```

You can prevent all the definitions from being imported into the importing module's namespace by using a special `import` syntax.

Listing 4.7   Importing modules into their own namespace

Imports the example module without importing any of its definitions into this file's namespace

This will no longer work because moduleVersion is no longer in this file's namespace.

The moduleVersion variable can be accessed by explicitly writing the module namespace.

```
from example import nil
echo(moduleVersion)
echo(example.moduleVersion)
```

When you use the `from` statement, the specific definitions that you want imported can be listed after the `import` keyword.

Listing 4.8   Importing only some of the definitions from a module

Imports moduleVersion into this file's namespace. All other public definitions need to be accessed via the example namespace.

The moduleVersion variable can again be accessed without explicitly writing the module namespace.

```
from example import moduleVersion
echo(moduleVersion)
echo(example.randomNumber)
```

The randomNumber variable must be qualified.

Certain definitions can be excluded using the except keyword.

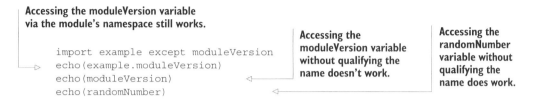

Listing 4.9 Excluding some definitions when importing

Accessing the moduleVersion variable via the module's namespace still works.

```
import example except moduleVersion
echo(example.moduleVersion)
echo(moduleVersion)
echo(randomNumber)
```

Accessing the moduleVersion variable without qualifying the name doesn't work.

Accessing the randomNumber variable without qualifying the name does work.

In Nim, it's idiomatic to import all modules so that all identifiers end up in the importing module's namespace, so you only need to explicitly specify the namespace when the name is ambiguous. This is different from Python, which requires every identifier that's imported to be accessed via the module's namespace unless the module is imported using the from x import * syntax.

Nim's default import behavior allows flexible Uniform Function Call Syntax (UFCS) and operator overloading. Another benefit is that you don't need to constantly retype the module names.

You might not recall the discussion on UFCS in chapter 1. It allows any procedure to be called on an object as if the function were a method of the object's class. The following listing shows UFCS in action.

Listing 4.10 Uniform Function Call Syntax

```
proc welcome(name: string) = echo("Hello ", name)

welcome("Malcolm")
"Malcolm".welcome()
```

Both syntaxes are valid and perform the same action.

You should now have a better understanding of Nim's module system. Let's go on to look at Nim's standard library in greater detail.

4.2 Overview of the standard library

Nim's standard library is split up into three major categories: pure, impure, and wrappers. This section will look at these categories in general. Later sections in this chapter explore a few specific modules from a couple of these categories.

4.2.1 Pure modules

A large proportion of Nim's standard library is composed of pure modules. These modules are written completely in Nim and require no dependencies; you should prefer them because of this.

The pure modules themselves are further split up into multiple categories, including the following:

- The core
- Collections and algorithms

- String handling
- Generic OS services
- Math libraries
- Internet protocols
- Parsers

4.2.2 *Impure modules*

Impure modules consist of Nim code that uses external C libraries. For example, the re module implements procedures and types for handling regular expressions. It's an impure library because it depends on PCRE, which is an external C library. This means that if your application imports the re module, it won't work unless the user installs the PCRE library on their system.

Shared libraries

Impure modules such as re use what's known as a shared library, typically a C library that's been compiled into a shared library file. On Windows, these files use the .dll extension, on Linux the .so extension, and on Mac OS the .dylib extension.[a]

When you import an impure module, your application will need to be able to find these shared libraries. They'll need to be installed via your OS's package manager or bundled with your application. On Linux, it's common to use a package manager; on Mac OS, both methods are fairly common; and on Windows, bundling the dependencies with your application is popular.

---

[a] See Wikipedia's "Dynamic linker" article: https://en.wikipedia.org/wiki/Dynamic_linker #Implementations.

4.2.3 *Wrappers*

Wrappers are the modules that allow these external C libraries to be used. They provide an interface to these libraries that, in most cases, matches the C interface exactly. Impure modules build on top of wrappers to provide a more idiomatic interface.

You can use wrappers directly, but doing so isn't easy because you'll need to use some of Nim's unsafe features, such as pointers and bit casts. This can lead to errors because in most cases you'll need to manage memory manually.

Impure modules define abstractions to provide a memory-safe interface that you can easily use in your source code without worrying about the low-level details of C.

4.2.4 *Online documentation*

We'll start looking at different modules in a moment, but I first want to mention that the Nim website contains documentation for the full standard library. A list of all the modules in the standard library can be found in the Nim documentation: http://nim-lang.org/docs/lib.html. This URL always shows the documentation for the latest release of Nim, and it contains links to documentation for each module.

The documentation for each module provides definitions and links to implementations of those definitions. It can, for example, link to a line of code where a procedure is implemented, showing you exactly how it functions.

Every part of Nim is open source, including its standard library, so you can look at the source of the standard library to see Nim code written by the Nim developers themselves. This allows you to truly understand the behavior of each part of the standard library, and you can even modify it to your liking.

Figure 4.5 shows what the documentation for the os module looks like.

The Nim documentation also includes a Nimble section,[1] with links to community-created modules. Nimble is a Nim package manager that makes the installation of these packages easy. You'll learn more about it in the next chapter.

The list of Nimble packages is split into official and unofficial lists. The official packages are ones that are officially supported by the core Nim developers, and as such they're far more stable than some of the unofficial packages. The official packages include modules that used to be part of the standard library but which have been transferred out in order to make the standard library a bit more lean.

We'll now look at the pure modules in a bit more detail. We'll start with the core modules.

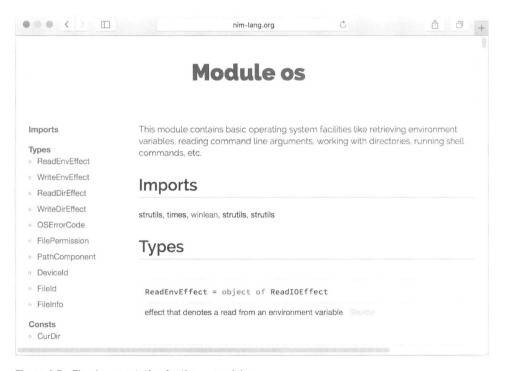

Figure 4.5   The documentation for the os module

---

[1] List of Nimble packages: https://nim-lang.org/docs/lib.html#nimble.

4.3   *The core modules*

The most important module in the core of the standard library is the system module. This is the only module that's implicitly imported, so you don't need to include import system at the top of each of your own modules. This module is imported automatically because it contains commonly used definitions.

The system module includes definitions for all the primitive types, such as int and string. Common procedures and operators are also defined in this module. Table 4.1 lists some examples.

Table 4.1   Some examples of definitions in the system module

Definitions	Purpose	Examples
+, -, *, /	Addition, subtraction, multiplication, division of two numbers.	`doAssert(5 + 5 == 10)` `doAssert(5 / 2 == 2.5)`
==, !=, >, <, >=, <=	General comparison operators.	`doAssert(5 == 5)` `doAssert(5 > 2)`

and, not, or	Bitwise and Boolean operations.	`doAssert(true and true)`
		`doAssert(not false)`
		`doAssert(true or false)`

add	Adds a value to a string or sequence.	`var text = "hi"`
		`text.add('!')`
		`doAssert(text == "hi!")`

len	Returns the length of a string or sequence.	`doAssert("hi".len == 2)`
shl, shr	Bitwise shift left and shift right.	`doAssert(0b0001 shl 1 == 0b0010)`
&	Concatenation operator; joins two strings into one.	`doAssert("Hi" & "!" == "Hi!")`
quit	Terminates the application with a specified error code.	`quit(QuitFailure)`
$	Converts the specified value into a string. This is defined in the system module for some common types.	`doAssert($5 == "5")`
repr	Takes any value and returns its string representation. This differs from $ because it works on any type; a custom repr doesn't need to be defined.	`doAssert(5.repr == "5")`
substr	Returns a slice of the specified string.	`doAssert("Hello".substr(0, 1) == "He")`
echo	Displays the specified values in the terminal.	`echo(2, 3.14, true, "a string")`
items	An iterator that loops through the items of a sequence or string.	`for i in items([1, 2]): echo(i)`

Table 4.1 Some examples of definitions in the `system` module *(continued)*

Definitions	Purpose	Examples
doAssert, assert	Raises an exception if the value specified is `false`. (`assert` calls are removed when compiled with `-d:release`. `doAssert` calls are always present.)	`doAssert(true)`

In addition to the definitions in table 4.1, the `system` module also contains types that map directly to C types. Remember that Nim compiles to C by default and that these types are necessary to interface with C libraries. Interfacing with C is an advanced topic; I'll go into it in more detail in chapter 8.

Whenever the `--threads:on` flag is specified when compiling, the system module includes the `threads` and `channels` modules. This means that all the definitions found in those modules are available through the `system` module. These modules implement threads that provide a useful abstraction for concurrent execution. Concurrency will be touched on in more detail in chapter 6.

Other modules in the core category include `threadpool` and `locks`, both of which implement different threading abstractions, and `macros`, which implements an API for metaprogramming.

The main module in the core that you'll be interested in is the `system` module. The others aren't as important, and you'll be using them only for specialized tasks like concurrency.

You should now have a basic idea of what some of the core modules implement, particularly the procedures and types defined in the implicitly imported `system` module. Next, let's look at the modules that implement data structures and common algorithms, and how they can be used.

4.4 Data structures and algorithms

A large proportion of data structures are defined in the `system` module, including ones you've already seen in chapter 2: `seq`, `array`, and `set`.

Other data structures are implemented as separate modules in the standard library. These modules are listed under the "Collections and algorithms" category in the standard library documentation. They include the `tables`, `sets`, `lists`, `queues`, `intsets`, and `critbits` modules.

Many of those modules have niche use cases, so we won't go into much detail about them, but we will talk about the `tables` and `sets` modules. We'll also look at some modules that implement different algorithms to deal with these data structures.

4.4.1   The tables module

Assume that you're writing an application that stores the average life expectancy of different kinds of animals. After adding all the data, you may wish to look up the average life expectancy of a specific animal. The data can be stored in many different data structures to accommodate the lookup.

One data structure that can be used to store the data is a sequence. The sequence type seq[T] defines a list of elements of type T. It can be used to store a dynamic list of elements of any type; *dynamic* refers to the fact that a sequence can grow to hold more items at runtime.

The following listing shows one way that the data describing the average life expectancy of different animals could be stored.

> **Listing 4.11   Defining a list of integers and strings**

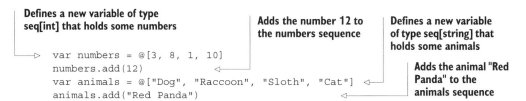

Defines a new variable of type seq[int] that holds some numbers

Adds the number 12 to the numbers sequence

Defines a new variable of type seq[string] that holds some animals

Adds the animal "Red Panda" to the animals sequence

```
var numbers = @[3, 8, 1, 10]
numbers.add(12)
var animals = @["Dog", "Raccoon", "Sloth", "Cat"]
animals.add("Red Panda")
```

In listing 4.11, the numbers variable holds the ages of each of the animals. The animals' names are then stored in the animals sequence. Each age stored in the numbers sequence has the same position as the animal it corresponds to in animals, but that's not intuitive and raises many issues. For example, it's possible to add an animal's average age expectancy to numbers without adding the corresponding animal's name into animals, and vice versa. A better approach is to use a data structure called a *hash table*.

A hash table is a data structure that maps keys to values. It stores a collection of (key, value) pairs, and the key appears only once in the collection. You can add, remove, and modify these pairs as well as look up values based on a key. Hash tables typically support keys of any type, and they're typically more efficient than any other lookup structure, which makes their use popular. Figure 4.6 shows how data about animals can be retrieved from a hash table by performing a lookup based on a key.

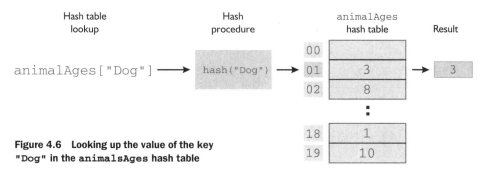

Figure 4.6   Looking up the value of the key "Dog" in the animalsAges hash table

The `tables` module implements a hash table, allowing you to write the following.

Listing 4.12 Creating a hash table

Hash tables are in the tables module, so it needs to be imported.

```
import tables
var animalAges = toTable[string, int](
  {
    "Dog": 3,
    "Raccoon": 8,
    "Sloth": 1,
    "Cat": 10
  })
animalAges["Red Panda"] = 12
```

Adds "Red Panda" to the animalAges hash table

Creates a new Table[string, int] out of the mapping defined in listing 4.11. The key and value types need to be specified because the compiler can't infer them in all cases.

Uses the {:} syntax to define a mapping from string to int

Several different types of hash tables are defined in the `tables` module: the generic version defined as `Table[A, B]`; the `OrderedTable[A, B]`, which remembers the insertion order; and the `CountTable[A]`, which simply counts the number of each key. The ordered and count tables are used far less often than the generic table because their use cases are more specific.

The `Table[A, B]` type is a generic type. In its definition, `A` refers to the type of the hash table's key, and `B` refers to the type of the hash table's value. There are no restrictions on the types of the key or the value, as long as there's a definition of a `hash` procedure for the type specified as the key. You won't run into this limitation until you attempt to use a custom type as a key, because a `hash` procedure is defined for most types in the standard library.

Listing 4.13 Using a custom type as a key in a hash table

The type keyword begins a section of code where types can be defined.

Defines a new Dog object with a name field of type string

```
import tables
type
  Dog = object
    name: string

var dogOwners = initTable[Dog, string]()
dogOwners[Dog(name: "Charlie")] = "John"
```

Creates a new instance of the Dog object and uses that as the key. Sets the value of that key in the dogOwners hash table to "John".

The initTable procedure can be used to initialize a new empty hash table.

Compiling listing 4.13 will result in the following output:

```
file.nim(7, 10) template/generic instantiation from here
lib/pure/collections/tableimpl.nim(92, 21)
    template/generic instantiation from here
lib/pure/collections/tableimpl.nim(43, 12)
    Error: type mismatch: got (Dog)
```

These errors are inside the standard library because that's where the call to hash(key) is made.

This refers to dogOwners [Dog(name: "Charlie")] = "John", where you're trying to use the Dog as the key.

```
but expected one of:                   ◁
hashes.hash(x: T)
hashes.hash(x: pointer)
hashes.hash(x: T)
hashes.hash(x: float)
hashes.hash(x: set[A])
hashes.hash(x: T)
hashes.hash(x: string)
hashes.hash(x: int)
hashes.hash(aBuf: openarray[A], sPos: int, ePos: int)
hashes.hash(x: int64)
hashes.hash(x: char)
hashes.hash(sBuf: string, sPos: int, ePos: int)
hashes.hash(x: openarray[A])
```

> Lists all the available definitions of
> the hash procedure. As you can see,
> there's no definition for the Dog
> type present in that list.

The compiler rejects the code with the excuse that it can't find the definition of a hash procedure for the Dog type. Thankfully, it's easy to define a hash procedure for custom types.

> **Listing 4.14   Defining a hash procedure for custom types**

```
import tables, hashes        ◁
type
  Dog = object
    name: string

proc hash(x: Dog): Hash =    ◁
  result = x.name.hash        ◁
  result = !$result           ◁

var dogOwners = initTable[Dog, string]()
dogOwners[Dog(name: "Charlie")] = "John"
```

> Imports the hashes module, which
> defines procedures for computing hashes

> Defines a hash procedure for the Dog type

> Uses the Dog's name field to compute a hash

> Uses the !$ operator to
> finalize the computed hash

The code in listing 4.14 shows in bold the additions that make the example compile. The hashes module is necessary to aid in computing a hash in the hash procedure. It defines the Hash type, the hash procedure for many common types including string, and the !$ operator. The !$ operator finalizes the computed hash, which is necessary when writing a custom hash procedure. The use of the !$ operator ensures that the computed hash is unique.

4.4.2   *The sets module*

Now let's have a quick look at another data structure: the set. The basic set type, introduced in chapter 2, is defined in the system module. This set type has a limitation—its base type is limited to an ordinal type of a certain size, specifically one of the following:

- int8, int16
- uint8/byte, uint16
- char
- enum

Attempting to define a set with any other base type, such as set[int64], will result in an error.

The sets module defines a HashSet[A] type that doesn't have this limitation. Just like the Table[A,B] type, the HashSet[A] type requires a hash procedure for the type A to be defined. The following listing creates a new HashSet[string] variable.

> **Listing 4.15 Modeling an access list using a HashSet**

Imports the sets module where the toSet procedure is defined

Defines a new HashSet[string] with a list of names

```
import sets
var accessSet = toSet(["Jack", "Hurley", "Desmond"])
if "John" notin accessSet:
  echo("Access Denied")
else:
  echo("Access Granted")
```

Checks if John is in the access set, and if he's not, displays the "Access Denied" message

If John is in the access set, displays the "Access Granted" message

Determining whether an element is within a set is much more efficient than checking whether it's within a sequence or array, because each element of a set doesn't need to be checked. This makes a very big difference when the list of elements grows, because the time complexity is $O(1)$ for sets and $O(n)$ for sequences.[2]

In addition to the HashSet[A] type, the sets module also defines an Ordered-Set[A] type that remembers the insertion order.

4.4.3 *The algorithms*

Nim's standard library also includes an algorithm module defining a selection of algorithms that work on some of the data structures mentioned so far, particularly sequences and arrays.

Among the most useful algorithms in the algorithm module is a sorting algorithm defined in the sort procedure. The procedure takes either an array or a sequence of values and sorts them according to a specified compare procedure.

Let's jump straight to an example that sorts a list of names, allowing you to display it to the user in alphabetical order, thereby making the process of searching the list much easier.

> **Listing 4.16 Sorting using the algorithm module**

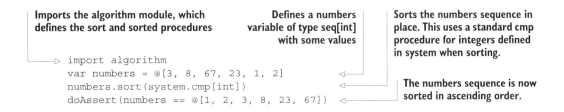

Imports the algorithm module, which defines the sort and sorted procedures

Defines a numbers variable of type seq[int] with some values

Sorts the numbers sequence in place. This uses a standard cmp procedure for integers defined in system when sorting.

```
import algorithm
var numbers = @[3, 8, 67, 23, 1, 2]
numbers.sort(system.cmp[int])
doAssert(numbers == @[1, 2, 3, 8, 23, 67])
```

The numbers sequence is now sorted in ascending order.

---

[2] For more info on time complexity, see the Wikipedia article: https://en.wikipedia.org/wiki/Time_complexity.

```
var names = ["Dexter", "Anghel", "Rita", "Debra"]
let sorted = names.sorted(system.cmp[string])
  doAssert(sorted == @["Anghel", "Debra", "Dexter", "Rita"])
  doAssert(names == ["Dexter", "Anghel", "Rita", "Debra"])
```

Returns a copy of the names array as a sequence with the elements sorted. This uses the standard cmp procedure for strings defined in system when sorting.

The names array has not been modified.

The sorted sequence contains the elements in ascending alphabetical order.

Defines a new names variable of type array[4, string] with some values

The code in listing 4.16 shows two different ways that both sequences and arrays can be sorted: using the sort procedure, which sorts the list in place, and using the sorted procedure, which returns a copy of the original list with the elements sorted. The former is more efficient because no copy of the original list needs to be made.

Note that the sorted procedure returns a seq[T] type, no matter what the input type is. This is why the sorted comparison must be done against a sequence literal.

Consider the system.cmp[int] procedure used in the sort call. Notice the lack of parentheses, (). Without them the procedure isn't called but is instead passed as a value to the sort procedure. The definition of the system.cmp procedure is actually pretty simple.

Listing 4.17 The definition of the generic cmp procedure

```
proc cmp*[T](x, y: T): int =
  if x == y: return 0
  if x < y: return -1
  else: return 1

doAssert(cmp(6, 5) == 1)
doAssert(cmp(5, 5) == 0)
doAssert(cmp(5, 6) == -1)
```

Defines a new generic cmp procedure taking two parameters and returning an integer

The sort procedure expects the specified cmp procedure to return a value that's larger than 0 when x > y.

Whereas when x == y, sort expects cmp to return exactly 0.

When x < y, sort expects cmp to return a value less than 0.

The cmp procedure is generic. It takes two parameters, x and y, both of type T. In listing 4.16, when the cmp procedure is passed to the sort procedure the first time, the T is bound to int because int is specified in the square brackets. In listing 4.17, the compiler can infer the T type for you, so there's no need to specify the types explicitly. You'll learn more about generics in chapter 8.

The cmp procedure will work for any type T as long as both the == and < operators are defined for it. The predefined cmp should be enough for most of your use cases, but you can also write your own cmp procedures and pass them to sort.

The algorithm module includes many other definitions that work on both arrays and sequences. For example, there's a reverse procedure that reverses the order of the elements of a sequence or array and a fill procedure that fills every position in an array with the specified value. For a full list of procedures, take a look at the algorithm module documentation: http://nim-lang.org/docs/algorithm.html.

4.4.4 Other modules

There are many other modules that implement data structures in Nim's standard library. Before you decide to implement a data structure yourself, take a look at the list of modules in Nim's standard library (http://nim-lang.org/docs/lib.html). It includes linked lists, queues, ropes, and much more.

There are also many more modules dedicated to manipulating data structures, such as the `sequtils` module, which includes many useful procedures for manipulating sequences and other lists. These procedures should be familiar to you if you have any previous experience with functional programming. For example, `apply` allows you to apply a procedure to each element of a sequence, `filter` returns a new list with elements that have fulfilled a specified predicate, and so on. To learn more about the `sequtils` module, take a look at its documentation: http://nim-lang.org/docs/sequtils.html.

This section provided some examples of the most useful data structures and algorithms in Nim's standard library. Let's now look at modules that allow us to make use of the services an OS provides.

4.5   Interfacing with the operating system

The programs that you create will usually require an OS to function. The OS manages your computer's hardware and software and provides common services for computer programs.

These services are available through a number of OS APIs, and many of the modules in Nim's standard library abstract these APIs to provide a single cross-platform Nim API that's easy to use in Nim code. Almost all of the modules that do so are listed under the "Generic Operating System Services" category in the standard library module list (https://nim-lang.org/docs/lib.html). These modules implement a range of OS services, including the following:

- Accessing the filesystem
- Manipulating file and folder paths
- Retrieving environment variables
- Reading command-line arguments
- Executing external processes
- Accessing the current system time and date
- Manipulating the time and date

Many of these services are essential to successfully implementing some applications. In the previous chapter, I showed you how to read command-line arguments and communicate with applications over a network. Both of these are services provided by the OS, but communicating with applications over a network isn't in the preceding list because it has its own category in the standard library. I'll talk about modules that deal with networks and internet protocols in section 4.7.

4.5.1   *Working with the filesystem*

A typical filesystem consists primarily of files and folders. This is something that the three major OSs thankfully agree on, but you don't need to look far to start seeing differences. Even something as simple as a file path isn't consistent. Take a look at table 4.2, which shows the file path to a file.txt file in the user's home directory.

Table 4.2   **File paths on different operating systems**

Operating system	Path to file in home directory
Windows	C:\Users\user\file.txt
Mac OS	/Users/user/file.txt
Linux	/home/user/file.txt

Note both the different directory separators and the different locations of what's known as the *home directory*. This inconsistency proves problematic when you want to write software that works on all three of these OSs.

The os module defines constants and procedures that allow you to write cross-platform code. The following example shows how to create and write to a new file at each of the file paths defined in table 4.2, without having to write different code for each of the OSs.

> **Listing 4.18   Write "Some Data" to file.txt in the home directory**

The os module defines the getHomeDir procedure as well as the / operator used on the second line.

```
import os
let path = getHomeDir() / "file.txt"
writeFile(path, "Some Data")
```

The getHomeDir proc returns the appropriate path to the home directory, depending on the current OS. The / operator is like the & concatenation operator, but it adds a path separator between the home directory and file.txt.

The writeFile procedure is defined in the system module. It simply writes the specified data to the file at the path specified.

To give you a better idea of how a path is computed, take a look at table 4.3.

Table 4.3   **The results of path-manipulation procedures**

Expression	Operating system	Result
getHomeDir()	Windows	C:\Users\username\
	Mac OS	/Users/username/
	Linux	/home/username/
getHomeDir() / "file.txt"	Windows	C:\Users\username\file.txt
	Mac OS	/Users/username/file.txt
	Linux	/home/username/file.txt

THE JOINPATH PROCEDURE   You can use the equivalent `joinPath` instead of the `/` operator if you prefer; for example, `joinPath(getHomeDir(), "file.txt")`.

The `os` module includes other procedures for working with file paths including `splitPath`, `parentDir`, `tailDir`, `isRootDir`, `splitFile`, and others. The code in listing 4.19 shows how some of them can be used. In each `doAssert` line, the right side of the `==` shows the expected result.

Listing 4.19   Path-manipulation procedures

Imports the os module to access the procedures used next.

Splits the path into a tuple containing a head and a tail

```
import os
doAssert(splitPath("usr/local/bin") == ("usr/local", "bin"))
doAssert(parentDir("/Users/user") == "/Users")
doAssert(tailDir("usr/local/bin") == "local/bin")
doAssert(isRootDir("/"))
doAssert(splitFile("/home/user/file.txt") == ("/home/user", "file", ".txt"))
```

Returns true if the specified directory is a root directory

Removes the first directory specified in the path and returns the rest

Returns the path to the parent directory of the path specified

Splits the specified file path into a tuple containing the directory, filename, and file extension

The `os` module also defines the `existsDir` and `existsFile` procedures for determining whether a specified directory or file exists. There are also a number of iterators that allow you to iterate over the files and directories in a specified directory path.

Listing 4.20   Displaying the contents of the home directory

Imports the os module to access the walkDir iterator and the getHomeDir procedure

Uses the walkDir iterator to go through each of the files in your home directory. The iterator will yield a value whenever a new file, directory, or link is found.

```
import os
for kind, path in walkDir(getHomeDir()):
  case kind
  of pcFile: echo("Found file: ", path)
  of pcDir: echo("Found directory: ", path)
  of pcLinkToFile, pcLinkToDir: echo("Found link: ", path)
```

When the path references a file, displays the message "Found file: " together with the file path

When the path references either a link to a file or a link to a directory, displays the message "Found link: " together with the link path

Checks what the path variable references: a file, a directory, or a link

When the path references a directory, displays the message "Found directory: " together with the directory path

The os module also implements many more procedures, iterators, and types for dealing with the filesystem. The Nim developers have ensured that the implementation is flexible and that it works on all OSs and platforms. The amount of functionality implemented in this module is too large to fully explore in this chapter, so I strongly recommend that you look at the os module's documentation yourself (http://nim-lang.org/docs/os.html). The documentation includes a list of all the procedures defined in the module, together with examples and explanations of how those procedures can be used effectively.

4.5.2 *Executing an external process*

You may occasionally want your application to start up another program. For example, you may wish to open your website in the user's default browser. One important thing to keep in mind when doing this is that the execution of your application will be blocked until the execution of the external program finishes. Executing processes is currently completely synchronous, just like reading standard input, as discussed in the previous chapter.

The osproc module defines multiple procedures for executing a process, and some of them are simpler than others. The simpler procedures are very convenient, but they don't always allow much customization regarding how the external process should be executed, whereas the more complex procedures do provide this.

The simplest way to execute an external process is using the execCmd procedure. It takes a command as a parameter and executes it. After the command completes executing, execCmd returns the exit code of that command. The standard output, standard error, and standard input are all inherited from your application's process, so you have no way of capturing the output from the process.

The execCmdEx procedure is almost identical to the execCmd procedure, but it returns both the exit code of the process and the output. The following listing shows how it can be used.

Listing 4.21 Using `execCmdEx` to determine some information about the OS

```
import osproc       ◁── Imports the osproc module where
                         the execCmdEx proc is defined

when defined(windows):                            ◁──  Checks whether this Nim code
  let (ver, _) = execCmdEx("cmd /C ver")    ◁──        is being compiled on Windows
else:
  let (ver, _) = execCmdEx("uname -sr")    ◁──

echo("My operating system is: ", ver)    ◁──
```

Checks whether this Nim code is being compiled on Windows

If this Nim code is being compiled on Windows, executes cmd /C ver using execCmdEx and unpacks the tuple it returns into two variables

Displays the output from the executed command

If this Nim code is not being compiled on Windows, executes uname -sr using execCmdEx and unpacks the tuple it returns into two variables

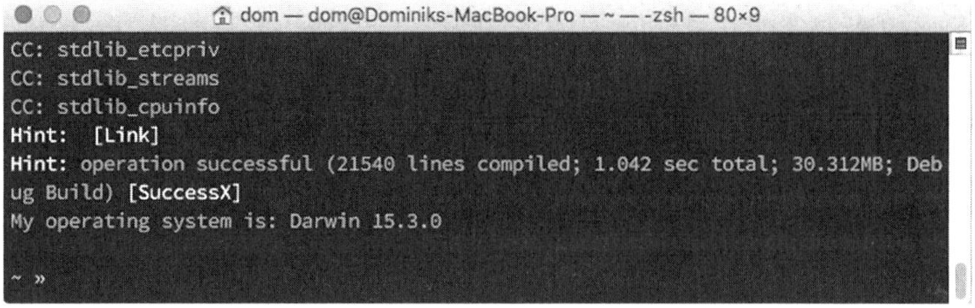

Figure 4.7 The output of listing 4.21

You can compile and run this application and see what's displayed. Figure 4.7 shows the output of listing 4.21 on my MacBook.

Keep in mind that this probably isn't the best way to determine the current OS version.

GETTING THE CURRENT OS There's an `osinfo` package available online that uses the OS API directly to get OS information (https://github.com/nim-lang/osinfo).

The compile-time if statement

In Nim, the `when` statement (introduced in chapter 2) is similar to an `if` statement, with the main difference being that it's evaluated at compile time instead of at runtime.

In listing 4.21, the `when` statement is used to determine the OS for which the current module is being compiled. The `defined` procedure checks at compile time whether the specified symbol is defined. When the code is being compiled for Windows, the `windows` symbol is defined, so the code immediately under the `when` statement is compiled, whereas the code in the `else` branch is not. On other OSs, the code in the `else` branch is compiled and the preceding code is ignored.

The scope rules for `when` are also a bit different from those for `if`. A `when` statement doesn't create a new scope, which is why it's possible to access the `ver` variable outside it.

Listing 4.21 also shows the use of an underscore as one of the identifiers in the unpacked tuple; it tells the compiler that you're not interested in a part of the tuple. This is useful because it removes warnings the compiler makes about unused variables.

That's the basics of executing processes using the `osproc` module, together with a bit of new Nim syntax and semantics. The `osproc` module contains other procedures that allow for more control of processes, including writing to the process's standard input and running more than one process at a time. Be sure to look at the documentation for the `osproc` module to learn more.

4.5.3   *Other operating system services*

There are many other modules that allow you to use the services provided by OSs, and they're part of the "Generic Operating System Services" category of the standard library. Some of them will be used in later chapters; others, you can explore on your own. The documentation for these modules is a good resource for learning more: http://nim-lang.org/docs/lib.html#pure-libraries-generic-operating-system-services

4.6   *Understanding and manipulating data*

Every program deals with data, so understanding and manipulating it is crucial. You've already learned some ways to represent data in Nim, both in chapter 2 and earlier in this chapter.

The most-used type for representing data is the `string` type, because it can represent just about any piece of data. An integer can be represented as `"46"`, a date as `"June 26th"`, and a list of values as `"2, Bill, King, Programmer"`.

Your programs need a way to understand and manipulate this data, and parsers can help with this. A parser will look at a value, in many cases a text value of type `string`, and build a data structure out of it. There is the possibility of the value being incorrect, so a parser will check for syntax errors while parsing the value.

The Nim standard library is full of parsers. There are so many of them that there's a full category named "Parsers." The parsers available in the standard library can parse the following: command-line arguments, configuration files in the `.ini` format, XML, JSON, HTML, CSV, SQL, and much more. You saw how to use the JSON parser in chapter 3; in this section, I'll show you how to use some of the other parsers.

The names of many of the modules that implement parsers begin with the word `parse`, such as `parseopt` and `parsexml`. Some of them have modules that implement a more intuitive API on top of them, such as these XML parsers: `xmldom`, `xmltree`, `xmldomparser`, and `xmlparser`. The latter two modules create a tree-like data structure out of the `parsexml` module's output. The former two modules are then used to manipulate the tree-like data structures. The `xmldom` module provides a web DOM–like API, whereas the `xmltree` module provides a more idiomatic Nim API. The `json` module defines both a high-level API for dealing with JSON objects and a low-level parser that parses JSON and emits objects that represent the current data being parsed.

4.6.1   *Parsing command-line arguments*

Describing how each of these modules can be used for parsing would require its own chapter. Instead, I'll present a specific data-parsing problem and show you some ways that this problem can be solved using the modules available in Nim's standard library.

The problem we'll look at is the parsing of command-line arguments. In chapter 3, you retrieved command-line arguments using the `paramStr()` procedure, and you used the returned `string` value directly. This worked well because the application didn't support any options or flags.

Let's say you want the application to support an optional `port` flag on the command line—one that expects a port number to follow. You may, for example, be writing a server application and want to give the user the option to select the port on which the server will run. Executing an application called `parsingex` with such an argument would look like this: `./parsingex --port=1234`. The `--port=1234` part can be accessed with a `paramStr()` procedure call, as follows.

Listing 4.22 Retrieving command-line arguments using `paramStr`

```
import os

let param1 = paramStr(1)
```

Imports the os module, which
defines the paramStr procedure

The command-line argument at index I will be
equal to "--port=I234", assuming the application
is executed as in the preceding discussion.

Now you've got a `string` value in the `param1` variable that contains both the flag name and the value associated with it. How do you extract those and separate them?

There are many ways, some less valid than others. I'll show you a couple of ways, and in doing so I'll show you many different ways that the `string` type can be manipulated and understood by your program.

Let's start by taking a substring of the original string value with the `substr` procedure defined in the `system` module. It takes a `string` value, a start index, and an end index, with both indexes represented as integers. It then returns a new copy of the string, starting at the first index specified and ending at the end index.

MORE WAYS TO MANIPULATE STRINGS Nim strings can be modified at runtime because they're mutable, which means they can be modified in place, without the need to allocate a new copy of the string. You can use the `add` procedure to append characters and other strings to them, and `delete` (defined in the `strutils` module) to delete characters from them.

Listing 4.23 Parsing the flag using `substr`

```
import os

let param1 = paramStr(1)
let flagName = param1.substr(2, 5)
let flagValue = param1.substr(7)
```

Gets the substring of
paraml from index 2
to index 5. This will
result in "port".

Gets the substring of
paraml from index 7 to
the end of the string.
This will result in "I234".

Figure 4.8 shows how the indexes passed to `substr` determine which substrings are returned.

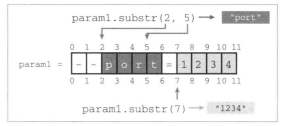

Figure 4.8   The `substr` procedure

The slice operator

A series of two dots, otherwise known as the `..` operator, can be used to create a `Slice` object. A `Slice` can then be fed into the `[]` operator, which will return a substring. This is similar to the `substr` procedure, but it supports reverse indexes using the `^` operator.

Same as using substr(2, 5); returns a substring from index 2 to index 5

Returns a substring from index 7 to the end of the string. The `^` operator counts back from the end of the string.

```
doAssert("--port=1234"[2 .. 5] == "port")
doAssert("--port=1234"[7 .. ^1] == "1234")
doAssert("--port=1234"[7 .. ^3] == "12")
```

Returns a substring from index 7 to the end of the string minus 2 characters

The code in listing 4.23 will work, but it is not very flexible. You might wish to support other flags, and to do that you will need to duplicate the code and change the indices.

In order to improve this, you can use the `strutils` module, which contains many definitions for working with strings. For example, `toUpperAscii` and `toLowerAscii` convert each character in a string to upper- or lowercase, respectively.[3] `parseInt` converts a string into an integer, `startsWith` determines whether a string starts with another string, and there are many others.

There's a specific procedure that can help you split up the flag string properly, and it's called `split`.

Listing 4.24　Parsing the flag using `split`

Imports the strutils module, where the split procedure is defined

Separates the param1 string value into multiple different strings at the location where an "=" character occurs. The split procedure returns a sequence of strings, in this case @["--port", "1234"].

```
import os, strutils

let param1 = paramStr(1)
let flagSplit = param1.split('=')
let flagName = flagSplit[0].substr(2)
let flagValue = flagSplit[1]
```

Grabs the second string in the sequence returned by split

Grabs the first string in the sequence returned by split and removes the first two characters

This is still poor-man's parsing, but it does work. There's no error handling, but the code should work for many different flags. But what happens when requirements change? Say, for example, one of your users prefers to separate the flag name from the value using the `:` symbol. This change is easy to implement because the `split`

---

[3]　The procedures are named this way because they don't support unicode characters. To get unicode support, you should use the `toUpper` and `toLower` procedures defined in the `unicode` module.

procedure accepts a set[char], so you can specify {'=', ':'} and the string will be split on both = and :.

The split procedure works very well for parsing something as simple as this example, but I'm sure you can imagine cases where it wouldn't be a good choice. For example, if your requirements change so that the flag name can now contain the = character, you'll run into trouble.

We'll stop here for now. You'll learn more about parsing in chapter 6, where you'll see how to use the parseutils module to perform more-advanced parsing.

Thankfully, you don't need to parse command-line arguments like this yourself. As I mentioned previously, the Nim standard library contains a parseopt module that does this for you. The following listing shows how it can be used to parse command-line arguments.

> **Listing 4.25   Parsing the flag using `parseopt`**

Imports the parseopt module, which defines the getOpt iterator

Iterates over each command-line argument. The getOpt iterator yields three values: the kind of argument that was parsed, the key, and the value.

```
import parseopt

for kind, key, val in getOpt():
  case kind
  of cmdArgument:
    echo("Got a command argument: ", key)
  of cmdLongOption, cmdShortOption:
    case key
    of "port": echo("Got port: ", val)
    else: echo("Got another flag --", key, " with value: ", val)
  of cmdEnd: discard
```

Checks the kind of argument that was parsed

If a simple flag with no value was parsed, displays just the flag name

The command-argument parsing has ended, so this line does nothing.

If a flag with a value was parsed, checks if it's --port and displays a specific message if it is, showing the port value. Otherwise, displays a generic message showing the flag name and value.

This code is a bit more verbose, but it handles errors, supports other types of flags, and goes through each command-line argument. This parser is quite tedious, and, unfortunately, the standard library doesn't contain any modules that build on top of it. There are many third-party modules that make the job of parsing and retrieving command-line arguments much easier, and these are available through the Nimble package manager, which I'll introduce in the next chapter.

Compile and run the code in listing 4.25. Try to pass different command-line arguments to the program and see what it outputs.

This section should have given you some idea of how you can manipulate the most common and versatile type: the string. I've talked about the different parsing modules available in Nim's standard library and showed you how one of them can be used to parse command-line arguments. I also introduced you to the strutils module, which contains many useful procedures for manipulating strings. Be sure to check out its documentation and the documentation for the other modules later.

4.7   *Networking and the internet*

The Nim standard library offers a large selection of modules that can be used for networking. You've already been introduced to the asynchronous event loop and the asynchronous sockets defined in the `asyncdispatch` and `asyncnet` modules, respectively. These modules provide the building blocks for many of the modules in the standard library's "Internet Protocols and Support" category.

The standard library also includes the `net` module, which is the synchronous equivalent of the `asyncnet` module. It contains some procedures that can be used for both asynchronous and synchronous sockets.

The more interesting modules are the ones that implement certain internet protocols, such as HTTP, SMTP, and FTP.[4] The modules that implement these protocols are called `httpclient`, `smtp`, and `asyncftpclient`, respectively. There's also an `asynchttpserver` module that implements a high-performance HTTP server, allowing your Nim application to serve web pages to clients such as your web browser.

The main purpose of the `httpclient` module is to request resources from the internet. For example, the Nim website can be retrieved as follows.

> **Listing 4.26   Requesting the Nim website using the `httpclient` module**

The asyncdispatch module defines an asynchronous event loop that's necessary to use the asynchronous HTTP client. It defines the waitFor procedure, which runs the event loop.

The httpclient module defines the asynchronous HTTP client and related procedures.

```
import asyncdispatch
import httpclient

let client = newAsyncHttpClient()
let response = waitFor client.get("http://nim-lang.org")
echo(response.version)
echo(response.status)
echo(waitFor response.body)
```

Creates a new instance of the AsyncHttpClient type

Displays the HTTP version that the server responded with (likely, "1.1")

Requests the Nim website using HTTP GET, which retrieves the website. The waitFor procedure runs the event loop until the get procedure is finished.

Displays the HTTP status that the server responded with. If the request is successful, it will be "200 OK".

Displays the body of the response. If the request is successful, this will be the HTML of the Nim website.

---

[4] For details on HTTP, SMTP, and FTP, be sure to view their respective Wikipedia articles.

The code in listing 4.26 will work for any resource or website. Today, the Nim website is served over SSL, you'll need to compile listing 4.26 with the `-d:ssl` flag in order to enable SSL support.

These modules are all fairly simple to use. Be sure to check out their documentation for details about the procedures they define and how those procedures can be used.

There may be protocols that the standard library misses, or custom protocols that you'd like to implement yourself. A wide range of networking protocols has been implemented as libraries outside the standard library by other Nim developers. They can be found using the Nimble package manager, which you'll learn about in the next chapter.

4.8 Summary

- A library is a collection of modules; modules, in turn, implement a variety of behaviors.
- Identifiers in Nim are private by default and can be exported using `*`.
- Modules are imported into the importing module's global namespace by default.
- The `from module import x` syntax can be used to selectively import identifiers from a module.
- The standard library is organized into pure, impure, and wrapper categories.
- The `system` module is imported implicitly and contains many commonly used definitions.
- The `tables` module implements a hash table that can be used to store a mapping between keys and values.
- The `algorithms` module defines a `sort` procedure that can be used for sorting arrays and sequences.
- The `os` module contains many procedures for accessing the computer's filesystem.
- Web pages can be retrieved using the `httpclient` module.

Package management

5

This chapter covers

- Understanding how Nimble helps you develop software
- Using Nimble packages to develop software
- Creating Nimble packages and publishing them

Today package managers have a central role in the development of software. This was not always the case; the Comprehensive Perl Archive Network, or CPAN, was one of the first large software repositories to have existed solely for a specific programming language. It consists of over 150,000 modules of Perl code, making it one of the biggest software module repositories from a single programming language. It's also one of the earliest examples of such a software repository; its success has influenced many others. Today, software repositories exist for just about all programming languages.

A *package* is an abstract term given to a collection of modules; these modules may form a library or an application. A *package manager* automates the process of downloading, installing, updating, and removing packages. Libraries contain implementations of different behavior, and can be invoked using a well-defined interface. These implementations are stored and exposed through one or more modules.

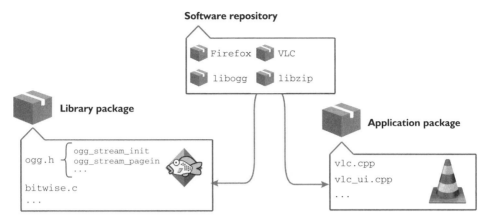

Figure 5.1   Comparison between packages, libraries, applications, and software repositories

Software repositories distribute a number of different packages, allowing those packages to be freely downloaded. You could download packages manually, but doing so would be tedious. For example, a package may have dependencies: other packages that need to be installed first for the package to work correctly. Package managers ensure that dependencies are correctly installed automatically. Figure 5.1 shows how packages, libraries, applications, and software repositories relate to each other.

Most programming languages have at least one package manager; some have multiple. Nim's package manager is important because it's a tool that gives you access to the hundreds of open source packages contained in Nim's package repository.

This chapter provides an overview of Nimble, the Nim package manager, including how to install and create packages. Be sure to also take a look at the Nimble documentation: https://github.com/nim-lang/nimble.

5.1   The Nim package manager

There are many package managers in existence today, but not all of them are designed for the same purpose. Package managers are primarily split into two categories: system-level and application-level.

System-level package managers are typically bundled with the OS. They allow the user to install a popular set of applications and libraries written in many different programming languages. Application-level package managers are more specific; they focus on libraries and applications written in a single programming language.

Imagine you got a brand-new computer, and you'd like to watch some movies on it. One of the most widely used applications for watching video is VLC, but it doesn't come preinstalled on computers. You can instruct a package manager to install VLC, together with any missing libraries VLC needs to function. A system-level package manager would be perfect for this.

Figure 5.2 System-level vs. application-level package managers

VLC comes with a library called libvlc; this library allows any application to play video with the same accuracy as VLC itself. If you wanted to make use of this library in your Nim application, you'd need a Nim package that implements a Nim interface to that library. Such a package would be installed via an application-level package manager.

Figure 5.2 shows examples of some common system-level and application-level package managers.

Package managers also differ in the way that they distribute packages. Some distribute packages in the form of binaries, whereas others distribute the source code. In the latter case, the packages must then be compiled on the user's computer using a compiler.

Nim's package manager is called *Nimble*. Nimble is an application-level package manager, and it distributes packages in the form of source code. This is similar to other application-level package managers such as Python's pip and NodeJS's npm. Nimble is already being used by many Nim programmers, even though it's not yet stable and there are still some features missing from it. This section will show you how the current version of Nimble (0.7.2 as of writing) can be used to manage Nim libraries and applications. Keep in mind that Nimble is evolving every day and that some of the things mentioned in this section may change in the future.

5.2 *Installing Nimble*

The good news is that you most likely have Nimble installed already. Nim installation packages have started to include Nimble since around version 0.15.0, so if you have Nim installed, you should have Nimble installed too.

You can easily check whether this is the case by running `nimble -v` in the terminal. If you see information about Nimble's version, you have Nimble installed; if you see something like "command not found: nimble," you don't.

Keep in mind that, in order to install packages, Nimble may execute an external application called Git, which you must also have installed and available in your path. For more details, look at the Nimble installation page on GitHub: https://github.com/nim-lang/nimble#installation.

5.3 The nimble command-line tool

You should now have Nimble installed on your system. Running `nimble` in a new terminal window should display a list of commands supported by Nimble. Figure 5.3 shows just a few of these.

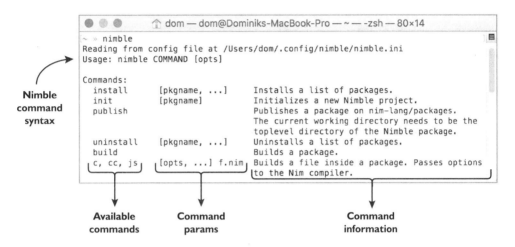

Figure 5.3 Some commands that Nimble supports

`nimble` will also show the order in which commands should be passed to Nimble. A single command is written after `nimble`, separated by a space. After that come the flags and parameters passed to that command, each separated by a space. For example, to search for any packages that relate to Linux, you can execute `nimble search linux`. You can also specify a `--ver` flag, which will show you the available versions of each package. Figure 5.4 shows the result of a search for "linux" with the `--ver` flag.

Note the "versions:" followed by a list of two different versions in figure 5.4. Those are the versions of the `daemonize` package that can be installed.

Nimble's command-line interface is the primary way of installing, searching for, upgrading, and removing packages. Before I show you how to install packages, though, let's look at what a package actually is.

5.4 What is a Nimble package?

Software is almost always composed of different types of files, including source code, images, sound, and more. For example, let's say you're creating a video game. Video games require a plethora of resources to function, and these need to be bundled together with the game's executable. A package offers a convenient way to bundle such files together with the software.

In the simplest sense, a minimal *Nimble package* is a directory containing a .nimble file and one or more Nim modules.

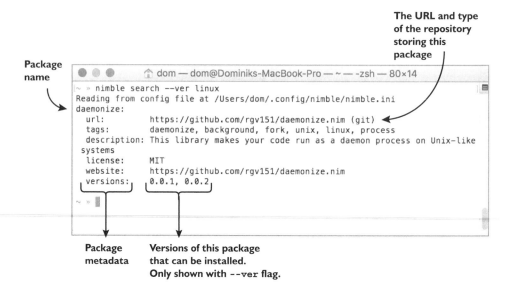

Figure 5.4 Searching for a "linux" package with version information

A .nimble file contains metadata about a package. It specifies a package's name, version, author, dependencies, and more. The *.nimble* part is just a file extension, and the filename of every .nimble file is the same as the name of the package. The following listing shows a simple example of a .nimble file.

Listing 5.1 MyPkg.nimble

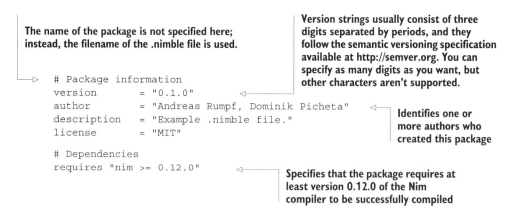

The .nimble files use a Nim-based format that supports a subset of Nim's features. In addition, the format contains some shortcuts for defining information about the package. You can freely define variables, procedures, and more within your .nimble files, and you can even import other modules into them.

Nimble also supports the definition of tasks, as follows:

```
task test, "Run the packages tests!":
  exec "nim c -r tests/mytest.nim"
```

Placing this snippet of code at the end of your .nimble file will allow you to execute `nimble test` to run your package's tests.

Figure 5.5 shows what the contents of a typical standalone Nimble package look like. The data specified in this MyPkg.nimble file is mandatory, and there are many other options you can specify in a .nimble file as well. I can't list them all here, but you'll learn about some of them later in this chapter. For a full list, check out the Nimble documentation on GitHub: https://github.com/nim-lang/nimble#readme.

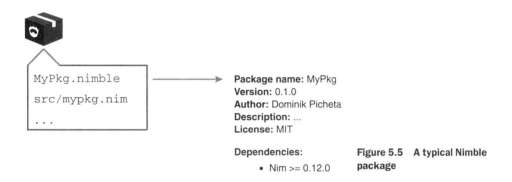

Package name: MyPkg
Version: 0.1.0
Author: Dominik Picheta
Description: ...
License: MIT

Dependencies:
- Nim >= 0.12.0

Figure 5.5   A typical Nimble package

Assuming you have a Nimble package somewhere on your local filesystem, you can easily open a terminal in the directory of that package and execute `nimble install`. When you do this, Nimble will attempt to install the package contained in the current directory. This is useful for local packages that you've created yourself. But what about packages that have been created by other developers? Do you need to download these manually?

Thankfully, the answer to that question is no. As part of the `install` command, a URL can be specified that points to the package you want to install. Currently, this URL must point to either a Git or Mercurial repository, which brings us to the definition of an *external* package: one that can be accessed over the internet. An external Nimble package is either a Git or Mercurial repository containing a .nimble file and one or more Nim modules.

What are Git and Mercurial?
Git and Mercurial are examples of distributed version control systems (DVCSs). A DVCS enables a team of software developers to work together on a software project, and by keeping track of the history of each file, it helps deal with situations where two or more developers end up editing the same files.

(continued)
A *repository* is where the history of a software project is stored. These repositories can be uploaded to a remote server and then subsequently downloaded using the `git` or `hg` command-line tools, for Git and Mercurial, respectively. This allows other developers to work on the project and upload their changes, which you can then download.

After a repository is downloaded, the histories of the files can be explored. You can, for example, see what the state of the repository was a week ago, or back when the repository was first created.

Git and Mercurial repositories may contain additional information, such as tags. Repositories containing Nimble packages must contain a tag that identifies each version of that package. Figure 5.6 shows how an external Nimble package's content can change between revisions.

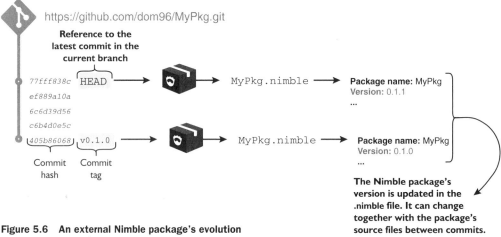

Figure 5.6   An external Nimble package's evolution

In the previous section, I showed you how the `search` command works. With the `--ver` flag, the `search` command lists the tags of each of the package repositories. Nimble interprets each tag as a version.

Nimble packages are coupled to repositories because most libraries and applications are already stored in repositories. Turning a repository into a Nimble package is easy—the repository just needs a .nimble file. Other package managers store their packages on a single centralized server, which has its advantages; this is something that Nimble will eventually also support.

5.5 *Installing Nimble packages*

The installation of Nimble packages is likely the most common task that you'll use Nimble for. You saw an example of the `install` command in the previous section. This command is the primary means of installing packages.

5.5.1 *Using the install command*

The `install` command is powerful. It can do any of the following:

- Install packages on your local filesystem
- Install packages from a specified URL
- Install a package by name
- Install a specific version of a package
- Install multiple packages at once

Installing local packages is simple. Just open a new terminal, `cd` into the directory of your local package (by typing `cd /home/user/MyPkg`, for example), and execute `nimble install`.

To install a package from a URL, open a new terminal and execute `nimble install <your_url_here>`, replacing the `<your_url_here>` with the URL of the package you want to install. Currently, the URL must point to a non-empty Git or Mercurial repository.

Nimble saves you the trouble of remembering a bunch of URLs for different packages. A package repository that contains a listing of packages created by the Nim community is available. Nimble downloads this listing, which contains some basic information about each package, such as the package's URL and name. Remember the `search` command? It searches through this listing, so any of the packages listed in your search results can be installed by specifying their names after the `install` command. For example, to install the `daemonize` package seen in the search results in figure 5.4, execute `nimble install daemonize`.

A specific version of a package can be installed by using the special `@` character after the name of a package. For example, to install version `0.0.1` of the `daemonize` package, execute `nimble install daemonize@0.0.1`. Alternatively, instead of a specific version, you can specify a version range. For example, if you want to install the latest version that's greater than version `0.0.1`, you can execute `nimble install daemonize@>=0.0.1`. Specifying a repository revision is also supported by using the `#` character after the `@` character, such as `nimble install daemonize@#b4be443`.

> **WARNING: SPECIAL CHARACTERS IN SHELLS** Depending on your shell, some of the characters, such as `@`, `>`, or `=`, may be treated as part of the shell's syntax. You may need to escape them or quote the package name and version like so: `nimble install "daemonize@>=0.1.0"`.

Specifying multiple parameters to the `install` command will cause Nimble to install more than one package. The parameters just need to be separated by a space.

5.5.2   *How does the install command work?*

To learn about what the `install` command does, let's look at the previous example command: `nimble install daemonize`. Try executing it now if you haven't already. You should see output similar to that in figure 5.7.

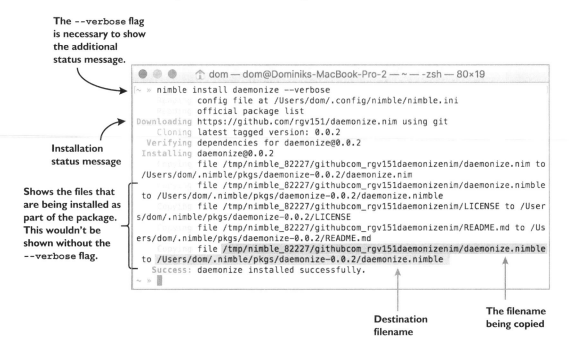

The `--verbose` flag is necessary to show the additional status message.

Installation status message

Shows the files that are being installed as part of the package. This wouldn't be shown without the `--verbose` flag.

Destination filename

The filename being copied

Figure 5.7   The output of `nimble install daemonize`

Nimble's output is currently rather verbose, but it tries to give as much information about the installation as possible. The output that you see in your version of Nimble may be a bit different from figure 5.7, but the key information should remain the same. The messages shown in figure 5.7 show each of the files from the `daemonize` package being copied into /Users/dom/.nimble/pkgs/daemonize-0.0.2/.

Scroll up in your terminal window, and you'll see what Nimble does first: it begins downloading the package. But before that, Nimble needs to know where to download the `daemonize` package from, and it determines this by consulting the package list. Figure 5.8 shows the full installation process and its many subprocesses.

The package list is currently hosted in a Git repository, and it can be accessed on GitHub at the following URL: https://github.com/nim-lang/packages. The package-list repository stores a packages.json file that lists metadata for different packages, including each package's name, URL, description, and more. Nimble can read this list, find the package you specified on the command line, and retrieve that package's URL. That way Nimble can determine the location of that package's repository and can easily download it. Figure 5.9 shows how the `daemonize` package is found in the packages.json file.

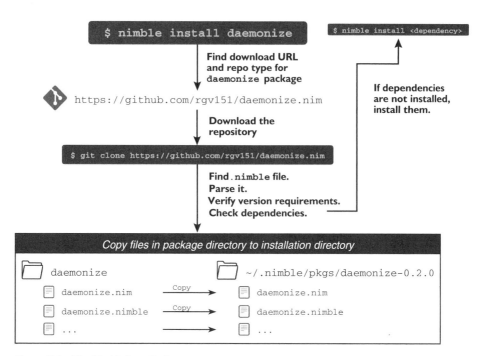

Figure 5.8   The Nimble installation process

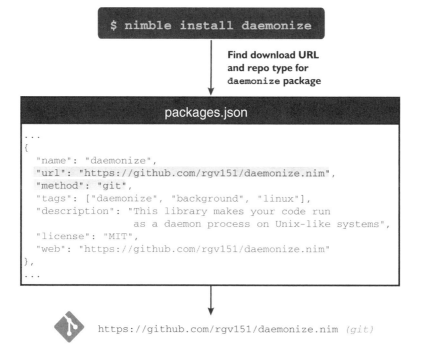

Figure 5.9   Finding information about the `daemonize` package in the packages.json file

PACKAGE LISTS   The package list stored in https://github.com/nim-lang/packages is the official Nimble package list. As of version 0.7.0, Nimble supports multiple package lists, so you can easily create and use your own package list in conjunction with the official one. The "Configuration" section of the Nimble readme explains how this can be done: https://github.com/nim-lang/nimble#configuration.

The download is done using either Git or Mercurial. As part of the download process, Nimble parses the tags on the remote repository and determines which satisfies the version requirements specified by the user. If more than one tag satisfies the version requirements, it picks the highest version. Figure 5.10 shows how Nimble decides which commit of a Nimble package to install.

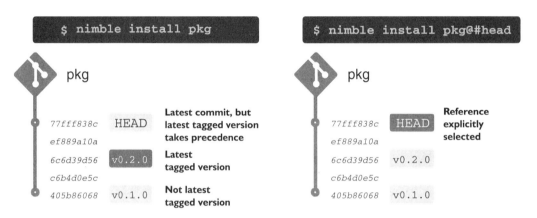

Figure 5.10   How Nimble decides which version of a package to install

Once the download is complete, the package's .nimble file is read, and Nimble verifies the validity of this file. Before installation can commence, the following must be checked:

- The `version` field specified in the .nimble file must correspond to the version that was tagged on the repository.
- The files that will be installed must follow a specific directory layout.
- The correct dependencies specified in the .nimble file must be installed.

Those are some of the most common checks that Nimble performs. If the first two fail, they'll result in an error and the package won't be installed. Missing dependencies will be installed automatically by Nimble. You'll learn more about these checks in the next section, where I'll show you how to create your own Nimble package.

Once the package is successfully validated, the installation commences, and Nimble copies all the files in the package to ~/.nimble/pkgs/pkg-ver, where *ver* is the version of the package and *pkg* is the name of the package.

That's a simple overview of the process involved in installing a Nimble package. This process can become more complicated depending on the options specified in the .nimble file.

5.6   *Creating a Nimble package*

You've likely encountered situations where some functionality in your application could be reused in another application. For example, in chapter 3, you developed a `protocol` module that defines procedures for encoding and decoding chat messages. You might want that module to be usable in other applications.

The easiest way to do so is to create a package out of that module. Your applications can then add that package as a dependency and use the same module easily.

Creating a Nimble package out of your Nim library or application has a number of advantages, such as making the installation of dependencies much easier and allowing others to use your package as a dependency for their own packages.

Creating a Nimble package is also fairly straightforward. All you need to do is create a .nimble file and you're good to go. Nimble's `init` command makes the creation of this file easy. The command will ask you some questions about the package and will create a .nimble file based on your responses. You'll likely still need to edit the resulting .nimble file manually to customize the options further, but once you understand what those options do, that's fairly straightforward.

Once you've created a local Nimble package, you might also want to open source it and publish it in Nimble's package list. To do this, you'll need to initialize a new Git or Mercurial repository. Later in this chapter, I'll show you how a Nimble package can be published.

Let's create a simple Nimble package.

5.6.1   *Choosing a name*

A package's name is very important. It needs to be as short as possible and ideally should describe what functionality the package implements.

> **PACKAGE NAME UNIQUENESS**   When picking a package name, it's a good idea to ensure that it's unique, especially if you intend to publish it to the Nimble package repository.

You must pick a name that doesn't contain any hyphens or at symbols (`-` or `@`). Those characters are treated uniquely by Nimble, so they're disallowed in package names.

The package that you'll create as part of this chapter will implement some very simple procedures for manipulating numbers. You can choose whatever package name you wish, but throughout this chapter I'll use the name `NimbleExample`. If you choose a different name, you'll need to adjust the chapter's example code accordingly.

To get started, create a NimbleExample directory somewhere on your filesystem. It will contain the Nimble package.

5.6.2   *A Nimble package's directory layout*

All Nimble packages must adhere to a specific directory layout. This layout is more important for libraries than applications because an application will be compiled, and in most cases all that needs to be installed will be the application's executable.

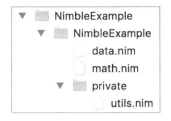

For libraries, the most important rule is to place all modules in a separate directory named after the package. So you need to create another NimbleExample directory inside the NimbleExample directory you've already created. Any modules placed inside that directory will be importable with the `NimbleExample/` prefix, like this: `import NimbleExample/module`.

Figure 5.11
The NimbleExample directory layout

One exception to this rule is that you can place a single module containing the primary functionality of your library in the root directory of your package, but it must share the name of your package. In this case, the module's filename would be Nimble-Example.nim. Figure 5.11 shows what the final directory structure of `NimbleExample` will look like.

For the purposes of this example, create the following math.nim file inside the secondary NimbleExample directory.

Listing 5.2   The `math` module

```
proc add*(a, b: int): int = a + b    ◁──┤
```
Defines a new add procedure taking two integers and returning the sum of those two integers. The procedure is exported using the *.

The code in listing 5.2 is pretty straightforward. It defines a new `add` procedure that adds two integers together. Note the `*` used to export the procedure; it ensures that the `add` procedure can be accessed from other modules. Save the code in listing 5.2 as math.nim in the NimbleExample/NimbleExample directory.

There's an additional convention for modules in a package that are destined to be used only by that package. They should be placed in a private directory, as is the case for the `utils` module defined in listing 5.3. Create a new directory named *private* in the NimbleExample/NimbleExample directory, and save the following code as utils.nim in NimbleExample/NimbleExample/private.

Listing 5.3   The `utils` module

```
proc mult*(a, b: int): int = a * b    ◁──┤
```
Defines a new mult procedure taking two integers and returning the result when those numbers are multiplied. The procedure is exported using the * that follows its name.

The code in listing 5.4 is a bit more complicated. It imports two modules defined in the `NimbleExample` package. The first is the `math` module defined in listing 5.2, and the other is the `utils` module defined in listing 5.3. Save the code in the following listing as data.nim in the NimbleExample/NimbleExample directory.

Listing 5.4 The data module

Imports the math module from the NimbleExample package

Imports the private utils module from the NimbleExample package

Uses the procedures defined in the utils and math modules to calculate the age. The age variable is exported using the *.

```
import NimbleExample/math
import NimbleExample/private/utils
let age* = mult(add(15, 5), 2)
```

The final directory layout should look like what you saw in figure 5.11. Ensure that your local directory layout is the same.

5.6.3 *Writing the .nimble file and sorting out dependencies*

Now that the modules are all in the correct directories, it's time to create the Nimble-Example.nimble file. You can execute `nimble init` in the outer NimbleExample directory to create this file automatically. Figure 5.12 shows an example of what `nimble init` asks and the answers needed to generate the NimbleExample.nimble file shown in listing 5.5.

Listing 5.5 The beginnings of NimbleExample.nimble

```
# Package

version     = "0.1.0"
author      = "Your Name"
description = "Simple package to learn about Nimble"
license     = "MIT"

# Dependencies

requires "nim >= 0.12.0"
```

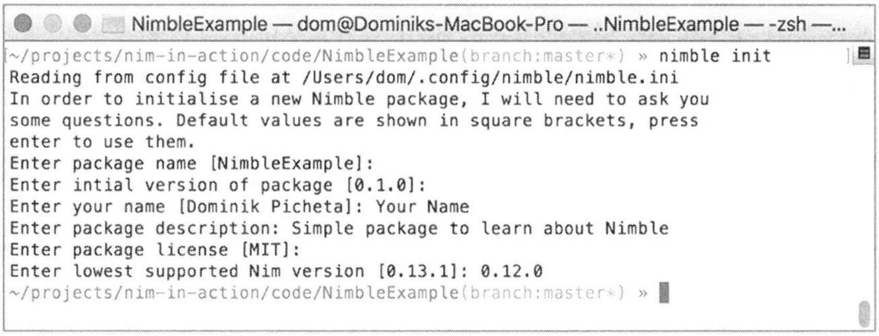

```
● ● ● 🖿 NimbleExample — dom@Dominiks-MacBook-Pro — ..NimbleExample — -zsh —...
~/projects/nim-in-action/code/NimbleExample(branch:master*) » nimble init
Reading from config file at /Users/dom/.config/nimble/nimble.ini
In order to initialise a new Nimble package, I will need to ask you
some questions. Default values are shown in square brackets, press
enter to use them.
Enter package name [NimbleExample]:
Enter intial version of package [0.1.0]:
Enter your name [Dominik Picheta]: Your Name
Enter package description: Simple package to learn about Nimble
Enter package license [MIT]:
Enter lowest supported Nim version [0.13.1]: 0.12.0
~/projects/nim-in-action/code/NimbleExample(branch:master*) » ▮
```

Figure 5.12 The `nimble init` command

After you execute `nimble init` or save the contents of listing 5.5 as NimbleExample
.nimble, you should be able to execute `nimble install`. That should successfully
install your package!

That's how simple it is to create a Nimble package. But creating a Nimble package
is just a small first step in developing Nimble packages. Packages evolve and requirements change, so how can Nimble help you during development?

For example, while developing a package, you may realize that you need the functionality of another Nim library. In many cases, this library will be a Nimble package.
For example, you may want to create a version of `add` for very large integers—ones
bigger than the biggest integer type in Nim's standard library. The `bigints` package
provides this functionality.

Open the math.nim file in the `NimbleExample` package, and change it so that its
contents are the same as those in the next listing. Changes are highlighted in bold.

Listing 5.6   Using the `bigints` package in the math module

```
import bigints
proc add*(a, b: int): int = a + b
proc add*(a, b: BigInt): BigInt = a + b
```

Imports the bigints module from the bigints
package. There's no need to explicitly state
the package name and module name.

Defines an add procedure
for the BigInt type defined
in the bigints module

Now try to compile it by executing `nim c NimbleExample/math`. The compiler should
output something similar to "math.nim(1, 8) Error: cannot open 'bigints'." This
points to the line of code that imports the `bigints` module. The compilation fails
because the `bigints` package hasn't been installed. Install it now by executing `nimble
install bigints` and compile `NimbleExample/math` again. This time the compilation
should succeed.

Does this mean that every user of the `NimbleExample` package will need to install
the `bigints` package manually? Currently, yes. But this is where the dependency specification in the NimbleExample.nimble file comes in—it allows Nimble to install the
dependencies automatically.

When compiling any Nim source code using the Nim compiler, every package that
you've installed using Nimble will be available to that source code. This is why importing the `bigints` module works as soon as you install the `bigints` package.

Nimble supports a handy c command that does exactly what the Nim compiler
does: it compiles the specified file. Try compiling the math.nim file using Nimble by
executing `nimble c NimbleExample/math` and note the results.

You may be surprised by the failure in execution, but it illustrates the key difference
between compiling with the Nim compiler directly, and compiling with Nimble. Nimble
doesn't let you import any modules whose packages you haven't specified as dependencies in your project's .nimble file, with the exception of the standard library modules.

> ### Global Nimble packages and the Nim compiler
>
> By default, when installing a package using Nimble, the package is installed into the current user's Nimble package store, which is located in ~/.nimble/. Every time you compile a Nim module using the Nim compiler, that module can import any of the modules belonging to any of the packages in Nimble's package store.
>
> If there are two versions of the same package installed, Nim will use the latest one.

Let's change the NimbleExample.nimble file so that it includes the `bigints` package as a dependency. The following listing shows what the NimbleExample.nimble file should now look like, with the differences highlighted in bold.

Listing 5.7 Adding a dependency on the `bigints` package

```
# Package

version       = "0.1.0"
author        = "Your Name"
description   = "Simple package to learn about Nimble"
license       = "MIT"

# Dependencies

requires "nim >= 0.12.0", "bigints"
```

The dependency on `bigints` in listing 5.7 specifies no requirements on the version of that package. As a result, Nimble will attempt to install the latest *tagged* version of that library, assuming one isn't already installed.

> **CUTTING-EDGE DEPENDENCIES** Inside your .nimble file's dependency specification, you can write #head after a package's name, like this: `requires "bigints#head"`. This will get Nimble to compile your package with the latest revision of that package available. This is similar to specifying @#head when installing packages on the command line, as shown in figure 5.9.

Once you change your NimbleExample.nimble file to match listing 5.7, you should be able to successfully compile the `math` module using Nimble. Nimble will even automatically install the `bigints` package for you if it detects that it's not installed. Figure 5.13 shows the difference between `nim c` and `nimble c`, depending on whether the `bigints` package has been installed.

You should now have a basic understanding of how Nimble handles dependencies, and you should know how to create more Nimble packages. But there's one piece of knowledge still missing: the process involved in publishing Nimble packages, which we'll discuss next.

But before you move on to the next section, here's a quick challenge. Write some simple tests for your Nimble package inside some of the package's modules. Remember to put your tests under a `when isMainModule:` statement; this statement ensures

Before `bigints` *package is installed*   *After* `bigints` *package is installed*

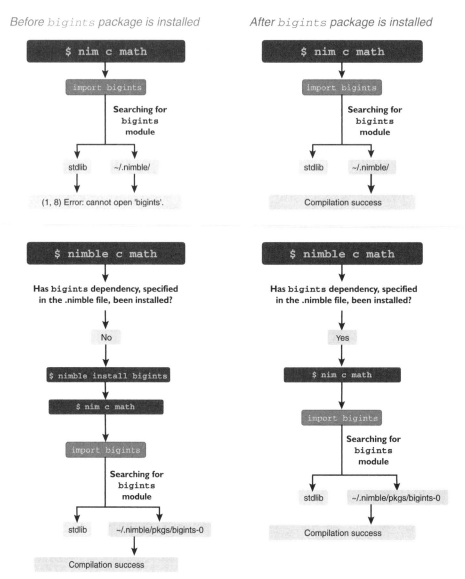

Figure 5.13 `nim c` vs. `nimble c`

that any code in its body is only executed when the `math` module is compiled directly. This ensures that tests aren't executed when the `math` module is imported in an application. Then, run those tests by using Nimble's c command. For example, `nimble c -r NimbleExample/math`, with the `-r` flag, will run the resulting executable automatically after compilation.

5.7 Publishing Nimble packages

The process of publishing a Nimble package to the official package list is fairly straightforward. But before your package is published, it must first be uploaded to a Git or Mercurial repository hosting service (such as GitHub or Bitbucket) and go through an approval process.

The first thing that you need to do is initialize a Git or Mercurial repository in your package's directory. We'll create a Git repository in this example because Git has been more widely adopted, but the choice of repository type doesn't matter much. It's mostly a matter of preference.

> **VERSION CONTROL** The details of distributed version control, Git, and Mercurial are outside the scope of this book. I recommend you read up on these technologies further if you're not familiar with them.

Before you get started, you'll need to create an account on http://github.com if you don't already have one.

After you have an account set up and are logged in, create a new Git repository on GitHub by clicking the New Repository button. If you can't find such a button, go to this URL: https://github.com/new. You should see something similar to the screenshot in figure 5.14.

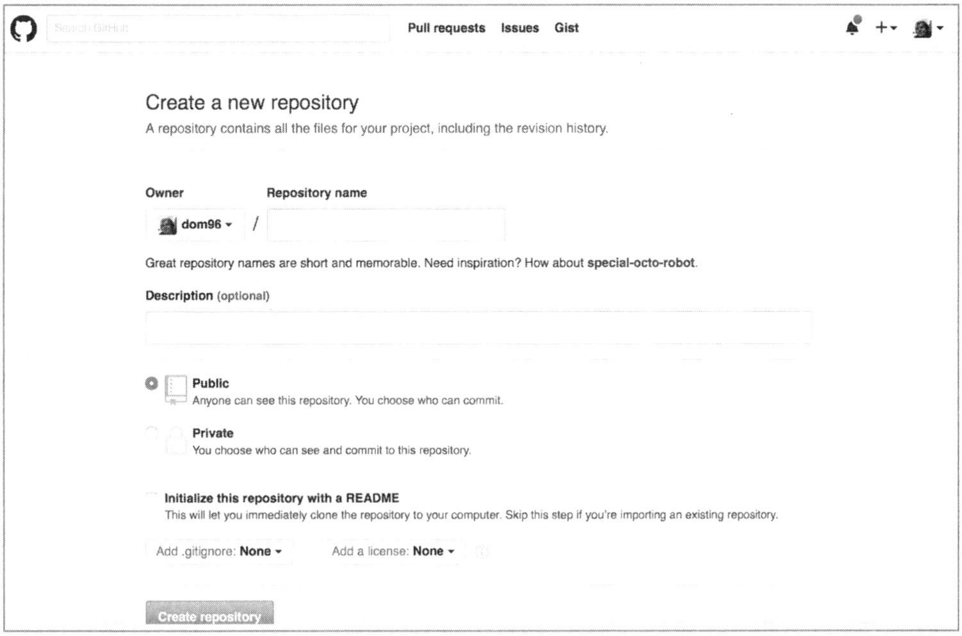

Figure 5.14   Creating a new repository on GitHub

Specify "NimbleExample" as the Repository Name, and then click the green Create Repository button. You'll be shown another web page that will let you know how to create a repository on the command line. The instructions on the web page are very generic. Listing 5.8 shows commands similar to the ones on the web page but tailored to successfully upload the `NimbleExample` package to GitHub. Execute these commands now.

Listing 5.8   Commands to upload the `NimbleExample` package to GitHub

```
git init
git add NimbleExample.nimble NimbleExample/data.nim NimbleExample/
    math.nim NimbleExample/private/utils.nim
git commit -m "first commit"
git remote add origin git@github.com:<your-user-name>/NimbleExample.git  ⊲─┐
git push -u origin master                                                  │
```

> Remember to change
> **<your-user-name>**
> to your GitHub username.

Once you successfully execute those commands, navigating to https://github.com/<your-user-name>/NimbleExample should show you a list of files. These files should include NimbleExample.nimble, the NimbleExample directory, and its contents.

There's only one thing left to do. The package is public, but Nimble has no way to find it yet because it hasn't been added to its package list. This means you won't be able to install it by executing `nimble install NimbleExample`.

Nimble can make use of multiple package lists, but the official package list at https://github.com/nim-lang/packages is the most widely used. A *pull request* is created whenever a user wants to add a package to this package list, and once that's done, the Nim community checks that the package can be added to the package list. Certain aspects of the package are checked, such as the package's name, to ensure it doesn't clash with the names of any other packages already on the list.

The pull request can be created manually or with the help of Nimble's `publish` command, which creates the pull request for you automatically.

Before publishing a package, it's a good idea to ensure that it can be installed successfully. Execute `nimble install` in the package's directory to verify that it can be installed successfully.

The package is then ready to be published. Execute `nimble publish` now, and follow the on-screen prompts. The process is somewhat complex as it requires you to create a new GitHub access token for Nimble. But once you do so, it streamlines the process of publishing Nimble packages significantly.

When your package is accepted and is added to the package list, you'll be able to install it by executing `nimble install NimbleExample`.

Remember that publishing a Nimble package is only done once. You don't need to publish the package again when you develop a new version of it. Instead, the version is tagged, as you'll see in the next section.

5.8   *Developing a Nimble package*

Software projects are typically given version numbers to identify their state. As software evolves, new developments are marked with increasing version numbers. Nimble packages are no different.

The `NimbleExample` package began its life as version `0.1.0`, and if it continues to be developed, it may someday reach version `1.0` or even `10.3`. Versions help the user distinguish and identify different states of your package.

Version information for your package is stored in your package's .nimble file using the `version` key. The version must consist of at least one digit, and multiple digits must be separated by periods. A full line specifying the version could look something like `version = "1.42.5"`.

5.8.1   *Giving version numbers meaning*

The way in which version numbers are assigned and incremented differs. In some cases, the version numbers have little meaning other than signifying that version `1.0` is newer than version `0.5`. In others, such as with semantic versioning, the version numbers tell you more about the API compatibility of different versions of software.

Semantic versioning is a convention for specifying a three-part version number: major version, minor version, and patch. The patch is incremented for minor bug fixes and changes that don't affect the API of the software. The minor version is incremented when backward-compatible additions are made to the software. The major version is incremented when the API of the software changes to something that's not backward compatible. The full semantic versioning specification is available at http://semver.org.

All Nimble packages should use this convention, so if you aren't familiar with it, be sure to learn about it.

5.8.2   *Storing different versions of a single package*

There are some things you need to keep in mind with versioning and Nimble packages.

A local Nimble package that doesn't have a Git or Mercurial repository associated with it has a specific version associated with it. This is the version in the .nimble file.

A local Nimble package that does have a Git or Mercurial repository associated with it is the same, but different versions of it can be retrieved because its repository contains a full history of the package. The retrieval must be done manually for local packages, whereas for remote packages, Nimble will automatically retrieve the specified version. All remote Nimble packages are currently stored in such repositories, and they can be downloaded to create a local repository containing each version of the Nimble package. Figure 5.15 shows the difference between a Nimble package with and without a Git repository.

When developing Nimble packages, it's important to remember one thing: Nimble uses the tags in the Nimble package's repository to retrieve a certain version.

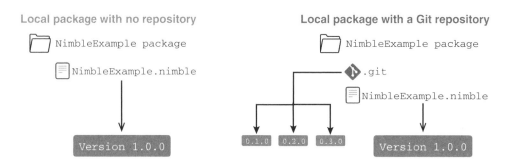

Figure 5.15   Local Nimble package with no repository vs. one with a Git repository

Whenever you want to release a new version of a package, you need to follow these steps:

1. Increment the version number in the .nimble file.
2. Commit these changes into your repository; for example, `git commit -am "Version 0.1.2"`.
3. Tag the commit you just made, using the new version number as the tag name; for example, `git tag v0.1.2`.
4. Upload the changes to the remote repository, making sure you upload the tags as well; for example, `git push origin master --tags`.

Performing step 1 first is very important. If the name of the tag doesn't match the version specified in the .nimble file at the point in history that the tag corresponds to, there will be an inconsistency, and Nimble will refuse to install the package.

The preceding steps for tagging versions are specific to Git. You'll find that in order to develop Nimble packages, you'll need at least a basic knowledge of Git or Mercurial.

5.9   *Summary*

- The Nim package manager is called Nimble.
- A Nimble package is any directory or repository, compressed or otherwise, containing a .nimble file and some Nim source code.
- A .nimble file contains information about a package, including its version, author, dependencies, and more.
- Nimble packages are installed using the `nimble install` command.
- Nimble packages can be installed from various sources, including the local filesystem, a Git or Mercurial URL, and a curated list of packages identified by name.
- Installing a package by name or from a URL will install the latest tagged version of it; the `tip` or the `HEAD` can be installed by appending `@#head` to the URL or package name.

- A Nimble package can be created using the `nimble init` command.
- A Nimble package can be published using the `nimble publish` command.
- New versions of packages are released by incrementing the version number in the .nimble file, creating a new commit, and then tagging it as the new version in Git or Mercurial.

Parallelism

Every computer program performs one or more computations, and these computations are usually performed *sequentially*. That is, the current computation has to complete before the next one starts. For example, consider a simple calculation, $(2 + 2) \times 4$, in which the addition must be computed first, to give 4, followed by the multiplication, to give 16. In that example, the calculation is performed sequentially.

Concurrency allows more than one computation to make progress without waiting for all other computations to complete. This form of computing is useful in many situations, such as in an I/O application like the chat application you developed in chapter 3. If executed sequentially, such applications waste time waiting on input or output operations to complete. Concurrency allows this time to be used for another task, drastically reducing the execution time of the application. You learned about concurrency in chapter 3; in this chapter, you'll learn about a related concept called *parallelism*.

Nim offers many built-in facilities for concurrency and parallelism including asynchronous I/O features in the form of futures and `await`, `spawn` for creating new threads, and more. You've already seen some of these used in chapter 3.

Parallelism in Nim is still evolving, which means that the features described in this chapter may change or be replaced by more-robust features. But the core concepts of parallelism in Nim should remain the same, and what you'll learn in this chapter will be applicable to other programming languages as well.

In addition to showing you Nim's parallelism features, this chapter will lead you through the implementation of a simple parser, which will show you different methods for creating parsers. Toward the end of the chapter, you'll optimize the parser so it's concurrent and can be run in parallel on multiple CPU cores.

6.1 Concurrency vs. parallelism

Nowadays, almost all OSs support multitasking, the ability to perform multiple tasks over a certain period of time. A task is usually known as a *process*, which is an instance of a computer program being executed. Each CPU executes only a single process at a time, but multitasking allows the OS to change the process that's currently being executed on the CPU without having to wait for the process to finish its execution. Figure 6.1 shows how two processes are executed concurrently on a multitasking OS.

Because CPUs are extremely fast, process A can be executed for 1 nanosecond, followed by process B for 2 nanoseconds, followed by process A for another nanosecond.[1] This gives the impression of multiple processes being executed at the same time, even though a CPU can only execute a single instruction at a time. This apparent simultaneous execution of multiple processes is called *concurrency*.

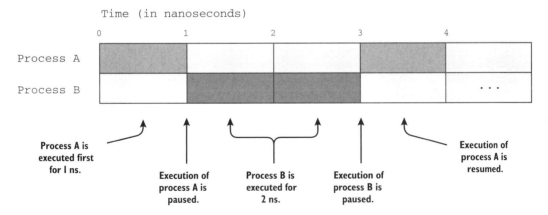

Figure 6.1 Concurrent execution of two processes

---

[1] For simplicity, I'll ignore the time taken for a context switch here.

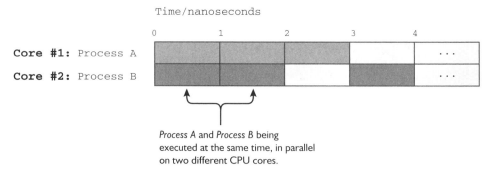

Figure 6.2   Parallel execution of two processes

In recent years, multicore CPUs have become popular. This kind of CPU consists of two or more independent units that can run multiple instructions simultaneously. This allows a multitasking OS to run two or more processes at the same time in *parallel*. Figure 6.2 shows how two processes are executed in parallel on a dual-core CPU.

Unlike a single-core CPU, a dual-core CPU can actually execute two processes at the same time. This type of execution is called *parallelism*, and it can only be achieved on multiple physical CPUs or via a simultaneous multithreading (SMT) technology such as Intel's Hyper-Threading (HT) Technology. Remember that despite the apparent similarities between concurrency and parallelism, the two are not the same.

In addition to processes, the OS also manages the execution of *threads*. A thread is a component of a process, and more than one can exist within the same process. It can be executed concurrently or in parallel, just like a process, although unlike processes, threads share resources such as memory among each other.

To make use of the full power of a multicore CPU, CPU-intensive computations must be parallelized. This can be done by using multiple processes, although threads are more appropriate for computations that require a large amount of data to be shared.

The asynchronous await that you saw used in chapter 3 is strictly concurrent. Because the asynchronous code always runs on a single thread, it isn't parallel, which means that it can't currently use the full power of multicore CPUs.

PARALLEL ASYNC AWAIT   It's very likely that a future version of Nim will include an asynchronous await that's parallel.

Unlike asynchronous await, spawn is parallel and has been designed specifically for CPU-intensive computations that can benefit from being executed on multicore CPUs.

PARALLELISM IN OTHER PROGRAMMING LANGUAGES   Some programming languages, such as Python and Ruby, don't support thread-level parallelism due to a global interpreter lock in their interpreter. This prevents applications that use threads from using the full power of multicore CPUs. There are ways around this limitation, but they require the use of processes that aren't as flexible as threads.

6.2   Using threads in Nim

Now that you've learned the difference between concurrency and parallelism, you're ready to learn how to use threads in Nim.

In Nim, there are two modules for working with threads. The `threads` module (http://nim-lang.org/docs/threads.html) exposes the ability to create threads manually. Threads created this way immediately execute a specified procedure and run for the duration of that procedure's runtime. There's also the `threadpool` module (http://nim-lang.org/docs/threadpool.html), which implements a *thread pool*. It exposes `spawn`, which adds a specified procedure to the thread pool's task queue. The act of spawning a procedure doesn't mean it will be running in a separate thread immediately, though. The creation of threads is managed entirely by the thread pool.

The sections that follow will explain all about the two different threading modules, so don't feel overwhelmed by the new terms I just introduced.

6.2.1   The threads module and GC safety

In this section, we'll look at the `threads` module. But before we start, I should explain how threads work in Nim. In particular, you need to know what *garbage collector safety* (GC safety) is in Nim. There's a very important distinction between the way threads work in Nim and in most other programming languages. Each of Nim's threads has its own isolated memory heap. Sharing of memory between threads is restricted, which helps to prevent race conditions and improves efficiency.

Efficiency is also improved by each thread having its own garbage collector. Other implementations of threads that share memory need to pause all threads while the garbage collector does its business. This can add problematic pauses to the application.

Let's look at how this threading model works in practice. The following listing shows a code sample that doesn't compile.

Listing 6.1   Mutating a global variable using a `Thread`

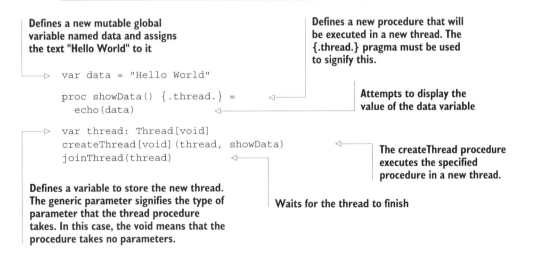

Defines a new mutable global variable named data and assigns the text "Hello World" to it

Defines a new procedure that will be executed in a new thread. The {.thread.} pragma must be used to signify this.

```
var data = "Hello World"

proc showData() {.thread.} =
  echo(data)

var thread: Thread[void]
createThread[void](thread, showData)
joinThread(thread)
```

Attempts to display the value of the data variable

The createThread procedure executes the specified procedure in a new thread.

Defines a variable to store the new thread. The generic parameter signifies the type of parameter that the thread procedure takes. In this case, the void means that the procedure takes no parameters.

Waits for the thread to finish

THE THREADS MODULE   The `threads` module is a part of the implicitly imported `system` module, so you don't need to import it explicitly.

This example illustrates what's disallowed by the GC safety mechanism in Nim, and you'll see later on how to fix this example so that it compiles.

Save the code in listing 6.1 as listing01.nim, and then execute `nim c --threads:on listing01.nim` to compile it. The `--threads:on` flag is necessary to enable thread support. You should see an error similar to this:

```
listing01.nim(3, 6) Error: 'showData' is not GC-safe as it accesses
  'data' which is a global using GC'ed memory
```

This error describes the problem fairly well. The global variable `data` has been created in the main thread, so it belongs to the main thread's memory. The `showData` thread can't access another thread's memory, and if it attempts to, it's not considered GC safe by the compiler. The compiler refuses to execute threads that aren't GC safe.

A procedure is considered GC safe by the compiler as long as it doesn't access any global variables that contain garbage-collected memory. An assignment or any sort of mutation also counts as an access and is disallowed. Garbage-collected memory includes the following types of variables:

- `string`
- `seq[T]`
- `ref T`
- Closure iterators and procedures, as well as types that include them

There are other ways of sharing memory between threads that are GC safe. You may, for example, pass the contents of `data` as one of the parameters to `showData`. The following listing shows how to pass data as a parameter to a thread; the differences between listings 6.2 and 6.1 are shown in bold.

Listing 6.2   Passing data to a thread safely

```
var data = "Hello World"

proc showData(param: string) {.thread.} =        A parameter of type string is
  echo(param)                                     specified in the procedure definition.

var thread: Thread[string]
createThread[string](thread, showData, data)
joinThread(thread)
```

A parameter of type string is specified in the procedure definition.

The void has been replaced by string to signify the type of parameter that the showData procedure takes.

The procedure argument is passed to echo instead of the global variable data.

The data global variable is passed to the createThread procedure, which will pass it on to showData.

Save the code in listing 6.2 as listing2.nim, and then compile it using `nim c --threads:on listing2.nim`. The compilation should be successful, and running the program should display "Hello World".

The createThread procedure can only pass one variable to the thread that it's creating. In order to pass multiple separate pieces of data to the thread, you must define a new type to hold the data. The following listing shows how this can be done.

Listing 6.3 Passing multiple values to a thread

```
type
  ThreadData = tuple[param: string, param2: int]

var data = "Hello World"

proc showData(data: ThreadData) {.thread.} =
  echo(data.param, data.param2)

var thread: Thread[ThreadData]
createThread[ThreadData](thread, showData, (param: data, param2: 10))
joinThread(thread)
```

EXECUTING THREADS

The threads created in the previous listings don't do very much. Let's examine the execution of these threads and see what happens when two threads are created at the same time and are instructed to display a few lines of text. In the following examples, two series of integers are displayed.

Listing 6.4 Executing multiple threads

```
var data = "Hello World"

proc countData(param: string) {.thread.} =
  for i in 0 .. <param.len:            ◄─── Iterates from 0 to the length of
    stdout.write($i)                         the param argument minus 1
  echo()                               ◄─── Displays the current iteration
                                            counter without displaying
                                            the newline character

var threads: array[2, Thread[string]]   ◄─── This time, there are two
createThread[string](threads[0], countData, data)   threads stored in an array.
createThread[string](threads[1], countData, data)
joinThreads(threads)                    ◄─── Creates a thread and assigns
                                            it to one of the elements in
                                            the threads array
```

Goes to the next line

Waits for all threads to finish

Save the code in listing 6.4 as listing3.nim, and then compile and run it. Listing 6.5 shows what the output will look like in most cases, and listing 6.6 shows what it may sometimes look like instead.

Listing 6.5 First possible output when the code in listing 6.4 is executed

```
00112233445566778899101
```

Listing 6.6   Second possible output when the code in listing 6.4 is executed

```
012345678910
012345678910
```

The execution of the threads depends entirely on the OS and computer used. On my machine, the output in listing 6.5 likely happens as a result of the two threads running in parallel on two CPU cores, whereas the output in listing 6.6 is a result of the first thread finishing before the second thread even starts. Your system may show different results. Figure 6.3 shows what the execution for both the first and second sets of results looks like.

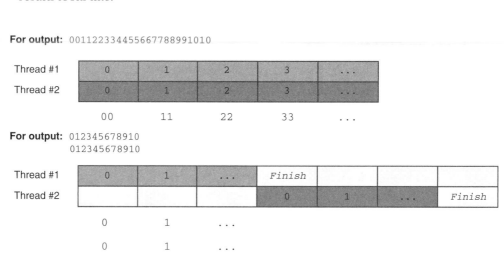

Figure 6.3   The two possible executions of listing 6.4

The threads created using the threads module are considerably resource intensive. They consume a lot of memory, so creating large numbers of them is inefficient. They're useful if you need full control over the threads that your application is using, but for most use cases the threadpool module is superior. Let's take a look at how the threadpool module works.

6.2.2   *Using thread pools*

The main purpose of using multiple threads is to parallelize your code. CPU-intensive computations should make use of as much CPU power as possible, which includes using the power of all the cores in a multicore CPU.

A single thread can use the power of a single CPU core. To use the power of all the cores, you could simply create one thread per core. The biggest problem then is making sure that those threads are all busy. You might have 100 tasks that don't all take the same amount of time to complete, and distributing them across the threads isn't a trivial job.

Alternatively, one thread per task could be created. But this creates problems of its own, in part because thread creation is very expensive. A large number of threads will consume a lot of memory due to OS overhead.

WHAT IS A THREAD POOL?

The `threadpool` module implements an abstraction that manages the distribution of tasks over a number of threads. The threads themselves are also managed by the thread pool.

The `spawn` command allows tasks, in the form of procedure invocations, to be added to the thread pool, which then executes the tasks in one of the threads it manages. The thread pool ensures that the tasks keep all the threads busy so that the CPU's power is utilized in the best way possible. Figure 6.4 shows how the thread pool manages tasks under the hood.

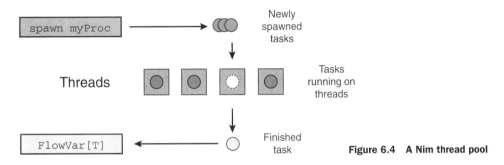

Figure 6.4   A Nim thread pool

USING SPAWN

The `spawn` procedure accepts an expression, which in most cases is a procedure call. `spawn` returns a value of the type `FlowVar[T]` that holds the return value of the procedure that was called. This is an advantage in comparison to the `threads` module, where threads can't return any values.

The following listing shows the `spawn` equivalent of the code in listing 6.4.

Listing 6.7   Executing multiple threads using `spawn`

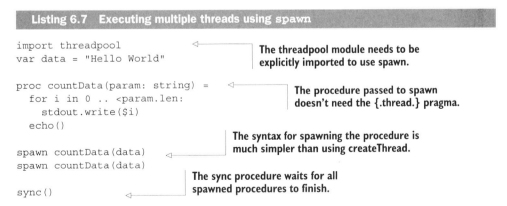

```
import threadpool          ◁          The threadpool module needs to be
var data = "Hello World"              explicitly imported to use spawn.

proc countData(param: string) =   ◁      The procedure passed to spawn
  for i in 0 .. <param.len:               doesn't need the {.thread.} pragma.
    stdout.write($i)
  echo()
                                 The syntax for spawning the procedure is
                                 much simpler than using createThread.
spawn countData(data)   ◁
spawn countData(data)
                             The sync procedure waits for all
                             spawned procedures to finish.
sync()          ◁
```

Save the code in listing 6.7 as listing4.nim, and then compile and run it. Keep in mind that the --threads:on flag still needs to be specified. The output should be mostly the same as the output shown in listings 6.5 and 6.6.

Procedures executed using spawn also have to be GC safe.

RETRIEVING RETURN VALUES FROM THE FLOWVAR TYPE

Let's look at an example that shows how to retrieve the return values from a spawned procedure. This involves dealing with the FlowVar[T] type.

FlowVar[T] can be thought of as a container similar to the Future[T] type, which you used in chapter 3. At first, the container has nothing inside it. When the spawned procedure is executed in a separate thread, it returns a value sometime in the future. When that happens, the returned value is put into the FlowVar container.

The following listing shows the readLine procedure from chapter 3, which uses a while loop to read text from the terminal without blocking.

Listing 6.8 Reading input from the terminal with spawn

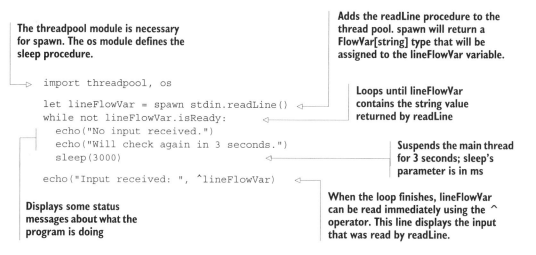

The threadpool module is necessary for spawn. The os module defines the sleep procedure.

Adds the readLine procedure to the thread pool. spawn will return a FlowVar[string] type that will be assigned to the lineFlowVar variable.

```
import threadpool, os

let lineFlowVar = spawn stdin.readLine()
while not lineFlowVar.isReady:
  echo("No input received.")
  echo("Will check again in 3 seconds.")
  sleep(3000)
echo("Input received: ", ^lineFlowVar)
```

Loops until lineFlowVar contains the string value returned by readLine

Suspends the main thread for 3 seconds; sleep's parameter is in ms

Displays some status messages about what the program is doing

When the loop finishes, lineFlowVar can be read immediately using the ^ operator. This line displays the input that was read by readLine.

Save listing 6.8 as listing5.nim, and then compile and run it. The application will wait until you enter some input into the terminal. It will check for input every 3 seconds.

Using the FlowVar type is straightforward. You can read the value inside it with the ^ operator, but this operator will block the thread it's used in until the FlowVar it's called on contains a value. You can check whether a FlowVar contains a value by using the isReady procedure. Listing 6.8 checks whether the lineFlowVar variable contains a value periodically, every 3 seconds.

Keep in mind that listing 6.8 is meant to demonstrate how the FlowVar[T] works. It's not meant to be very practical, because the program will only check for input every 3 seconds.

In this example, you could just as well call readLine on the main thread, since there's nothing else running on it. A more realistic example might replace the `sleep(3000)` statement with another procedure that does some useful work on the main thread. For example, you might draw your application's user interface or call the asynchronous I/O event loop's `poll` procedure, as in chapter 3.

6.2.3 *Exceptions in threads*

The ways exceptions behave in separate threads may be surprising. When a thread crashes with an unhandled exception, the application will crash with it. It doesn't matter whether you read the value of the `FlowVar` or not.

> **FUTURE VERSIONS** This behavior will change in a future version of Nim, so that exceptions aren't raised unless you read the value of the `FlowVar`.

The following listing shows this behavior in action.

Listing 6.9 Exceptions in a spawned procedure

```
import threadpool

proc crash(): string =
  raise newException(Exception, "Crash")

let lineFlowVar = spawn crash()
sync()
```

Save listing 6.9 as listing6.nim, and then compile and run it. You should see a traceback in the output pointing you to the `raise` statement in the `crash` procedure.

> **THE RAISES PRAGMA** The raises pragma can be used to ensure that your threads handle all exceptions. To make use of it, you can define the `crash` procedure like so: `proc crash(): string {.raises: [].} = …`. This will mark the `crash` procedure as raising no exceptions. Exceptions that are allowed to be raised by the procedure can be specified in the square brackets.

In summary, the simplicity of both passing arguments to a spawned procedure and receiving the procedure's result makes `spawn` good for tasks that have a relatively short runtime. Such tasks typically produce results at the end of their execution, and as such don't need to communicate with other threads until their execution stops.

For long-running tasks that need to communicate with other threads periodically, the `createThread` procedure defined in the `threads` module should be used instead.

6.3 *Parsing data*

Now that you know how to use threads in Nim, let's look at a practical example of how they can be used. The example in this section involves parsers and shows a practical use case involving Nim's concurrency and parallelism features.

A lot of data is generated every day from many different sources and intended for many different applications. Computers are very useful tools for processing this data, but in order for that data to be consumed, the computers must understand the format the data is stored in.

A *parser* is a software component that takes data as input and builds a data structure out of it. The input data is typically in the form of text. In chapter 3, you looked at the JSON data format and at how it was parsed, using the `json` module, into a data structure that could then be queried for specific information.

There often comes a time when you need to write a custom parser for a simple data format. There are many ways such a task can be tackled in Nim.

In this section, I'll show you how to write a parser for Wikipedia's page-view data.[2] This data is useful for many different applications, but in this section we'll create an application that will find the most popular page in the English Wikipedia. In the process, you'll do the following:

- Learn the structure and format of the Wikipedia page-counts files
- Use different techniques to write a parser for the page-counts format
- Read large files by breaking them up into conveniently sized *chunks* or fragments

WIKIPEDIA API   Wikipedia recently introduced a Pageview API (https://wikitech .wikimedia.org/wiki/Analytics/PageviewAPI) that supplements the raw page-view data and makes finding the most popular page in the English Wikipedia much easier. If you're writing an application that needs to find the most popular pages on Wikipedia, you may want to use the API instead. Parsing the raw data manually is less efficient, but you'll find the example applicable to other tasks.

At the end of this section, I'll also show you how to parallelize the parser, allowing it to perform better on systems with multicore CPUs.

6.3.1   *Understanding the Wikipedia page-counts format*

The raw page-count data can be downloaded from Wikipedia here: https://dumps .wikimedia.org/other/pagecounts-all-sites/.

The data files are organized into specific years and months. For example, the page-count data for January 2016 is available at https://dumps.wikimedia.org/other/ pagecounts-all-sites/2016/2016-01/. The data is then further subdivided into days and hours. Each file at the preceding URL represents the visitors within a single hour. The files are all gzipped to reduce their size.

Download the following file and then extract it: https://dumps.wikimedia .org/other/pagecounts-all-sites/2016/2016-01/pagecounts-20160101-050000.gz.

FOR WINDOWS USERS   On Windows, you may need to install 7-Zip or another application for extracting gzipped archives.

The file may take a while to download, depending on your internet speed. It's around 92 MB before extraction, and around 428 MB after extraction, so it's a fairly large file. The parser will need to be efficient to parse that file in a timely manner.

---

[2]   https://wikitech.wikimedia.org/wiki/Analytics/Data/Pagecounts-all-sites.

The file is filled with lines of text separated by newline characters. Each line of text consists of the following four fields separated by spaces:

```
domain_code page_title count_views total_response_size
```

`domain_code` contains an abbreviated domain name; for example, en.wikipedia.org is abbreviated as `en`. `page_title` contains the title of the page requested; for example, `Dublin` for http://en.wikipedia.org/wiki/Dublin. `count_views` contains the number of times the page has been viewed within the hour. Finally, `total_response_size` is the number of bytes that have been transferred due to requests for that page.

For example, consider the following line:

```
en Nim_(programming_language) 1 70231
```

This means that there was one request to http://en.wikipedia.org/wiki/Nim_(programming_language) that accounted in total for 70,231 response bytes.

The file I asked you to download is one of the smaller files from January 2016. It contains data about the Wikipedia pages visited from January 1, 2016, 4:00 a.m. UTC, to January 1, 2016, 5:00 a.m. UTC.

6.3.2 *Parsing the Wikipedia page-counts format*

There are many different options when it comes to parsing the page-counts format. I'll show you how to implement a parser using three different methods: regular expressions, the `split` procedure, and the `parseutils` module.

PARSING USING REGULAR EXPRESSIONS

A common way to parse data is using regular expressions (regexes), and if you've ever dealt with string processing in any way, you've likely come across them. Regular expressions are very popular, and often when developers need to parse a string, they immediately jump to using regular expressions.

Regular expressions are by no means a magical solution to every parsing problem. For example, writing a regular expression to parse arbitrary HTML is virtually impossible.[3] But for parsing a simple data format like the Wikipedia page-counts format, regular expressions work well.

> **LEARNING ABOUT REGULAR EXPRESSIONS** Explaining regular expressions in depth is beyond the scope of this chapter. If you aren't familiar with them, I encourage you to read up on them online.

Regular expressions are supported in Nim via the `re` module. It defines procedures and types for using regular expressions to parse and manipulate strings.

> **WARNING: EXTERNAL DEPENDENCY** The `re` module is an impure module, which means it depends on an external C library. In re's case, the C library is called PCRE, and it must be installed alongside your application for your application to function properly.

---

[3] That doesn't stop people from trying: http://stackoverflow.com/questions/1732348/regex-match-open-tags-except-xhtml-self-contained-tags.

Let's focus on parsing a single line first. The following listing shows how you can do that with the re module.

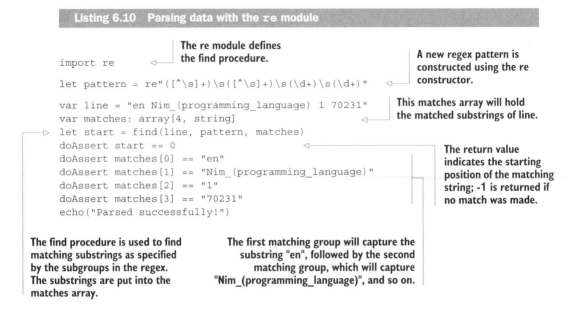

Listing 6.10   Parsing data with the `re` module

```
import re        ◁──┐  The re module defines
                      the find procedure.

let pattern = re"([^\s]+)\s([^\s]+)\s(\d+)\s(\d+)"   ◁──┐  A new regex pattern is
                                                            constructed using the re
var line = "en Nim_(programming_language) 1 70231"         constructor.
var matches: array[4, string]                ◁──┐  This matches array will hold
                                                   the matched substrings of line.
let start = find(line, pattern, matches)
doAssert start == 0                      ◁──────────────┐  The return value
doAssert matches[0] == "en"                               indicates the starting
doAssert matches[1] == "Nim_(programming_language)"       position of the matching
doAssert matches[2] == "1"                                string; -1 is returned if
doAssert matches[3] == "70231"                            no match was made.
echo("Parsed successfully!")
```

The find procedure is used to find matching substrings as specified by the subgroups in the regex. The substrings are put into the matches array.

The first matching group will capture the substring "en", followed by the second matching group, which will capture "Nim_(programming_language)", and so on.

> **WARNING: THE RE CONSTRUCTOR** Constructing a regular expression is an expensive operation. When you're performing multiple regex matches with the same regular expression, make sure you reuse the value returned by the re constructor.

Save listing 6.10 as listing7.nim, and then compile and run it. The program should compile and run successfully, displaying "Parsed successfully!"

> **PCRE PROBLEMS** If the program exits with an error similar to `could not load: pcre.dll`, you're missing the PCRE library and must install it.

The code for parsing strings with regular expressions is straightforward. As long as you know how to create regular expressions, you should have no trouble using it.

The re module also includes other procedures for parsing and manipulating strings. For example, you can replace matched substrings using the replace procedure. Take a look at the documentation for the re module for more information (http://nim-lang.org/docs/re.html).

PARSING THE DATA MANUALLY USING SPLIT

You can also parse data manually in many different ways. This approach provides multiple advantages but also a few disadvantages. The biggest advantage over using regular expressions is that your application will have no dependency on the PCRE library. Manual parsing also makes it easier to control the parsing process. In some cases, the biggest disadvantage is that it takes more code to parse data manually.

For such a simple data format as the Wikipedia page-counts format, you can use the `split` procedure defined in the `strutils` module. The following listing shows how `split` can be used to parse "en Nim_(programming_language) 1 70231."

Listing 6.11 Parsing using `split`

The strutils module defines the split procedure.

By default, the split procedure splits the string when it finds whitespace. The returned sequence will be @["en", "Nim_(programming_language)", "I", "70231"].

```
import strutils

var line = "en Nim_(programming_language) 1 70231"
var matches = line.split()
doAssert matches[0] == "en"
doAssert matches[1] == "Nim_(programming_language)"
doAssert matches[2] == "1"
doAssert matches[3] == "70231"
```

The contents of the resulting matches variable are the same as in listing 6.10.

This solution will work very well for this use case, but for more-complex data formats, you may want a solution that's more flexible. The most flexible way to parse a string is to iterate over every character in that string using a `while` loop. This method of parsing is very verbose, but it's useful in certain circumstances, such as when parsing more-complex data formats like HTML. Nim's `parseutils` module defines procedures that make parsing using such methods much easier.

PARSING DATA MANUALLY USING PARSEUTILS

The following listing shows how the `parseutils` module can be used to parse "en Nim_(programming_language) 1 70231."

Listing 6.12 Parsing using `parseutils`

Imports parseutils, which defines parseUntil

Defines a counter to keep track of the program's current position in the string

Copies characters starting at index i from the line string to the string specified in the second argument, until line[i] == ' '. The returned value is the number of characters captured, and it's used to increment i.

```
import parseutils

var line = "en Nim_(programming_language) 1 70231"

var i = 0
var domainCode = ""
i.inc parseUntil(line, domainCode, {' '}, i)
i.inc
var pageTitle = ""
i.inc parseUntil(line, pageTitle, {' '}, i)
i.inc
var countViews = 0
i.inc parseInt(line, countViews, i)
i.inc
var totalSize = 0
i.inc parseInt(line, totalSize, i)
```

Skips whitespace character by simply incrementing i

Defines a string or int variable where the parsed token will be stored

Parses an int starting at index i in the line string. The parsed int is stored in the second argument. The returned value is the number of characters captured.

```
doAssert domainCode == "en"
doAssert pageTitle == "Nim_(programming_language)"
doAssert countViews == 1
doAssert totalSize == 70231
```

The code in listing 6.12 is far more complex than the previous listing, but it allows for far greater flexibility.

The `parseutils` module also defines many other procedures that are useful for parsing. They're mostly convenience wrappers over a `while` loop. For example, the equivalent code for `i.inc parseUntil(line, domainCode, {' '}, i)` is the following:

```
while line[i] != ' ':
  domainCode.add(line[i])
  i.inc
```

Because of the flexibility of this parser, the code can parse the last two fields into integers in a single step. That's instead of having to first separate the fields and then parse the integer, which is inefficient.

In summary, the `split` procedure is the simplest approach, but it's slower than `parseutils` because it needs to create a sequence and new strings to hold the matches. In comparison, the parsing code that uses `parseutils` only needs to create two new strings and two new integers; there's no overhead associated with the creation of a sequence.

The regex parsing code is also simpler than `parseutils`, but it suffers from the PCRE dependency and is also slower than the `parseutils` parser.

This makes the `parseutils` parser the best solution for this use case, even though it's slightly more complex and significantly more verbose. Its speed will come in handy when parsing the 7,156,099 lines in the pagecounts-20160101-050000 file.

6.3.3   *Processing each line of a file efficiently*

The Wikipedia page-counts files are large. Each measures around 500 MB and contains around 10 million lines of data. The pagecounts-20160101-050000 file that I asked you to download measures 428 MB and contains 7,156,099 lines of page-count data.

In order to parse this file efficiently, you'll need to consume the file in fragments. Reading the full file into your program's memory would consume at least 428 MB of RAM, and the actual consumption would likely be far larger due to various overheads. That's why it's a good idea to read large files by breaking them up into conveniently sized, smaller fragments, otherwise known as *chunks*.

USING AN ITERATOR TO READ A FILE IN FRAGMENTS

Nim defines an iterator called `lines` that iterates over each line in a file. This iterator doesn't need to copy the full file's contents into the program's memory, which makes it very efficient. The `lines` iterator is defined in the `system` module.

The following listing shows how the `lines` iterator can be used to read lines from the pagecounts-20160101-050000 file.

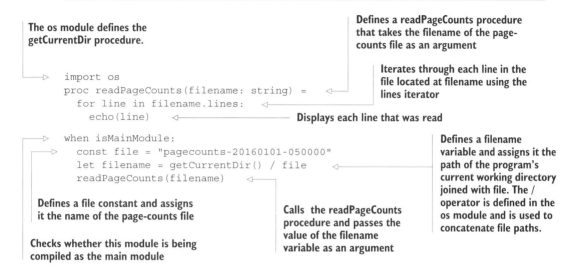

Listing 6.13 Iterating over each line in a file

The os module defines the getCurrentDir procedure.

Defines a readPageCounts procedure that takes the filename of the page-counts file as an argument

Iterates through each line in the file located at filename using the lines iterator

```
import os
proc readPageCounts(filename: string) =
  for line in filename.lines:
    echo(line)
```

Displays each line that was read

```
when isMainModule:
  const file = "pagecounts-20160101-050000"
  let filename = getCurrentDir() / file
  readPageCounts(filename)
```

Defines a filename variable and assigns it the path of the program's current working directory joined with file. The / operator is defined in the os module and is used to concatenate file paths.

Defines a file constant and assigns it the name of the page-counts file

Calls the readPageCounts procedure and passes the value of the filename variable as an argument

Checks whether this module is being compiled as the main module

Save listing 6.13 as sequential_counts.nim, and then compile and run it. The program will take around a minute to execute because it will display each line of the page-counts file. You may terminate it by pressing Ctrl-C. As it runs, you can observe the memory usage, which should remain low.

PARSING EACH LINE

You can now add the parsing code from listing 6.12 to the code in listing 6.13. Listing 6.14 shows how the parser can be integrated into listing 6.13, with the changes highlighted in bold.

Listing 6.14 Parsing each line in a file

```
import os, parseutils
proc parse(line: string, domainCode, pageTitle: var string,
           countViews, totalSize: var int) =
  var i = 0
  domainCode.setLen(0)
  i.inc parseUntil(line, domainCode, {' '}, i)
  i.inc
  pageTitle.setLen(0)
  i.inc parseUntil(line, pageTitle, {' '}, i)
  i.inc
  countViews = 0
  i.inc parseInt(line, countViews, i)
  i.inc
  totalSize = 0
  i.inc parseInt(line, totalSize, i)
proc readPageCounts(filename: string) =
  var domainCode = ""
  var pageTitle = ""
```

The variables in which the parsed tokens are stored are passed by reference. This is efficient because new strings don't have to be allocated for each call to parse.

The length of the string is reset to 0. This is much more efficient than assigning "" because setLen reuses memory instead of allocating new strings.

The integer variables are simply reset to 0.

```
    var countViews = 0
    var totalSize = 0
    for line in filename.lines:
      parse(line, domainCode, pageTitle, countViews, totalSize)
      echo("Title: ", pageTitle)

when isMainModule:
  const file = "pagecounts-20160101-050000"
  let filename = getCurrentDir() / file
  readPageCounts(filename)
```

Calls the parse procedure and passes it the current line together with variables where tokens can be stored

Displays the title of each page that was found in the page-counts file

Replace the code in sequential_counts.nim with the code in listing 6.14. The following listing shows what some of the output from sequential_counts.nim may look like.

Listing 6.15   The output of sequential_counts.nim

```
...
Title: List_of_digital_terrestrial_television_channels_(UK)
Title: List_of_diglossic_regions
Title: List_of_dignitaries_at_the_state_funeral_of_John_F._Kennedy
Title: List_of_dimensionless_quantities
Title: List_of_diners
Title: List_of_dinosaur_genera
Title: List_of_dinosaur_specimens_with_nicknames
Title: List_of_dinosaurs
...
```

The code in listing 6.14 employs a number of optimizations. First, the biggest slowdowns in Nim applications are often caused by too many variables being allocated and deallocated. The parse procedure could return the parsed tokens, but that would result in a new string being allocated for each iteration. Instead, the parse procedure here accepts a mutable reference to two strings and two ints, which it then fills with the parsed tokens. A file that takes 9.3 seconds to parse without this optimization takes 7.8 seconds to parse with the optimization. That's a difference of 1.5 seconds.

The use of setLen is another optimization. It ensures that the string isn't reallocated but is instead reused. The parse procedure is executed at least 7 million times, so a tiny optimization creates massive gains in total execution speed.

FINDING THE MOST POPULAR ARTICLE

Now that the parsing code has been introduced, all that's left is to find the most popular article on the English Wikipedia. The following listing shows the finished sequential_counts application with the latest changes shown in bold.

Listing 6.16   The finished sequential_counts.nim

```
import os, parseutils

proc parse(line: string, domainCode, pageTitle: var string,
    countViews, totalSize: var int) =
  var i = 0
```

```
    domainCode.setLen(0)
    i.inc parseUntil(line, domainCode, {' '}, i)
    i.inc
    pageTitle.setLen(0)
    i.inc parseUntil(line, pageTitle, {' '}, i)
    i.inc
    countViews = 0
    i.inc parseInt(line, countViews, i)
    i.inc
    totalSize = 0
    i.inc parseInt(line, totalSize, i)

proc readPageCounts(filename: string) =
  var domainCode = ""
  var pageTitle = ""
  var countViews = 0
  var totalSize = 0
  var mostPopular = ("", "", 0, 0)
  for line in filename.lines:
    parse(line, domainCode, pageTitle, countViews, totalSize)
    if domainCode == "en" and countViews > mostPopular[2]:
      mostPopular = (domainCode, pageTitle, countViews, totalSize)

  echo("Most popular is: ", mostPopular)

when isMainModule:
  const file = "pagecounts-20160101-050000"
  let filename = getCurrentDir() / file
  readPageCounts(filename)
```

Defines a tuple to store the four parsed fields for the most popular page

Checks whether the current line contains information about a page from the English Wikipedia and whether its view count is greater than that of the currently most popular page

If it's greater, saves it as the new most popular page

WARNING: RELEASE MODE Ensure that you compile sequential_counts.nim in release mode by passing the `-d:release` flag to the Nim compiler. Without that flag, the execution time of the application will be significantly longer.

Replace the contents of sequential_counts.nim with the code in listing 6.16, and then compile it in release mode and run it. After a few seconds, you should see output similar to the following.

Listing 6.17 Output for sequential_counts.nim

```
Most popular is: (Field0: en, Field1: Main_Page, Field2: 271165, Field3: 4791
    147476)
```

The most popular page in the English Wikipedia is in fact the main page! This makes a lot of sense, and although it's obvious in hindsight, it's trivial to edit the code you've written to find more-interesting statistics. I challenge you to edit sequential_counts .nim and play around with the data. You can try finding the top-10 most popular pages in the English Wikipedia, or you can download different page-counts files and compare the results.

You should now have a good understanding of how you can parse data effectively. You've learned what bottlenecks you should look out for in your Nim applications and how to fix them. The next step is to parallelize this parser so that its execution time is even lower on multicore CPUs.

6.4   *Parallelizing a parser*

In order for the program to be parallel, it must make use of threads. As mentioned previously, there are two ways that threads can be created in Nim: using the `threads` module, or using the `threadpool` module. Both will work, but the `threadpool` module is more appropriate for this program.

6.4.1   *Measuring the execution time of sequential_counts*

Before we parallelize the code, let's measure how long `sequential_counts` takes to execute.

This can be done very easily on UNIX-like OSs by using the `time` command. Executing `time ./sequential_counts` should output the execution time of sequential_counts.nim. On a MacBook Pro with an SSD and a dual-core 2.7 GHz Intel Core i5 CPU, which includes hyperthreading, the execution time is about 2.8 seconds.

On Windows, you'll need to open a new Windows PowerShell window, and then use the `Measure-Command` command to measure the execution time. Executing `Measure-Command {./sequential_counts.exe}` should output the execution time.

The program currently runs in a single thread and is very CPU-intensive. This means its speed can be significantly improved by making it parallel.

6.4.2   *Parallelizing sequential_counts*

Create a new parallel_counts.nim file. This is the file that we'll populate with code from now on.

How can the `threadpool` module be used to parallelize this code? You may be tempted to `spawn` the `parse` procedure, but this won't work because it needs `var` parameters that can't safely be passed to a spawned procedure. It also wouldn't help much, because a single call to `parse` is relatively quick.

Before you can parallelize this code, you must first change the way that the page-counts file is read. Instead of reading each line separately, you need to read the file in larger fragments. But what size fragment should you read?

Consider the following scenario. The page-counts file begins with the following lines:

```
en Main_Page 123 1234567
en Nim_(programming_language) 100 12415551
```

If the fragment size is so small that only `"en Main_Page"` is read, the program will fail because the size of the fragment is insufficient.

Alternatively, a fragment might contain valid data at the start, but it may end with a line that was not fully read, such as `"en Main_Page 123 1234567\nen Nim_"`. This data will need to be split after every newline (`"\n"`), and each line will need to be parsed separately. The last line in this example will lead to an error, because it's not complete. A solution is to find where the last line ends, and then defer parsing the line that hasn't been fully read until the next time a fragment of the file is read.

Here's how parallel_counts.nim should work:

- Instead of reading lines, a large fragment of text should be read.
- A new procedure called parseChunk should be created.
- The parseChunk procedure should receive a fragment of text, go through each line, and pass the line to the parse procedure.
- At the same time, it should check which of the parsed pages are the most popular.
- The parseChunk procedure should be spawned. A *slice* of the fragment should be passed to parseChunk, and the slice should not contain any incomplete lines.
- The incomplete line should be saved. Once the next fragment is read, the incomplete line should be prepended to the newly read fragment.

TERMINOLOGY   The term *chunk* is synonymous with the term *fragment*, and throughout this chapter both will be used interchangeably. A *slice* means a subset of the full data, such as a substring.

Listings 6.18, 6.19, and 6.20 show different sections of a parallel_counts.nim file that implements this solution.

6.4.3 *Type definitions and the parse procedure*

Listing 6.18 starts with the top section of the file, which is not much different from the sequential version. This section includes the import statement, some new type definitions, and the original parse procedure. A new Stats type is defined to store page-count statistics about a specific page; this type will be used to store the most popular page in each spawned procedure. The Stats type will be returned from the spawned procedure, so it must be a ref type because spawn currently can't spawn procedures that return custom value types. A new procedure called newStats is also defined, which constructs a new empty Stats object. There's also the definition of $, which converts a Stats type to a string.

Listing 6.18 The top section of parallel_counts.nim

The threadpool module is required for spawn, and the strutils module is required for the % operator.

Defines a new Stats type that will hold information about a page's statistics. The type has to be defined as a ref because a procedure that returns a non-ref type can't be spawned.

```
import os, parseutils, threadpool, strutils

type
  Stats = ref object
    domainCode, pageTitle: string
    countViews, totalSize: int

proc newStats(): Stats =
    Stats(domainCode: "", pageTitle: "", countViews: 0, totalSize: 0)
```

The Stats type defines fields for each of the parsed tokens.

Defines a new procedure called newStats that acts as a constructor for the Stats type

```
proc `$`(stats: Stats): string =
  "(domainCode: $#, pageTitle: $#, countViews: $#, totalSize: $#)" % [
    stats.domainCode, stats.pageTitle, $stats.countViews, $stats.totalSize
  ]

proc parse(line: string, domainCode, pageTitle: var string,
    countViews, totalSize: var int) =
  if line.len == 0: return
  var i = 0
  domainCode.setLen(0)
  i.inc parseUntil(line, domainCode, {' '}, i)
  i.inc
  pageTitle.setLen(0)
  i.inc parseUntil(line, pageTitle, {' '}, i)
  i.inc
  countViews = 0
  i.inc parseInt(line, countViews, i)
  i.inc
  totalSize = 0
  i.inc parseInt(line, totalSize, i)
```

> Defines a $ operator for the Stats type so that it can be converted to a string easily. In practice, this means that echo can display it.

> The parse procedure is the same.

6.4.4   *The parseChunk procedure*

Listing 6.19 shows the middle section of the parallel_counts.nim file. It defines a new procedure called parseChunk, which takes a string parameter called chunk and returns the most popular English Wikipedia page in that fragment. The fragment consists of multiple lines of page-count data.

The procedure begins by initializing the result variable; the return type is a ref type that must be initialized so that it's not nil. The rest of the procedure is similar to the readPageCounts procedure in the sequential_counts.nim file. It defines four variables to store the parsed tokens, and then it iterates through the lines in the chunk using the splitLines iterator, and parses each of the lines.

Listing 6.19   The middle section of parallel_counts.nim

> The parseChunk procedure is very similar to the readPageCounts procedure in sequential_counts.nim.

> Initializes the result variable with a new value of the Stats type

> Calls the parse procedure on each line inside the chunk to parse into the 4 fields: domainCode, pageTitle, countViews, and totalSize

> Iterates over every line in chunk

> Creates variables to store the parsed tokens.

```
proc parseChunk(chunk: string): Stats =
  result = newStats()
  var domainCode = ""
  var pageTitle = ""
  var countViews = 0
  var totalSize = 0
  for line in splitLines(chunk):
    parse(line, domainCode, pageTitle, countViews, totalSize)
    if domainCode == "en" and countViews > result.countViews:
      result = Stats(domainCode: domainCode, pageTitle: pageTitle,
                     countViews: countViews, totalSize: totalSize)
```

> Checks if the parsed page is in the English Wikipedia and whether it got more views than the page stored in result

> If that's the case, result is assigned the parsed page.

6.4.5   *The parallel readPageCounts procedure*

Listing 6.20 shows the `readPageCounts` procedure, which has been modified significantly since the last time you saw it in listing 6.16. It now takes an optional parameter called `chunkSize` that determines how many characters it should read each iteration. But the procedure's implementation is what differs most. The file is opened manually using the `open` procedure, followed by definitions of variables required to properly store the results of the fragment-reading process.

     The fragment-reading process is complicated by the fact that the code needs to keep track of unfinished lines. It does so by moving backwards through the contents of `buffer`, which stores the fragment temporarily, until it finds a newline character. The `buffer` string is then sliced from the start of the fragment to the end of the last full line in the fragment. The resulting slice is then passed to the `parseChunk` procedure, which is spawned in a new thread using `spawn`.

     The end of the fragment that hasn't yet been parsed is then moved to the beginning of the `buffer`. In the next iteration, the length of the characters that will be read will be `chunkSize` minus the length of the buffer that wasn't parsed in the last iteration.

Listing 6.20   The last section of parallel_counts.nim

The open procedure is now used to open a file. It returns a File object that's stored in the file variable.

Defines a new buffer string of length equal to chunkSize. Fragments will be stored here.

The readPageCounts procedure now includes a chunkSize parameter with a default value of 1_000_000. The underscores help readability and are ignored by Nim.

Defines a new responses sequence to hold the FlowVar objects that will be returned by spawn

```nim
proc readPageCounts(filename: string, chunkSize = 1_000_000) =
  var file = open(filename)
  var responses = newSeq[FlowVar[Stats]]()
  var buffer = newString(chunkSize)
  var oldBufferLen = 0
  while not endOfFile(file):
    let reqSize = chunksize - oldBufferLen
    let readSize = file.readChars(buffer, oldBufferLen, reqSize) + oldBufferLen
    var chunkLen = readSize

    while chunkLen >= 0 and buffer[chunkLen - 1] notin NewLines:
      chunkLen.dec
```

Calculates the number of characters that need to be read

Decreases the chunkLen variable until chunkLen - 1 points to any newline character

Creates a variable to store the fragment length that will be parsed

Loops until the full file is read

Defines a variable to store the length of the last buffer that wasn't parsed

Uses the readChars procedure to read the reqSize number of characters. This procedure will place the characters that it reads starting at oldBufferLen, which will ensure that the old buffer isn't overwritten. The oldBufferLen is added because that's the length of the old buffer that was read previously.

Creates a new thread to execute the parseChunk procedure and passes a slice of the buffer that contains a fragment that can be parsed. Adds the FlowVar[string] returned by spawn to the list of responses.

Assigns the part of the fragment that wasn't parsed to the beginning of buffer

```
responses.add(spawn parseChunk(buffer[0 .. <chunkLen]))
oldBufferLen = readSize - chunkLen
buffer[0 .. <oldBufferLen] = buffer[readSize - oldBufferLen .. ^1]

var mostPopular = newStats()
for resp in responses:                 ◁————— Iterates through each response
  let statistic = ^resp
  if statistic.countViews > mostPopular.countViews:
    mostPopular = statistic

echo("Most popular is: ", mostPopular)

file.close()

when isMainModule:
  const file = "pagecounts-20160101-050000"
  let filename = getCurrentDir() / file
  readPageCounts(filename)
```

Blocks the main thread until the response can be read and then saves the response value in the statistics variable

Checks if the most popular page in a particular fragment is more popular than the one saved in the mostPopular variable. If it is, overwrites the mostPopular variable with it.

Ensures that the file object is closed

The parallel version is unfortunately more complex, but the complexity is mostly restricted to the readPageCounts procedure, where the algorithm for reading the file in fragments adds great complexity to the program. In terms of the line count, though, the parallel version is only about twice as long.

6.4.6   *The execution time of parallel_counts*

Merge listings 6.18, 6.19, and 6.20 into a single parallel_counts.nim file. Then compile and run the program. Make sure you pass both the --threads:on flag as well as the -d:release flag to Nim when compiling. Measure the execution time using the techniques described in section 6.4.1.

On a MacBook Pro with an SSD and a dual core 2.7 GHz Intel Core i5 CPU that includes hyperthreading, the execution time is about 1.2 seconds, which is less than half of the 2.8 seconds that the sequential version took to execute. That's a considerable difference!

On UNIX-like systems, the time command allows you to verify that the parallel version is in fact parallel by looking at its CPU usage. For example, the time command outputs ./parallel_counts 4.30s user 0.25s system 364% cpu 1.251 total, showing that parallel_counts was using 364% of the available CPU. In comparison, sequential_counts almost always shows around 99% CPU usage. This high CPU usage percentage proves that parallel_counts is using all cores together with hyperthreading.

Now that you've seen how to parallelize a parser, you should have a better idea about how to parallelize Nim code in general. The last sections of this chapter will teach you about race conditions and how to avoid them.

6.5 *Dealing with race conditions*

You don't typically need to worry about race conditions when writing concurrent code in Nim because of the restriction that Nim puts on GC-safe procedures: memory belonging to another thread can't be accessed in a spawned procedure or a procedure marked using the {.thread.} pragma.

A race condition occurs when two or more threads attempt to read and write to a shared resource at the same time. Such behavior can result in unpredictable results that often are difficult to debug. This is one of the reasons why Nim prevents the sharing of some resources between threads. Nim instead prefers data to be shared using alternative methods such as *channels*, which prevent race conditions.

Sometimes these methods aren't appropriate for certain use cases, such as when lots of data needs to be modified by the thread. Because of this, Nim also supports shared memory. Sharing memory via global variables is easy as long as you only want to share value types. Sharing reference types is much harder because you must make use of Nim's manual memory-management procedures.

> **WARNING: SHARED MEMORY** Using shared memory is risky because it increases the chances for race conditions in your code. Also, you must manage the memory yourself. I advise you to only use shared memory if you're certain that it's required and if you know what you're doing. In future versions of Nim, using shared memory will likely become safer and much easier.

Listing 6.21 implements a simple program that increments the value of a global variable inside two threads running in parallel. The result is a race condition.

Listing 6.21 Race condition with shared memory

The threadpool module
defines the spawn procedure.

```
import threadpool          ◁──     Defines a global variable called counter

var counter = 0            ◁──       Iterates from 0 to x-1

proc increment(x: int) =
  for i in 0 .. <x:        ◁──     Defines a new local variable called value
    var value = counter    ◁──     and assigns it the value of counter
    value.inc                      Sets the value of the global counter
    counter = value        ◁──     variable to the value of "value"

spawn increment(10_000)            Spawns two new threads that will call the increment
spawn increment(10_000)            procedure with 10_000 as the argument
sync()                     ◁──
echo(counter)              ◁──     Waits until all the threads are finished
```

Increments
value └▷

Displays the value of the counter

In this example, the `increment` procedure is GC safe because the global variable `counter` it accesses is of type `int`, which is a value type. The `increment` procedure increments the global `counter` variable x times. The procedure is spawned twice, which means that there will be two `increment` procedures executing at the same time. The fact that they're both reading, incrementing, and then writing the incremented value to the global `counter` variable in discrete steps means that some increments may be missed.

> **SHARING MEMORY THAT MUST BE ALLOCATED ON THE HEAP**   Value types, such as integers, can exist on the stack (or in the executable's data section if the value is stored in a global variable), but reference types such as `string`, `seq[T]` and `ref T` can't. Nim supports the sharing of reference types, but it won't manage the memory for you. This may change in a future version of Nim, but currently you must use a procedure called `allocShared` defined in the `system` module to allocate shared memory manually.

Save listing 6.21 as race_condition.nim, and then compile it without the `-d:release` flag and run it. Run it a couple of times and note the results. The results should appear random, and should almost never display the expected value of 20,000. Figure 6.5 shows what the execution of listing 6.21 looks like.

Preventing race conditions is very important because whenever a bug occurs due to a race condition, it's almost always nondeterministic. The bug will be very difficult to reproduce, and once it is reproduced, debugging it will be even harder because the mere act of doing so may cause the bug to disappear.

Now that you know what race conditions are, let's look at ways to prevent them.

6.5.1   *Using guards and locks to prevent race conditions*

Just like most languages, Nim provides synchronization mechanisms to ensure that resources are only used by a single thread at a time.

One of these mechanisms is a *lock*. It enforces limits on access to a resource, and it's usually paired with a single resource. Before that resource is accessed, the lock is acquired, and after the resource is accessed, it's released. Other threads that try to access the same resource must attempt to acquire the same lock, and if the lock has already been acquired by another thread, the acquire operation will block the thread until the lock is released. This ensures that only one thread has access to the resource.

Locks work very well, but they aren't assigned to any variables by default. They can be assigned using a *guard*. When a variable is guarded with a specific lock, the compiler will ensure that the lock is locked before allowing access. Any other access will result in a compile-time error.

Synchronized execution

Thread #1		Thread #2		counter
Executed code	value	Executed code	value	
`value = counter`	0		0	0
increment	1		0	0
`counter = value`	1		0	1
	1	`value = counter`	1	1
	1	increment	2	1
	1	`counter = value`	2	2

Thread #2 does nothing until thread #1 is finished.

After thread #1 is finished, thread #2 performs its work and thread #1 does nothing.

Thread #1 sets its local `value` variable to 0. Thread #2 sets it to 1 after `counter` was updated by thread #1.

The result is correct.

Unsynchronized execution

Thread #1		Thread #2		counter
Executed code	value	Executed code	value	
`value = counter`	0	`value = counter`	0	0
	0	increment	1	0
	0	`counter = value`	1	1
increment	1		1	1
`counter = value`	1		1	1

Both threads end up setting `counter` to 1.

Both threads set their local `value` variable to 0.

Two increment operations end up incrementing only by 1.

Figure 6.5 Synchronized and unsynchronized execution of listing 6.21

The following listing shows how a new Lock, together with a guard, can be defined.

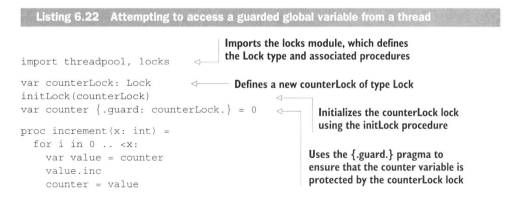

Listing 6.22 Attempting to access a guarded global variable from a thread

```
import threadpool, locks          Imports the locks module, which defines
                                   the Lock type and associated procedures

var counterLock: Lock             Defines a new counterLock of type Lock
initLock(counterLock)
var counter {.guard: counterLock.} = 0    Initializes the counterLock lock
                                          using the initLock procedure
proc increment(x: int) =
  for i in 0 .. <x:               Uses the {.guard.} pragma to
    var value = counter           ensure that the counter variable is
    value.inc                     protected by the counterLock lock
    counter = value
```

```
spawn increment(10_000)
spawn increment(10_000)
sync()
echo(counter)
```

Save listing 6.22 as unguarded_access.nim, and then compile it. The compilation should fail with "unguarded_access.nim(9, 17) Error: unguarded access: counter." This is because the counter variable is protected by the guard, which ensures that any access to counter must occur after the counterLock lock is locked. Let's fix this error by locking the counterLock lock.

> **Listing 6.23   Incrementing a global variable with a lock**

```
import threadpool, locks

var counterLock: Lock
initLock(counterLock)
var counter {.guard: counterLock.} = 0

proc increment(x: int) =
  for i in 0 .. <x:
    withLock counterLock:        ◁——   The code that accesses the counter
      var value = counter               variable is now inside a withLock
      value.inc                         section. This locks the lock and
      counter = value                   ensures that it's unlocked after the
                                        code under the withLock body ends.
spawn increment(10_000)
spawn increment(10_000)
sync()
echo(counter)
```

Save the code in listing 6.23 as parallel_incrementer.nim, and then compile and run it. The file should compile successfully and its output should always be 20000, which means that the race condition is fixed! The fact that the compiler verifies that every guarded variable is locked properly ensures the safe execution of the code. It also helps prevent bugs from appearing accidentally in the future, when new code is added or existing code is changed.

6.5.2   *Using channels so threads can send and receive messages*

Despite all Nim's efforts to make locks as safe as possible, they may not always be the safest choice. And for some use cases, they may simply be inappropriate, such as when threads share very few resources. Channels offer an alternative form of synchronization that allows threads to send and receive messages between each other.

A channel is an implementation of a *queue*—a first-in-first-out (FIFO) data structure. This means that the first value to be added to the channel will be the first one to be removed. The best way to visualize such a data structure is to imagine yourself queuing for food at a cafeteria. The first person to queue is also the first person to get their food. Figure 6.6 shows a representation of a FIFO channel.

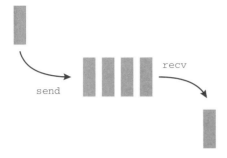

Figure 6.6 Representation of a FIFO channel

Nim implements channels in the `channels` module of the standard library. This module is part of `system`, so it doesn't need to be explicitly imported.

A channel is created as a global variable, allowing every thread to send and receive messages through it. Once a channel is defined, it must be initialized using the `open` procedure. Listing 6.24 defines and initializes a new `chan` variable of type `Channel` `[string]`. You can specify any type inside the square brackets, including your own custom types.

Listing 6.24 Initializing a channel using `open`

```
var chan: Channel[string]
open(chan)
```

Values can be sent using the `send` procedure and received using the `recv` procedure. The following listing shows how to use both procedures.

Listing 6.25 Sending and receiving data through a channel

```
import os, threadpool          ◁   The os module defines the sleep procedure.
var chan: Channel[string]          The threadpool module is needed for spawn.
open(chan)

proc sayHello() =                  The sayHello procedure will sleep its thread for 1
  sleep(1000)              ◁       second before sending a message through chan.
  chan.send("Hello!")
                                   Executes the sayHello procedure in another thread
spawn sayHello()          ◁
doAssert chan.recv() == "Hello!"  ◁——— Blocks the main thread until a "Hello!" is received
```

The `recv` procedure will block until a message is received. You can use the `tryRecv` procedure to get nonblocking behavior; it returns a tuple consisting of a Boolean, which indicates whether or not data was received, and the actual data.

To give you a better idea of how channels work, let's implement listing 6.23 with channels instead of locks. The following listing shows parallel_incrementer.nim implemented using channels.

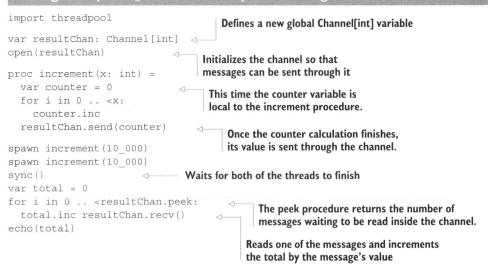

Listing 6.26   parallel_incrementer.nim implemented using channels

```
import threadpool

var resultChan: Channel[int]        ◁ ──┐  Defines a new global Channel[int] variable
open(resultChan)                    ◁ ──    Initializes the channel so that
                                            messages can be sent through it
proc increment(x: int) =
  var counter = 0                   ◁ ──┐  This time the counter variable is
  for i in 0 .. <x:                        local to the increment procedure.
    counter.inc
    resultChan.send(counter)        ◁ ──┐  Once the counter calculation finishes,
                                            its value is sent through the channel.
spawn increment(10_000)
spawn increment(10_000)
sync()                              ◁ ──    Waits for both of the threads to finish
var total = 0
for i in 0 .. <resultChan.peek:     ◁ ──┐  The peek procedure returns the number of
  total.inc resultChan.recv()       ◁ ──    messages waiting to be read inside the channel.
echo(total)
```

Reads one of the messages and increments
the total by the message's value

The global `counter` variable is replaced by a global `resultChan` channel. The `increment` procedure increments a local `counter` variable x times, and then it sends `counter`'s value through the channel. This is done in two different threads.

The main thread waits for the two threads to finish, at which point it reads the messages that have been sent to the `resultChan`. Figure 6.7 shows the execution of listing 6.26.

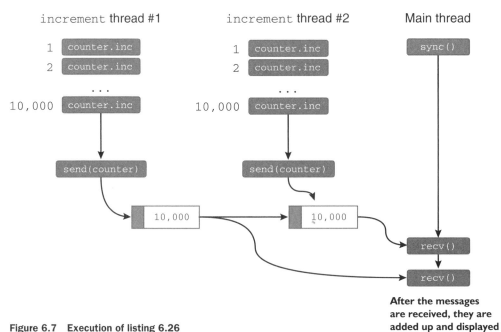

Figure 6.7   Execution of listing 6.26

6.6 *Summary*

- The apparent execution of processes at the same time is called *concurrency*, whereas true simultaneous execution of processes is called *parallelism.*
- Each thread in Nim has a separate heap that's managed by a separate garbage collector.
- Threads can be created using the `createThread` procedure defined in the `threads` module.
- A procedure can be added to a thread pool using the `spawn` procedure defined in the `threadpool` module.
- GC safety, which is enforced by the compiler, ensures that garbage-collected data isn't shared between threads.
- Data parsing can be performed using regular expressions, the `split` procedure, or the `parseutils` module.
- Threads can be used to parallelize a parser.
- Locks or channels can be used to synchronize the execution of threads to prevent race conditions.

Building a Twitter clone

This chapter covers

- Developing a Twitter clone in Nim
- Storing and querying for data in a SQL database
- Generating HTML and sending it to the user's browser
- Deploying your web application

Web applications have become extremely popular in recent years because of their convenience and the widespread use of web browsers. Many people have taken advantage of this to become millionaires, developing the likes of Twitter, Facebook, and Google.

Large web applications consisting of many components are typically written in several different programming languages, chosen to match the requirements of the components. In most cases, the core infrastructure is written in a single language, with a few small specialized components being written in one or two different programming languages. YouTube, for example, uses C, C++, Java, and Python for its many different components, but the core infrastructure is written in Python.

Thanks to the great speed of development that Python provides, YouTube was able to evolve by quickly responding to changes and implementing new ideas rapidly. In specialized cases, C extensions were used to achieve greater performance.

Smaller web applications are typically written in a single programming language. The choice of language differs, but it's typically a scripting language like Python, Ruby, or PHP. These languages are favored for their expressive and interpreted characteristics, which allow web applications to be iterated on quickly.

Unfortunately, applications written in those languages are typically slow, which has resulted in problems for some major websites. For example, Twitter, which was initially written in Ruby, has recently moved to Scala because Ruby was too slow to handle the high volume of tweets posted by users every day.

Websites can also be written in languages such as C++, Java, and C#, which are compiled. These languages produce very fast applications, but developing in them is not as fast as in Python or other scripting languages. This is likely due to the slow compile times in those languages, which means that you must spend more time waiting to test your application after you've made changes to it. Those languages are also not as expressive as Python or other scripting languages.

Nim is a hybrid. It's a compiled language that takes inspiration from scripting languages. In many ways, it's as expressive as any scripting language and as fast as any compiled language. Compilation times in Nim are also very fast, which makes Nim a good language for developing efficient web applications.

This chapter will lead you through the development of a web application. Specifically, it will show you how to develop a web app that's very similar to Twitter. Of course, developing a full Twitter clone would take far too much time and effort. The version developed in this chapter will be significantly simplified.

You'll need some knowledge of SQL for this chapter. Specifically, you'll need to understand the structure and semantics of common SQL statements, including `CREATE TABLE` and `SELECT`.

7.1 Architecture of a web application

Developers make use of many different architectural patterns when designing a web application. Many web frameworks are based on the very popular model-view-controller (MVC) pattern and its variants. One example of an MVC framework is Ruby on Rails.

MVC is an architectural pattern that has been traditionally used for graphical user interfaces (GUIs) on the desktop. But this pattern also turned out to be very good for web applications that incorporate a user-facing interface. The MVC pattern is composed of three distinct components that are independent of each other: the *model*, which acts as a data store; the *view*, which presents data to the user; and the *controller*, which gives the user the ability to control the application. Figure 7.1 shows how the three different components communicate.

Consider a simple calculator application consisting of a number of buttons and a display. In this case, the *model* would be a simple database that stores the numbers that

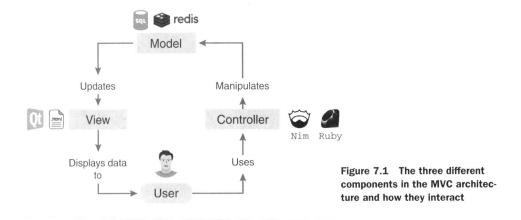

Figure 7.1   **The three different components in the MVC architecture and how they interact**

have been typed into the calculator, the *view* would be the display that shows the result of the current calculation, and the *controller* would detect any button presses and control the view and model accordingly. Figure 7.2 shows a simple graphical calculator with the different components labeled.

It's a good idea to design web applications using the MVC pattern, especially when writing very large applications. This pattern ensures that your code doesn't mix database code, HTML generation code, and logic code together, leading to easier maintenance for large web applications. Depending on the use case, variations on this pattern can also be used, separating code more or less strictly. Stricter separation would mean separating the web application into more components than just the model, view, and controller, or separating it into further subgroups derived from the model, view, or controller.

When you design the architecture of a web application, you may already naturally separate your code into logical independent units. Doing so can achieve the same benefits as using the MVC pattern, with the additional benefit of making your codebase more specific to the problem you're solving. It isn't always necessary to abide by

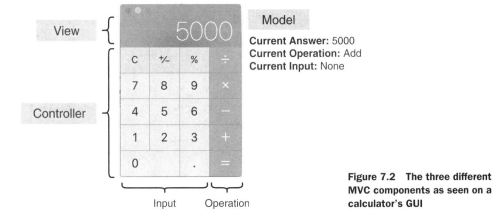

Figure 7.2   **The three different MVC components as seen on a calculator's GUI**

architectural patterns, and there are some web frameworks that are pattern agnostic. This type of framework is more suited for small web applications, or applications that don't need to incorporate all the components of the MVC pattern.

Sinatra is one example of a framework that doesn't enforce the MVC pattern. It's written in Ruby, just like Ruby on Rails, but it has been designed to be minimalistic. In comparison to Ruby on Rails, Sinatra is much lighter because it lacks much of the functionality that's common in full-fledged web application frameworks:

- Accounts, authentication, and authorization
- Database abstraction layers
- Input validation and sanitation
- Templating engines

This makes Sinatra very simple to work with, but it also means that Sinatra doesn't support as many features out of the box as Ruby on Rails does. Sinatra instead encourages developers to work on additional packages that implement the missing functionality.

The term *microframework* is used to refer to minimalistic web application frameworks like Sinatra. Many microframeworks exist, some based on Sinatra and written in various programming languages. There's even one written in Nim called Jester.

Jester is a microframework heavily based on Sinatra. At the time of writing, it's one of the most popular Nim web frameworks. We'll use Jester to develop the web application in this chapter, as it's easy to get started with and it's the most mature of the Nim web frameworks. Jester is hosted on GitHub: https://github.com/dom96/jester. Later on in this chapter, you'll see how to install Jester using the Nimble package manager, but first I'll explain how a microframework like Jester can be used to write web applications.

7.1.1 Routing in microframeworks

Full-fledged web frameworks usually require a big application structure to be created before you can begin developing the web application. Microframeworks, on the other hand, can be used immediately. All that's needed is a simple definition of a route. The following listing shows a simple route definition in Jester.

Listing 7.1 A / route defined using Jester

```
routes:
  get "/":
    resp "Hello World!"
```

To better understand what a *route* is, let me first explain how your web browser retrieves web pages from web servers. Figure 7.3 shows an HTTP request to twitter .com.

When you're browsing the internet and you navigate to a website or web page, your web browser requests that page using a certain URL. For example, when navigating to the front page of Twitter, your web browser first connects to twitter.com and

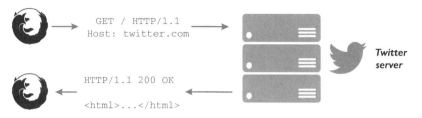

Figure 7.3   An HTTP request to twitter.com

then asks the Twitter server to send it the contents of the front page. The exchange occurs using the HTTP protocol and looks something like the following.

Listing 7.2   A simple HTTP GET request

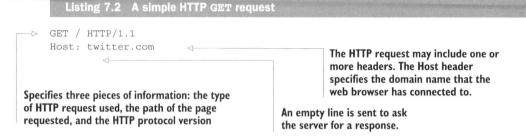

```
GET / HTTP/1.1
Host: twitter.com
```

The HTTP request may include one or more headers. The Host header specifies the domain name that the web browser has connected to.

Specifies three pieces of information: the type of HTTP request used, the path of the page requested, and the HTTP protocol version

An empty line is sent to ask the server for a response.

Note the similarities between the information in listing 7.2 and listing 7.1. The two important pieces of information are the GET, which is a type of HTTP request, and the /, which is the path of the web page requested. The / path is a special path that refers to the front page.

In a web application, the path is used to distinguish between different routes. This allows you to respond with different content depending on the page requested. Jester receives HTTP requests similar to the one in listing 7.2, and it checks the path and executes the appropriate route. Figure 7.4 shows this operation in action.

An ordinary web application will define multiple routes, such as /register, /login, /search, and so on. The web application that you'll develop will include similar routes. Some routes will perform certain actions, such as tweeting, whereas others will simply retrieve information.

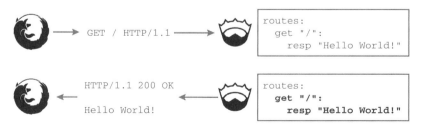

Figure 7.4   HTTP requests and routing in Jester

7.1.2   *The architecture of Tweeter*

Tweeter is what we'll call the simplified version of Twitter that you'll develop in this chapter. Obviously, implementing all of Twitter's features would take far too much time and effort. Instead, Tweeter will consist of the following features:

- Posting messages up to 140 characters
- Subscribing to another user's posts, called *following* in Twitter and many other social media websites
- Viewing the messages posted by users you're following

Some of Twitter's features that won't be implemented are

- User authentication: the user will simply type in their username and log in with no registration required
- Search, including hashtags
- Retweeting, replying to messages, or liking messages

That's a pretty small set of features, but it should be more than enough to teach you the basics of web development in Nim. Through these features, you'll learn several things:

- How web application projects are structured
- How to store data in a SQL database
- How to use Nim's templating language
- How to use the Jester web framework
- How the resulting application can be deployed on a server

The architecture of Tweeter will roughly follow the MVC architectural pattern explained earlier.

The following information will need to be stored in a database:

- Posted messages, and the users who posted them
- The username of each user
- The names of the users that each user is following

When you're developing web applications, it's useful to abstract database operations into a separate module. In Tweeter, this module will be called `database` and it will define procedures for reading from and writing to a database. This maps well onto the *model* component in the MVC architecture.

HTML will need to be generated based on the data provided by the `database` module. You'll create two separate views containing procedures to generate HTML: one for the front page and the other for the timelines of different users. For example, a `renderMain` procedure will generate an HTML page, and a `renderUser` procedure will generate a small bit of HTML representing a user.

Finally, the main source code file that includes the routes will act as the controller. It will receive HTTP requests from the web browser, and, based on those requests, it will perform the following actions:

- Retrieve the appropriate data from the database
- Build the HTML code based on that data
- Send the generated HTML code back to the requesting web browser

Figure 7.5 shows the process of developing these three components and their features.

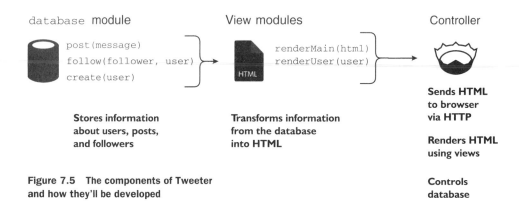

Figure 7.5   **The components of Tweeter and how they'll be developed**

7.2   *Starting the project*

The previous section described how web applications in general are designed and specifically how Tweeter will be designed, so you should have a reasonable idea of what you'll be building in this chapter. This section describes the first steps in beginning the project, including the following:

- Setting up Tweeter's directory structure
- Initializing a Nimble package
- Building a simple Hello World Jester web application

Just like in chapter 3, we'll start by creating the directories and files necessary to hold the project. Create a new Tweeter directory in your preferred code directory, such as C:\code\Tweeter or ~/code/Tweeter. Then create a src directory inside that, and a Nim source code file named tweeter.nim inside the src directory. This directory structure is shown in the following listing.

Listing 7.3   **Tweeter's directory structure**

```
Tweeter
└── src
    └── tweeter.nim
```

The web framework that this project will use is Jester. This is an external dependency that will need to be downloaded in order for Tweeter to compile. It could be downloaded manually, but that's not necessary, because Jester is a Nimble package, which means that Nimble can download it for you.

Chapter 5 showed you how to use Nimble, and in this chapter you'll use Nimble during development. To do so, you'll need to first create a .nimble file. You may recall that Nimble's `init` command can be used to generate one quickly.

To initialize a .nimble file in your project's directory, follow these steps:

1 Open a new terminal window.
2 `cd` into your project directory by executing something like `cd ~/code/Tweeter`. Make sure you replace `~/code/Tweeter` with the location of your project.
3 Execute `nimble init`.
4 Answer the prompts given by Nimble. You can use the default values for most of them by simply pressing Enter.

If you've done everything correctly, your terminal window should look something like figure 7.6.

```
● ● ●        Tweeter — dom@Dominiks-MacBook-Pro — ~/code/Tweeter — -zsh — 80×12
[~/code/Tweeter » nimble init
Reading from config file at /Users/dom/.config/nimble/nimble.ini
In order to initialise a new Nimble package, I will need to ask you
some questions. Default values are shown in square brackets, press
enter to use them.
Enter package name [Tweeter]:
Enter intial version of package [0.1.0]:
Enter your name [Dominik Picheta]:
Enter package description: A simple Twitter clone developed in Nim in Action.
Enter package license [MIT]:
Enter lowest supported Nim version [0.13.1]:
~/code/Tweeter »
```

Figure 7.6 Successful initialization of a Nimble package

Now, open the Tweeter.nimble file that was created by Nimble. It should look similar to the following.

Listing 7.4 The Tweeter.nimble file

```
# Package

version       = "0.1.0"
author        = "Dominik Picheta"
description   = "A simple Twitter clone developed in Nim in Action."
license       = "MIT"

# Dependencies

requires "nim >= 0.13.1"
```

As you can see in the last line, in order for the `Tweeter` package to successfully compile, the Nim compiler's version must be at least `0.13.1`. The `requires` line specifies the dependency requirements of the `Tweeter` package. You'll need to edit this line to introduce a requirement on the `jester` package. Simply edit the last line so that it reads `requires "nim >= 0.13.1", "jester >= 0.0.1"`. Alternatively, you can add `requires "jester >= 0.0.1"` at the bottom of the Tweeter.nimble file.

You'll also need to add `bin = @["tweeter"]` to the Tweeter.nimble file to let Nimble know which files in your package need to be compiled. You should also instruct Nimble not to install any Nim source files, by adding `skipExt = @["nim"]` to the file. Your Tweeter.nimble file should now contain the following lines.

Listing 7.5   The final Tweeter.nimble file

```
# Package

version       = "0.1.0"
author        = "Dominik Picheta"
description   = "A simple Twitter clone developed in Nim in Action."
license       = "MIT"

bin = @["tweeter"]
skipExt = @["nim"]

# Dependencies

requires "nim >= 0.13.1", "jester >= 0.0.1"
```

Now, open up tweeter.nim again, and write the following code in it.

Listing 7.6   A simple Jester test

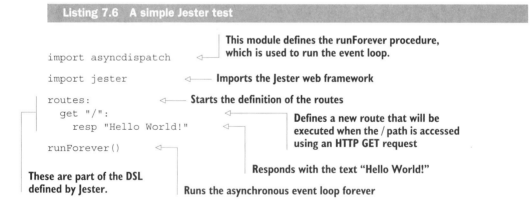

```
import asyncdispatch          ◁──┐  This module defines the runForever procedure,
                                 │  which is used to run the event loop.

import jester              ◁──── Imports the Jester web framework

routes:               ◁──── Starts the definition of the routes
    get "/":                      ◁─────┐
        resp "Hello World!"    ◁──┐     │  Defines a new route that will be
                                  │     │  executed when the / path is accessed
runForever()      ◁───┐          │     │  using an HTTP GET request
                      │          │
These are part of the DSL        │     Responds with the text "Hello World!"
defined by Jester.               └── Runs the asynchronous event loop forever
```

Go back to your terminal and execute `nimble c -r src/tweeter`. Your terminal should show something like what you see in figure 7.7.

Compiling your project using Nimble will ensure that all dependencies of your project are satisfied. If you haven't previously installed the Jester package, Nimble will install it for you before compiling Tweeter.

As you can see in figure 7.7, Jester lets you know in its own whimsical way about the URL that you can use to access your web application. Open a new tab in your favorite

```
roc. [User]
/Users/dom/.nimble/pkgs/jester-0.1.0/jester.nim(230, 10) Hint: 'setMatches' is d
eclared but not used [XDeclaredButNotUsed]
/Users/dom/.nimble/pkgs/jester-0.1.0/jester.nim(77, 3) Hint: 'Callback' is decla
red but not used [XDeclaredButNotUsed]
lib/pure/asyncdispatch.nim(1468, 7) Hint: Processing match as an async proc. [Us
er]
Hint:   [Link]
Hint: operation successful (39912 lines compiled; 0.949 sec total; 65.665MB; Deb
ug Build) [SuccessX]
INFO Jester is making jokes at http://localhost:5000
```

Figure 7.7   **The successful compilation and execution of** `tweeter`

web browser and navigate to the URL indicated by Jester, typically http://local-host:5000/. At that URL, you should see the "Hello World" message shown in figure 7.8. Your web application will continue running and responding to as many requests as you throw at it. You can terminate it by pressing Ctrl-C.

With Nimble's help, you were able to get started with Jester relatively quickly, and you now have a good starting point for developing Tweeter. Your next task will involve working on the `database` module.

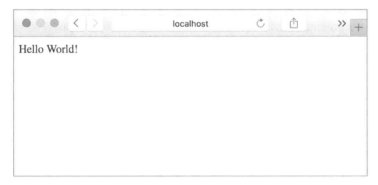

Figure 7.8   **"Hello World!" from Jester**

7.3   *Storing data in a database*

Tweeter will use a `database` module to implement the storage and querying of infor-mation related to the messages and users. This module will be designed in such a way that it can easily be extended to use a different database implementation later.

Because Nim is still relatively young, it doesn't support as many databases as some of the more popular programming languages such as C++ or Java. It does, however, sup-port many of the most popular ones, including Redis, which is a key-value database;

MongoDB, which is a document-oriented database; MySQL, which is a relational database; and many more.

If you're familiar with databases, you'll know that both Redis and MongoDB are what's known as NoSQL databases. As the name suggests, these databases don't support SQL for making queries on the database. Instead, they implement their own language, which typically isn't as mature or sophisticated as SQL.

It's likely that you have more experience with relational databases than any of the many different types of NoSQL databases, so you'll be happy to hear that Nim supports three different SQL databases out of the box. MySQL, SQLite, and PostgreSQL are all supported via the `db_mysql`, `db_sqlite`, and `db_postgres` modules, respectively.

Tweeter will need to store the following information in its database:

- Messages posted by users with metadata including the user that posted the message and the time it was posted
- Information about specific users, including their usernames and the names of users that they're following

All the databases I mentioned can be used to store this information. The choice of database depends on the requirements. Throughout this chapter, I use a SQL database for development, and specifically SQLite because it's far easier to get started with than MySQL or PostgreSQL.

MYSQL AND POSTGRESQL SUPPORT Both MySQL and PostgreSQL are supported by Nim in the same way that SQLite is. Changing between different database backends is trivial. As far as code changes go, simply importing `db_mysql` or `db_postgres` instead of `db_sqlite` should be enough.

7.3.1 Setting up the types

Let's begin by setting up the types in the `database` module. First, you'll need to create a new database.nim file in Tweeter's src directory. You can then define types in that file. These types will be used to store information about specific messages and users.

The next listing shows what those definitions look like.

> Listing 7.7 The types that store a Tweeter message and user information

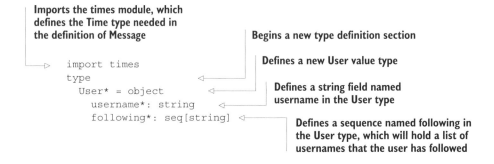

Imports the times module, which defines the Time type needed in the definition of Message

Begins a new type definition section

Defines a new User value type

Defines a string field named username in the User type

Defines a sequence named following in the User type, which will hold a list of usernames that the user has followed

```
import times
type
  User* = object
    username*: string
    following*: seq[string]
```

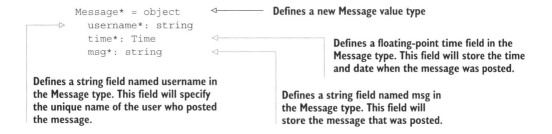

```
Message* = object          ◁──────── Defines a new Message value type
    username*: string
    time*: Time            ◁
    msg*: string           ◁
```

Defines a floating-point time field in the Message type. This field will store the time and date when the message was posted.

Defines a string field named username in the Message type. This field will specify the unique name of the user who posted the message.

Defines a string field named msg in the Message type. This field will store the message that was posted.

The User type will represent information about a single specific user, and the Message type will similarly represent information about a single specific message. To get a better idea of how messages will be represented, look at the sample Twitter message shown in figure 7.9.

Dominik Picheta
@d0m96

Hello to all Nim in Action readers!

6:16 PM - 23 Feb 2016

Figure 7.9   A sample Twitter message

An instance of the Message type can be used to represent the data in that message, as shown in the next listing.

Listing 7.8   Representing the data in figure 7.9 using an instance of Message

```
var message = Message(
  username: "d0m96",
  time: parse("18:16 - 23 Feb 2016", "H:mm - d MMM yyyy").toTime,   ◁
  msg: "Hello to all Nim in Action readers!"
)
```

The parse procedure is defined in the times module. It can parse a given time in the specified format and return a TimeInfo object that holds that time.

Figure 7.9 doesn't include information about the people I follow, but we can speculate and create an instance of the User type for it anyway.

Listing 7.9   Representing a user using an instance of User

```
var user = User(
  username: "d0m96",
  following: @["nim_lang", "ManningBooks"]
)
```

The database module needs to provide procedures that return such objects. Once those objects are returned, it's simply a case of turning the information stored in those objects into HTML to be rendered by the web browser.

7.3.2 Setting up the database

Before the procedures for querying and storing data can be created, the database schema needs to be created and a new database initialized with it.

For the purposes of Tweeter, this is pretty simple. The User and Message types map pretty well to User and Message tables. All that you need to do is create those tables in your database.

> **ORM** You may be familiar with object-relational mapping libraries, which mostly automate the creation of tables based on objects. Unfortunately, Nim doesn't yet have any mature ORM libraries that could be used. Feel free to play around with the libraries that have been released on Nimble.

I'll use SQLite for Tweeter's database. It's easy to get started with, as the full database can be embedded directly in your application's executable. Other database software needs to be set up ahead of time and configured to run as a separate server.

The creation of tables in the database is a one-off task that's only performed when a fresh database instance needs to be created. Once the tables are created, the database can be filled with data and then queried. I'll show you how to write a quick Nim script that will create the database and all the required tables.

Create a new file called createDatabase.nim inside Tweeter's src directory. The next listing shows the code that you should start off with.

Listing 7.10   Connecting to a SQLite database

```
import db_sqlite

var db = open("tweeter.db", "", "", "")

db.close()
```

> The open procedure creates a new database at the location specified. In this case, it will create a tweeter.db file in createDatabase's working directory.

The db_sqlite module's API has been designed so that it's compatible with the other database modules, including db_mysql and db_postgres. This way, you can simply change the imported module to use a different database. That's also why the open procedure in the db_sqlite module has three parameters that aren't used.

The code in listing 7.10 doesn't do much except initialize a new SQLite database at the specified location, or open an existing one, if it exists. The open procedure returns a DbConn object that can then be used to talk to the database.

The next step is creating the tables, and that requires some knowledge of SQL. Figure 7.10 shows what the tables will look like after they're created.

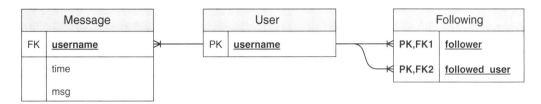

Figure 7.10   The database tables

The following listing shows how to create the tables that store the data contained in the User and Message objects.

Listing 7.11   Creating tables in a SQLite database

The sql procedure converts a string literal into a
SqlQuery string that can then be passed to exec.

Creates a new table, as long as the
database doesn't already contain it

```
import db_sqlite

var db = open("tweeter.db", "", "", "")

db.exec(sql"""
  CREATE TABLE IF NOT EXISTS User(
    username text PRIMARY KEY
  );
""")

db.exec(sql"""
  CREATE TABLE IF NOT EXISTS Following(
    follower text,
    followed_user text,
    PRIMARY KEY (follower, followed_user)
    FOREIGN KEY (follower) REFERENCES User(username),
    FOREIGN KEY (followed_user) REFERENCES User(username)
  );
""")
```

Specifies that the User table should
contain a username field and that it
should be a primary key[1]

Creates a new table, as
long as the database
doesn't already contain it

Contains the username of the user
that the follower is following

Contains the username of the follower

Creates a foreign-key constraint,
ensuring that the data added to the
database is correct

Specifies that the follower and followed_user
fields are, together, the primary key

---

[1]   In some cases, it may be faster to use an integer as the primary key. This isn't done here for simplicity.

The sql procedure converts a string literal into a SqlQuery string that can then be passed to exec.

```
db.exec(sql"""
  CREATE TABLE IF NOT EXISTS Message(
    username text,
    time integer,
    msg text NOT NULL,
    FOREIGN KEY (username) REFERENCES User(username)
  );
""")

echo("Database created successfully!")

db.close()
```

Contains the username of the user who posted the message

Creates a new table, as long as the database doesn't already contain it

Contains the time when the message was posted, stored as UNIX time, the number of seconds since 1970-01-01 00:00:00 UTC

Contains the actual message text; a NOT NULL key constraint is also present to ensure that it's not null

Whew. That's a lot of SQL. Let me explain it in a bit more detail.

Each `exec` line executes a separate piece of SQL, and an error is raised if that SQL isn't executed successfully. Otherwise, a new SQL table is successfully created with the specified fields. After the code in listing 7.11 is finished executing, the resulting database will contain three different tables. The `Following` table is required because SQLite doesn't support arrays.

The table definitions contains many table constraints, which prevent invalid data from being stored in the database. For example, the `FOREIGN KEY` constraints present in the `Following` table ensure that the `followed_user` and `follower` fields contain usernames that are already stored in the `User` table.

Save the code in listing 7.11 in your createDatabase.nim file, and then compile and run it by executing `nimble c -r src/createDatabase`. You should see a "Database created successfully!" message and a tweeter.db file in Tweeter's directory.

Your database has been created, and you're now ready to start defining procedures for storing and retrieving data.

7.3.3 Storing and retrieving data

The createDatabase.nim file is now finished, so you can switch back to the database.nim file. This section explains how you can begin adding data into the database and how to then get the data back out.

Let's start with storing data in the database. These three actions in Tweeter will trigger data to be added to the database:

- Posting a new message
- Following a user
- Creating an account

The database module should define procedures for those three actions, as follows:

```
proc post(message: Message)
proc follow(follower: User, user: User)
proc create(user: User)
```

Each procedure corresponds to a single action. Figure 7.11 shows how the `follow` procedure will modify the database.

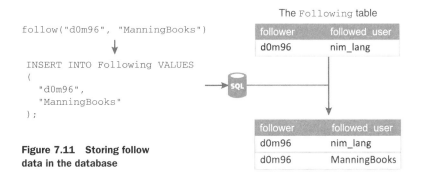

Figure 7.11 Storing follow data in the database

Each of those procedures simply needs to execute the appropriate SQL statements to store the desired data. And in order to do that, the procedures will need to take a DbConn object as a parameter. The DbConn object should be saved in a custom `Database` object so that it can be changed if required in the future. The following listing shows the definition of the `Database` type.

Listing 7.12 The `Database` type

```
import db_sqlite
type
  Database* = ref object
    db: DbConn

proc newDatabase*(filename = "tweeter.db"): Database =
  new result
  result.db = open(filename, "", "", "")
```

Add the import statement, the type definition, and the corresponding constructor to the top of your database.nim file. After you do so, you'll be ready to implement the post, `follow`, and `create` procedures.

The following listing shows how they can be implemented.

Listing 7.13   Implementing the `post`, `follow`, and `create` procedures

```
proc post*(database: Database, message: Message) =
  if message.msg.len > 140:
    raise newException(ValueError, "Message has to be less than 140 characters.")

  database.db.exec(sql"INSERT INTO Message VALUES (?, ?, ?);",
    message.username, $message.time.toSeconds().int, message.msg)

proc follow*(database: Database, follower: User, user: User) =
  database.db.exec(sql"INSERT INTO Following VALUES (?, ?);",
    follower.username, user.username)

proc create*(database: Database, user: User) =
  database.db.exec(sql"INSERT INTO User VALUES (?);", user.username)
```

Inserts a row into the specified table. The question marks are replaced with the values passed in after the SQL statement. The exec procedure ensures that the values are escaped to prevent SQL injections.

The time, which has type Time, is converted into the number of seconds since the UNIX epoch by calling toSeconds. The float result is then converted into an int.

Verifies that the message length isn't greater than 140 characters. If it is, raises an exception.[2]

The code in listing 7.13 is fairly straightforward, and the annotations explain the important parts of the code. These procedures should work perfectly well, but you should still test them. In order to do so, you'll need a way to query for data.

This gives us a good excuse to implement the procedures needed to get information from the database. As before, let's think about the actions that will prompt the retrieval of data from the database.

The primary way that the user will interact with Tweeter will be via its front page. Initially, the front page will ask the user for their username, and Tweeter will need to check whether that username has already been created. A procedure called `findUser` will be defined to check whether a username exists in the database. This procedure should return a new `User` object containing both the user's username and a list of users being followed. If the username doesn't exist, an account for it will be created, and the user will be logged in.

At that point, the user will be shown a list of messages posted by the users that they follow. A procedure called `findMessages` will take a list of users and return the messages that those users posted, in chronological order.

Each of the messages shown to the user will contain a link to the profile of the user who posted it. Once the user clicks that link, they'll be shown messages posted only by that user. The `findMessages` procedure will be flexible enough to be reused for this purpose.

---

[2] This won't handle Unicode accurately, as `len` doesn't return the number of Unicode characters in the string. You may wish to look at the `unicode` module to fix this.

Let's define those two procedures. The following listing shows their definitions and implementations.

Listing 7.14 Implementing the `findUser` and `findMessages` procedures

Finds a row with the specified username in the database

This procedure returns a Boolean that determines whether the user was found. The User object is saved in the user parameter.

Finds the usernames of people that the user with the specified username is following

False is returned when the database doesn't contain the username specified.

```
import strutils
proc findUser*(database: Database, username: string, user: var User): bool =
  let row = database.db.getRow(
    sql"SELECT username FROM User WHERE username = ?;", username)
  if row[0].len == 0: return false
  else: user.username = row[0]

  let following = database.db.getAllRows(
    sql"SELECT followed_user FROM Following WHERE follower = ?;", username)
  user.following = @[]
  for row in following:
    if row[0].len != 0:
      user.following.add(row[0])

  return true

proc findMessages*(database: Database, usernames: seq[string],
    limit = 10): seq[Message] =
  result = @[]
  if usernames.len == 0: return
  var whereClause = " WHERE "
  for i in 0 .. <usernames.len:
    whereClause.add("username = ? ")
    if i != <usernames.len:
      whereClause.add("or ")

  let messages = database.db.getAllRows(
    sql("SELECT username, time, msg FROM Message" &
      whereClause &
      "ORDER BY time DESC LIMIT " & $limit),
    usernames)
  for row in messages:
    result.add(Message(username: row[0], time: fromSeconds(row[1].parseInt),
      msg: row[2]))
```

Iterates through each row that specifies who the user is following, and adds each username to the list named following

This procedure takes an optional limit parameter. Its default value is 10, and it specifies the number of messages that this procedure will return.

Initializes the seq[Message] so that items can be added to it

Asks the database to return a list of all the messages from usernames in chronological order, limited to the value of limit

Adds "username = ?" to the whereClause for each username specified in usernames. This ensures that the SQL query returns messages from each of the usernames specified.

Iterates through each of the messages and adds them to the resultant sequence. The returned time integer, which is the number of seconds since the UNIX epoch, is converted into a Time object by the fromSeconds procedure.

Add these procedures to your database.nim file. Make sure you also import the `strutils` module, which defines `parseInt`.

These procedures are significantly more complicated than those implemented in listing 7.13. The `findUser` procedure makes a query to find the specified user, but it then also makes another query to find who the user is following. The `findMessages` procedure requires some string manipulation to build part of the SQL query because the number of usernames passed into this procedure can vary. Once the `WHERE` clause of the SQL query is built, the rest is fairly simple. The SQL query also contains two keywords: the `ORDER BY` keyword instructs SQLite to sort the resulting messages based on the time they were posted, and the `LIMIT` keyword ensures that only a certain number of messages are returned.

7.3.4   Testing the database

The `database` module is now ready to be tested. Let's write some simple unit tests to ensure that all the procedures in it are working correctly.

You can start by creating a new directory called tests in Tweeter's root directory. Then, create a new file called database_test.nim in the tests directory. Type `import database` into database_test.nim, and then try to compile it by executing `nimble c tests/database_test.nim`.

The compilation will fail with "Error: cannot open 'database'." This is due to the unfortunate fact that neither Nim nor Nimble has any way of finding the `database` module. This module is hidden away in your src directory, so it can't be found.

To get around this, you'll need to create a new file called database_test.nim.cfg in the tests directory. Inside it, write `--path:"../src"`. This will instruct the Nim compiler to look for modules in the src directory when compiling the `database_test` module. Verify that the database_test.nim file now compiles.

The test will need to create its own database instance so that it doesn't overwrite Tweeter's database instance. Unfortunately, the code for setting up the database is in the `createDatabase` module. You're going to have to move the bulk of that code into the `database` module so that `database_test` can use it. The new createDatabase.nim file will be much smaller after you add the procedures shown in listing 7.15 to the database module. Listing 7.16 shows the new createDatabase.nim implementation.

Listing 7.15   The `setup` and `close` procedures destined for database.nim

```
proc close*(database: Database) =          ◁
  database.db.close()

proc setup*(database: Database) =          ◁
  database.db.exec(sql"""
    CREATE TABLE IF NOT EXISTS User(
      username text PRIMARY KEY
    );
  """)

  database.db.exec(sql"""
```

The close procedure closes the database and returns any allocated resources to the OS.

The setup procedure initializes the database with the User, Following, and Message tables.

```
  CREATE TABLE IF NOT EXISTS Following(
    follower text,
    followed_user text,
    PRIMARY KEY (follower, followed_user),
    FOREIGN KEY (follower) REFERENCES User(username),
    FOREIGN KEY (followed_user) REFERENCES User(username)
  );
""")

database.db.exec(sql"""
  CREATE TABLE IF NOT EXISTS Message(
    username text,
    time integer,
    msg text NOT NULL,
    FOREIGN KEY (username) REFERENCES User(username)
  );
""")
```

Listing 7.16   The new implementation of createDatabase.nim

```
import database

var db = newDatabase()
db.setup()
echo("Database created successfully!")
db.close()
```

Add the code in listing 7.15 to database.nim, and replace the contents of createDatabase.nim with the code in listing 7.16.

Now that this small reorganization of code is complete, you can start writing test code in the database_test.nim file. The following listing shows a simple test of the database module.

Listing 7.17   A test of the `database` module

```
import database

import os, times

when isMainModule:
  removeFile("tweeter_test.db")          ◁──  Removes the old test database
  var db = newDatabase("tweeter_test.db")  ◁──  Creates a new
  db.setup()                                     tweeter_test.db database
                                          ◁──  Creates the tables in the SQLite database
  db.create(User(username: "d0m96"))
  db.create(User(username: "nim_lang"))   }  Tests user creation

  db.post(Message(username: "nim_lang", time: getTime() - 4.seconds,
      msg: "Hello Nim in Action readers"))
  db.post(Message(username: "nim_lang", time: getTime(),
      msg: "99.9% off Nim in Action for everyone, for the next minute only!"))
```

Posts two messages 4 seconds apart, with the first message posted in the past and the second in the present

```
var dom: User
doAssert db.findUser("d0m96", dom)        ◁──── Tests the findUser procedure. It should
var nim: User                                    return true in both cases because the d0m96
doAssert db.findUser("nim_lang", nim)     ◁──── and nim_lang users have been created.
db.follow(dom, nim)
                                          ◁───┐
doAssert db.findUser("d0m96", dom)            │ Tests the follow procedure

let messages = db.findMessages(dom.following)      ◁──────────────────┐
echo(messages)
doAssert(messages[0].msg == "99.9% off Nim in Action for everyone,
    for the next minute only!")
doAssert(messages[1].msg == "Hello Nim in Action readers")
echo("All tests finished successfully!")
```

Rereads the user information for   **Tests the findMessages procedure**
d0m96 to ensure that the
"following" information is correct

This test is very large. It tests the database module as a whole, which is necessary to test it fully. Try to compile it yourself, and you should see the two messages displayed on your screen followed by "All tests finished successfully!"

That's it for this section. The database module is complete, and it can store information about users including who they're following and the messages they post. The module can also read that data back. All of this is exposed in an API that abstracts the database away and defines only the procedures needed to build the Tweeter web application.

7.4   *Developing the web application's view*

Now that the database module is complete, it's time to start developing the web component of this application.

The database module provides the data needed by the application. It's the equivalent of the model component in the MVC architectural pattern. The two components that are left are the view and the controller. The controller acts as a link joining the view and model components together, so it's best to implement the view first.

In Tweeter's case, the view will contain multiple modules, each defining one or more procedures that will take data as input and return HTML as output. The HTML will represent the data in a way that can be rendered by a web browser and displayed appropriately to the user.

One of the view procedures will be called renderUser. It will take a User object and generate HTML, which will be returned as a string. Figure 7.12 is a simplified illustration of how this procedure, together with the database module and the controller, will display the information about a user to the person accessing the web application.

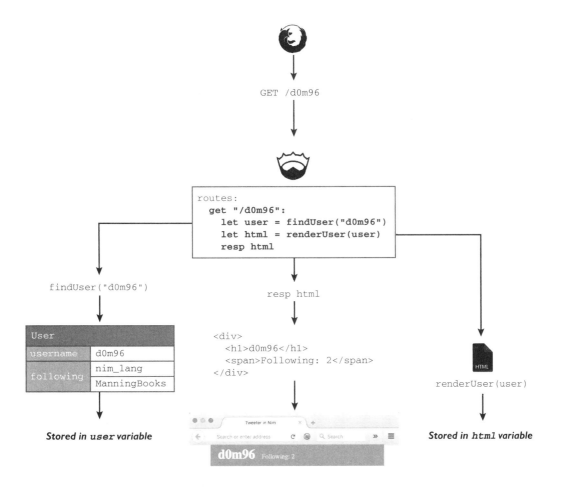

Figure 7.12 The process of displaying information about a user in the web browser

There are many ways to implement procedures that convert information into HTML, like the renderUser procedure. One way is to use the % string formatting operator to build up a string based on the data:

```
import strutils
proc renderUser(user: User): string =
  return "<div><h1>$1</h1><span>Following: $2</span></div>" %
          [user.username, $user.following.len]
```

Unfortunately, this is very error prone, and it doesn't ensure that special characters such as ampersands or < characters are escaped. Not escaping such characters can cause invalid HTML to be generated, which would lead to invalid data being shown to the user. More importantly, this can be a major security risk!

Nim supports two methods of generating HTML that are more intuitive. The first is defined in the `htmlgen` module. This module defines a DSL for generating HTML. Here's how it can be used:

```nim
import htmlgen
proc renderUser(user: User): string =
  return `div`(
    h1(user.username),
    span("Following: ", $user.following.len)
  )
```

The backticks (`` ` ``) around the div are needed because "div" is a keyword.

The username passed to h1 becomes the `<h1>` tag's content.

Only strings are accepted, so the length must be explicitly converted to a string using the $ operator.

This method of generating HTML is great when the generated HTML is small. But there's another more powerful method of generating HTML called *filters*. The following listing shows filters in action.

Listing 7.18   Using a Nim filter to generate HTML

```nim
#? stdtmpl(subsChar = '$', metaChar = '#')
#import "../database"
#
#proc renderUser*(user: User): string =
#  result = ""
<div id="user">
  <h1>${user.username}</h1>
  <span>${$user.following.len}</span>
</div>
#end proc
#
#when isMainModule:
#  echo renderUser(User(username: "d0m96", following: @[]))
#end when
```

This line, the filter definition, allows you to customize the behavior of the filter.

This file assumes that it's placed in a views subdirectory. This is why the ".." is necessary to import "database".

In filters, it's important to ensure that all lines are prefixed with #.

Keywords delimit where the procedure ends because indentation doesn't work well in templates such as these.

Each line that doesn't begin with # is converted to result.add by the compiler.

In the filter, an ordinary procedure is created, and in it you need to initialize the result variable.

Filters allow you to mix Nim code together with any other code. This way, HTML can be written verbatim and Nim code can still be used. Create a new folder called views in the src directory of Tweeter, and then save the contents of listing 7.18 into views/user.nim. Then, compile the file. You should see the following output:

```html
<div id="user">
  <h1>d0m96</h1>
  <span>0</span>
</div>
```

Filters are very powerful and can be customized extensively.

WARNING: AN IMPORTANT FILTER GOTCHA   When writing filters, be sure that all the empty lines are prefixed with #. If you forget to do so, you'll get errors such as "undeclared identifier: result" in your code.

Figure 7.13 shows the view that the renderUser procedure will create.

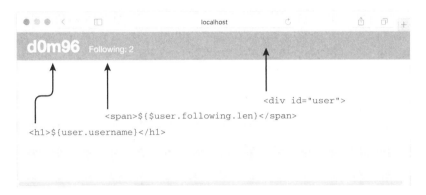

Figure 7.13   The view created by listing 7.18

The code shown in listing 7.18 still suffers from the same problems as the first example in this section: it doesn't escape special characters. But thanks to the filter's flexibility, this can easily be repaired, as follows.

Listing 7.19   Escaping special characters in views/user.nim

```
#? stdtmpl(subsChar = '$', metaChar = '#', toString = "xmltree.escape")    ⟵
#import "../database"
#import xmltree
#
#proc renderUser*(user: User): string =
#   result = ""
<div id="user">
  <h1>${user.username}</h1>
  <span>Following: ${$user.following.len}</span>
</div>
#end proc
#
#when isMainModule:
#   echo renderUser(User(username: "d0m96<>", following: @[]))    ⟵
#end when
```

> This parameter specifies the operation applied to each expression, such as ${user.username}. Here, the toString parameter is overwritten with a new xmltree.escape string to escape the expression.

The xmltree module that defines escape needs to be imported.

The username of the user is now d0m96<> to test the escape mechanism.

FILTER DEFINITIONS   You can learn more about how to customize filters by taking a look at their documentation: http://nim-lang.org/docs/filters.html.

Save this file in views/user.nim and note the new output. Everything should be as before, except for the <h1> tag, which should read <h1>d0m96<></h1>. Note how the <> is escaped as <>.

7.4.1   *Developing the user view*

The vast majority of the user view is already implemented in the view/user.nim file. The procedures defined in this view will be used whenever a specific user's page is accessed.

The user's page will display some basic information about the user and all of the user's messages. Basic information about the user is already presented in the form of HTML by the renderUser procedure.

The renderUser procedure needs to include Follow and Unfollow buttons. Instead of making the renderUser procedure more complicated, let's overload it with a new renderUser procedure that takes an additional parameter called currentUser. The following listing shows its implementation. Add it to the view/user.nim file.

> **Listing 7.20   The second `renderUser` procedure**

This procedure definition is almost identical to the previous renderUser procedure. The difference is in the parameters, in this case the addition of the currentUser parameter.

Checks to see if the currently logged-in user is already following the specified user. If not, creates a Follow button.

Adds a form that contains a Follow or Unfollow button. The form is submitted to the /follow route.

```
#proc renderUser*(user: User, currentUser: User): string =
#   result = ""
<div id="user">
  <h1>${user.username}</h1>
  <span>Following: ${$user.following.len}</span>
  #if user.username notin currentUser.following:
  <form action="follow" method="post">
    <input type="hidden" name="follower" value="${currentUser.username}">
    <input type="hidden" name="target" value="${user.username}">
    <input type="submit" value="Follow">
  </form>
  #end if
</div>
#
#end proc
```

Hidden fields are used to pass information to the /follow route.

Figure 7.14 shows what the follow button will look like once its rendered.

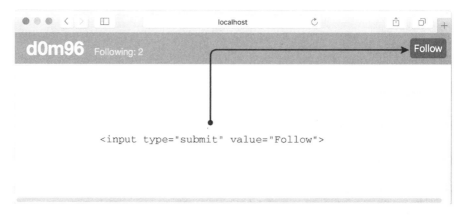

```
<input type="submit" value="Follow">
```

Figure 7.14   The Follow button constructed by `renderUser` in listing 7.20

Now, let's implement a `renderMessages` procedure. The next listing shows the full implementation of the `renderMessages` procedure, together with the `renderUser` procedures implemented in the previous section.

Listing 7.21 Final views/user.nim with the new `renderMessages` procedure

```
#? stdtmpl(subsChar = '$', metaChar = '#', toString = "xmltree.escape")
#import "../database"
#import xmltree
#import times
#
#proc renderUser*(user: User): string =
#  result = ""
<div id="user">
  <h1>${user.username}</h1>
  <span>Following: ${$user.following.len}</span>
</div>
#end proc
#
#proc renderUser*(user: User, currentUser: User): string =
#  result = ""
<div id="user">
  <h1>${user.username}</h1>
  <span>Following: ${$user.following.len}</span>
  #if user.username notin currentUser.following:
  <form action="follow" method="post">
    <input type="hidden" name="follower" value="${currentUser.username}">
    <input type="hidden" name="target" value="${user.username}">
    <input type="submit" value="Follow">
  </form>
  #end if
</div>
#
#end proc
#
#proc renderMessages*(messages: seq[Message]): string =
#  result = ""
<div id="messages">
  #for message in messages:
    <div>
      <a href="/${message.username}">${message.username}</a>
      <span>${message.time.getGMTime().format("HH:mm MMMM d',' yyyy")}</span>
      <h3>${message.msg}</h3>
    </div>
  #end for
</div>
#end proc
```

The times module is imported so that the time can be formatted.

The new renderMessages procedure takes a list of messages and returns a single string.

As before, result is initialized so that text can be appended to it by the filter.

The for loop is explicitly finished by the "end for" keywords.

Message text is added last.

Adds the username to the HTML first.

Iterates through all messages. All the following HTML code will be added verbatim in each iteration.

The procedure will first emit a new <div> tag.

The time when the message was created is formatted and added to the HTML.

```
#
#when isMainModule:
#  echo renderUser(User(username: "d0m96<>", following: @[]))
#  echo renderMessages(@[                              ◁
#    Message(username: "d0m96", time: getTime(), msg: "Hello World!"),
#    Message(username: "d0m96", time: getTime(), msg: "Testing")
#  ])
#end when
```

**The renderMessages procedure
is tested with some messages.**

Replace the contents of your views/user.nim file with the contents of listing 7.21.
Then compile and run it. You should see something similar to the following:

```
<div id="user">
  <h1>d0m96&lt;&gt;</h1>
  <span>Following: 0</span>
</div>

<div id="messages">
    <div>
      <a href="/d0m96">d0m96</a>
      <span>12:37 March 2, 2016</span>
      <h3>Hello World!</h3>
    </div>
    <div>
      <a href="/d0m96">d0m96</a>
      <span>12:37 March 2, 2016</span>
      <h3>Testing</h3>
    </div>
</div>
```

Figure 7.15 shows what the rendered message will look like.

And that's it for the user view. All you need to do now is build the remaining views.

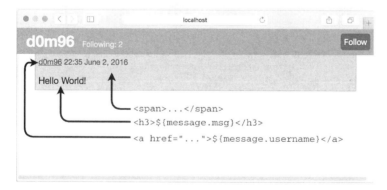

Figure 7.15   A message produced by `renderMessages`

7.4.2 Developing the general view

The user view will be used for a specific user's page. All that remains to be created is the front page. The front page will either show a login form or, if the user has logged in, it will show the messages posted by the people that the user follows.

This general view will be used as the front page of Tweeter, so for simplicity we'll implement the procedures in a new file called general.nim. Create this file in the views directory now.

One important procedure that we haven't implemented yet is one that will generate the main body of the HTML page. Let's implement this now as a renderMain procedure and add it to the new general.nim file. The following listing shows the implementation of renderMain.

Listing 7.22 Implementing the `renderMain` procedure

```
#? stdtmpl(subsChar = '$', metaChar = '#')       ◁──  The toString parameter is no
#import xmltree                                        longer set in the filter definition.
#
#proc `$!`(text: string): string = escape(text)  ◁──  Defines a new operator that can
#end proc                                              be used to escape text easily
#
#proc renderMain*(body: string): string =        ◁──  Defines the renderMain procedure,
#  result = ""                                         which simply generates a new HTML
<!DOCTYPE html>                                        document and inserts the body of
<html>                                                 the page inside the <div> tag
  <head>
    <title>Tweeter written in Nim</title>
    <link rel="stylesheet" type="text/css" href="style.css">
  </head>

  <body>
    <div id="main">
      ${body}
    </div>
  </body>

</html>
#end proc
```

The code is fairly straightforward. The renderMain procedure takes a parameter called body containing the HTML code that should be inserted into the body of the HTML page. In comparison to listing 7.21, the toString parameter is no longer used to ensure that the body isn't escaped. Instead, a new operator called $! has been introduced. This operator is simply an alias for the escape procedure. This means that you can easily decide which of the strings you're embedding will be escaped and which won't be.

Now that the renderMain procedure has been implemented, it's time to move on to implementing the remaining two procedures: renderLogin and renderTimeline. The first procedure will show a simple login form, and the second will show the user their timeline. The *timeline* is the messages posted by people that the user is following.

Let's start with `renderLogin`. The following listing shows how it can be implemented.

Listing 7.23   The implementation of `renderLogin`

```
#proc renderLogin*(): string =
#  result = ""
<div id="login">
  <span>Login</span>
  <span class="small">Please type in your username...</span>
  <form action="login" method="post">
    <input type="text" name="username">
    <input type="submit" value="Login">
  </form>
</div>
#end proc
```

This procedure is very simple because it doesn't take any arguments. It simply returns a piece of static HTML representing a login form. Figure 7.16 shows what this looks like when rendered in a web browser. Add this procedure to the bottom of the general .nim file.

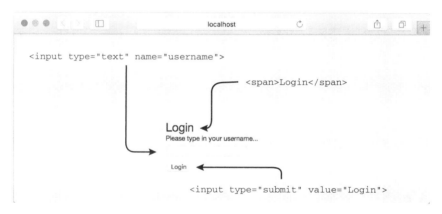

Figure 7.16   The rendered login page

The `renderTimeline` procedure, shown next, is also fairly straightforward, even though it takes two parameters. Add this procedure to the bottom of general.nim, and make sure that you also import `"../database"` and user at the top of the file.

Listing 7.24   The implementation of `renderTimeline`

```
#proc renderTimeline*(username: string, messages: seq[Message]): string =
#  result = ""
<div id="user">
  <h1>${$!username}'s timeline</h1>
</div>
<div id="newMessage">
  <span>New message</span>
```

```
  <form action="createMessage" method="post">
    <input type="text" name="message">
    <input type="hidden" name="username" value="${$!username}">
    <input type="submit" value="Tweet">
  </form>
</div>
${renderMessages(messages)}
#end proc
```

> The **$!** operator is used here to ensure that username is escaped.

> The **renderMessages** procedure is called, and its result is inserted into the generated HTML.

The preceding implementation is fairly simple. It first creates a `<div>` tag that holds the title, and then a `<div>` tag that allows the user to tweet a new message. Finally, the renderMessages procedure defined in the user module is called.

For completeness, here's the full general.nim code.

```
#? stdtmpl(subsChar = '$', metaChar = '#')
#import "../database"
#import user
#import xmltree
#
#proc `$!`(text: string): string = escape(text)
#end proc
#
#proc renderMain*(body: string): string =
#  result = ""
<!DOCTYPE html>
<html>
  <head>
    <title>Tweeter written in Nim</title>
    <link rel="stylesheet" type="text/css" href="style.css">
  </head>

  <body>
    ${body}
  </body>

</html>
#end proc
#
#proc renderLogin*(): string =
#  result = ""
<div id="login">
  <span>Login</span>
  <span class="small">Please type in your username...</span>
  <form action="login" method="post">
    <input type="text" name="username">
    <input type="submit" value="Login">
  </form>
</div>
#end proc
#
#proc renderTimeline*(username: string, messages: seq[Message]): string =
```

```
#  result = ""
<div id="user">
  <h1>${$!username}'s timeline</h1>
</div>
<div id="newMessage">
  <span>New message</span>
  <form action="createMessage" method="post">
    <input type="text" name="message">
    <input type="hidden" name="username" value="${$!username}">
    <input type="submit" value="Tweet">
  </form>
</div>
${renderMessages(messages)}
#end proc
```

With that, the view components are complete, and Tweeter is very close to being finished. All that's left is the component that ties the database and views together.

7.5   *Developing the controller*

The controller will tie the `database` module and the two different views together. Compared to the three modules you've already implemented, the controller will be much smaller. The bulk of the work is now essentially behind you.

You've already created a file, tweeter.nim, that implements the controller. Open this file now, so that you can begin editing it.

This file currently contains one route: the / route. You'll need to modify this route so that it responds with the HTML for the login page. To do so, start by importing the different modules that you implemented in the previous section: `database`, `views/user`, and `views/general`. You can use the following code to import these modules:

```
import database, views/user, views/general
```

Once you've done that, you can modify the / route so that it sends the login page to the user's web browser:

```
get "/":
  resp renderMain(renderLogin())
```

Save your newly modified tweeter.nim file, and then compile and run it. Open a new web browser tab and navigate to http://localhost:5000. You should see a login form, albeit a very white one. It might look similar to figure 7.17.

Let's add some CSS style to this page. If you're familiar with CSS and are confident in your web design abilities, I encourage you to write some CSS yourself to create a nice design for Tweeter's login page.

> **SHARE YOUR CSS**   If you do end up designing your own Tweeter, please share what you come up with on Twitter with the hashtag #NimInActionTweeter. I'd love to see what you come up with. If you don't have Twitter, you can also post it on the Nim forums or the Manning forums at http://forum.nim-lang .org and https://forums.manning.com/forums/nim-in-action, respectively.

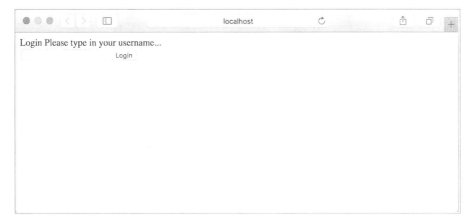

Figure 7.17 **The unstyled login form**

If you're more like myself and don't have any web design abilities whatsoever, you can use the CSS available at the following URL: https://github.com/dom96/nim-in-action-code/blob/master/Chapter7/Tweeter/public/style.css.

The CSS file should be placed in a directory named *public*. Create this directory now, and save your CSS file as style.css. When a page is requested, Jester will check the public directory for any files that match the page requested. If the requested page exists in the public directory, Jester will send that page to the browser.

> **STATIC FILE DIRECTORY** The public directory is known as the static file directory. This directory is set to `public` by default, but it can be configured using the `setStaticDir` procedure or in a settings block. For more information on static file config in Jester, see the documentation on GitHub: https://github.com/dom96/jester#static-files.

Once you've placed the CSS file in the public directory, refresh the page. You should see that the login page is now styled. It should look something like the screen in figure 7.18 (or it may look better if you wrote your own CSS).

Type in a username, and click the Login button. You'll see an error message reading "404 Not Found." Take a look at your terminal and see what Jester displayed there. You should see something similar to figure 7.19.

Note the last line, which reads as follows:

```
DEBUG post /login
DEBUG   404 Not Found {Content-type: text/html;charset=utf-8, Content-Length: 178}
```

This specifies that an HTTP post request was made to the /login page. A route for the /login page hasn't yet been created, so Jester responds with a "404 Not Found" error.

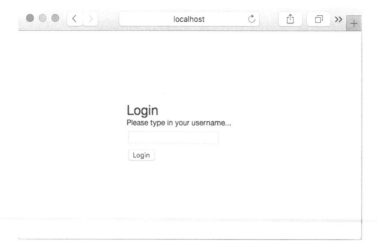

Figure 7.18   The login page

7.5.1   Implementing the /login route

Let's implement the /login route now. Its implementation is short.

Listing 7.26   The /login route

```
post "/login":
    setCookie("username", @"username", getTime().getGMTime() + 2.hours)
    redirect("/")
```

Specifies a new POST route on the path /login. Any HTTP POST requests on /login will activate this route, and the code in its body will be executed.

Asks Jester to redirect the user's web browser to the front page

Sets a new cookie with a key of "username" and tells it to expire in 2 hours. The cookie's value is set to the username that the user typed into the login box on the front page.

```
Tweeter — nimble c -r src/tweeter — nimble — tweeter • nimble c -r src/tweeter — 85×10
57f8ae083af2cf4}
DEBUG get /favicon.ico
DEBUG    404 Not Found {Content-type: text/html;charset=utf-8, Content-Length: 178}
DEBUG get /apple-touch-icon-precomposed.png
DEBUG    404 Not Found {Content-type: text/html;charset=utf-8, Content-Length: 178}
DEBUG get /apple-touch-icon.png
DEBUG    404 Not Found {Content-type: text/html;charset=utf-8, Content-Length: 178}
DEBUG post /login
DEBUG    404 Not Found {Content-type: text/html;charset=utf-8, Content-Length: 178}
```

Figure 7.19   Debug information from Jester

Add the code in listing 7.26 to tweeter.nim, and make sure it's indented just like the other route. You'll also need to import the `times` module. The preceding code may seem a bit magical, so let me explain it in more detail.

The code does two simple things: it sets a cookie and then redirects the user to the front page of Tweeter.

A cookie is a piece of data stored in a user's browser. It's composed of a key, a value, and an expiration date. The cookie created in this route stores the username that was typed in by the user just before the Login button was clicked. This username was sent together with the HTTP request when the Login button was clicked. It's referred to by `"username"` because that's the `name` of the `<input>` tag that was created in the `renderLogin` procedure. The value of `"username"` is accessed in Jester using the `@` operator.

The expiration date of the cookie is calculated using a special + operator that adds a `TimeInterval` to a `TimeInfo` object. In this case, it creates a date that's 2 hours in the future. At the end of the code, the route finishes by redirecting the user to the front page.

Recompile tweeter.nim, run it, and test it out. You should now be able to type in a new username, click Login, and see the web browser navigate to the front page automatically. Notice what's happening in your terminal, and particularly the following line:

```
DEBUG post /login
DEBUG   303 See Other {Set-Cookie: username=test; Expires=Wed,
02 Mar 2016 21:57:29 UTC, Content-Length: 0, Location: /}
```

The last line is actually the response that Jester sent, together with the HTTP headers, which include a `Set-Cookie` header. Figure 7.20 shows this in action. The cookie is set, but the user is redirected back to the front page.

Figure 7.20   The current login process

7.5.2   *Extending the / route*

The cookie is set, but the user is still shown the front page without actually being logged in. Let's fix that. The following listing shows a modified version of the / route that fixes this problem.

Listing 7.27   The / route

Creates a new database instance that will open the database saved in tweeter.db. This is done inside a global variable so that every route can access it.

```
let db = newDatabase()            ◁──┘

routes:                                     Checks if the cookie has been set
  get "/":                                       Checks if the username
    if request.cookies.hasKey("username"):  ◁──┘   already exists in the
      var user: User                                        database
      if not db.findUser(request.cookies["username"], user):  ◁──┘
        user = User(username: request.cookies["username"], following: @[])
        db.create(user)
      let messages = db.findMessages(user.following)
      resp renderMain(renderTimeline(user.username, messages))   ◁────
    else:
      resp renderMain(renderLogin())   ◁──┐
```

Retrieves the messages posted by the users that the logged-in user is following

If the cookie isn't set, shows the login page

Uses the renderTimeline procedure to render the user's timeline, and then passes the result to renderMain, which returns a fully rendered web page

If the username doesn't exist in the database, creates it

Modify tweeter.nim by replacing the / route with the code in listing 7.27. Then recompile and run Tweeter again. Navigate to http://localhost:5000, type `test` into the Login text box, and click Login. You should now be able to see test's timeline, which should look similar to the screenshot in figure 7.21.

Congratulations, you've almost created your very own Twitter clone!

Figure 7.21   A simple timeline

7.5.3 *Implementing the /createMessage route*

Let's keep going. The next step is to implement the tweeting functionality. Clicking the Tweet button will try to take you to the /createMessage route, resulting in another 404 error.

The following listing shows how the /createMessage route can be implemented.

Listing 7.28 The /createMessage route

```
post "/createMessage":
  let message = Message(
    username: @"username",
    time: getTime(),
    msg: @"message"
  )
  db.post(message)
  redirect("/")
```

This route initializes a new `Message` and uses the `post` procedure defined in the database module to save the message in the database. It then redirects the browser to the front page.

Add this code to the bottom of your routes. Then recompile, run Tweeter, and navigate to http://localhost:5000. After logging in, you should be able to start tweeting. Unfortunately, you'll quickly notice that the tweets you create aren't appearing. This is because your username isn't passed to the `findMessages` procedure in the / route.

To fix this problem, change `let messages = db.findMessages(user.following)` to `let messages = db.findMessages(user.following & user.username)`. Recompile and run Tweeter again. You should now be able to see the messages you've created. Figure 7.22 shows an example of what that will look like.

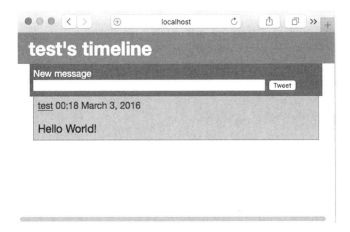

Figure 7.22   A timeline with messages

7.5.4   *Implementing the user route*

The username in the message is clickable; it takes you to the user page for that specific username. In this example, clicking the `test` username should take you to http://localhost:5000/test, which will result in a 404 error because a route for /test hasn't yet been created.

This route is a bit different, because it should accept any username, not just `test`. Jester features patterns in route paths to support such use cases. The following listing shows how a route that shows any user's timeline can be implemented.

Listing 7.29   The user route

```
get "/@name":
    var user: User
    if not db.findUser(@"name", user):
        halt "User not found"

    let messages = db.findMessages(@[user.username])
    resp renderMain(renderUser(user) & renderMessages(messages))
```

Anything that follows the @ character in a path is a variable. Jester will activate this route when the path is /test, or /foo, or /<insert_anything_here>.

The renderUser procedure is used to render the timeline of the specified user, and the renderMessages procedure is then used to generate the HTML for the user's messages.

Inside the route, the @ operator is used to retrieve the value of the "name" variable in the path. The User object for that username value is then retrieved.

If the user isn't found, the route finishes early with the specified message. The halt procedure is similar to a return.

Add the route in listing 7.29 into tweeter.nim, recompile, run Tweeter again, and navigate to the front page: http://localhost:5000/.

You'll note that the page no longer has any style associated with it. What happened? Unfortunately, the route you've just added also matches /style.css, and because a user with that name doesn't exist, a 404 error is returned.

This is easy to fix. Jester provides a procedure called `cond` that takes a Boolean parameter, and if that parameter is false, the route is skipped. Simply add `cond '.' notin @"name"` at the top of the route to skip the route if a period (.) is inside the value of the `name` variable. This will skip the route when /style.css is accessed, and it will fall back to responding with the static file.

Test this by recompiling tweeter.nim and running it again. You should see that the stylesheet has been restored when you navigate to http://localhost:5000/. Log in using the `test` username, and click on the username in your message again. You should see something resembling figure 7.23.

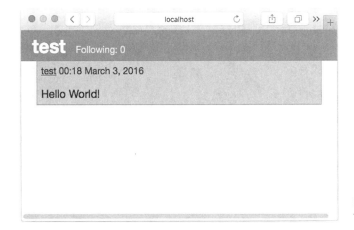

Figure 7.23   Another user's timeline

7.5.5   *Adding the Follow button*

There's one important feature missing from the user's timeline page. That's the Follow button, without which users can't follow each other. Thankfully, the user view already contains support for it. The route just needs to check the cookies to see if a user is logged in.

This operation to check if a user is logged in is becoming common—the / route also performs it. It would make sense to put this code into a procedure so that it's reusable. Let's create this procedure now. Add the following userLogin procedure above your routes and outside the routes block, inside the tweeter.nim file.

Listing 7.30   The userLogin procedure

```
proc userLogin(db: Database, request: Request, user: var User): bool =
  if request.cookies.hasKey("username"):
    if not db.findUser(request.cookies["username"], user):
      user = User(username: request.cookies["username"], following: @[])
      db.create(user)
    return true
  else:
    return false
```

The userLogin procedure checks the cookies for a username key. If one exists, it reads the value and attempts to retrieve the user from the database. If no such user exists, the user will be created. The procedure performs the same actions as the / route.

The new implementations of the / and user routes are fairly easy. The following listing shows the new implementation of the two routes.

Listing 7.31   The new implementations of the / and user routes

```
get "/":
  var user: User
```

```
    if db.userLogin(request, user):
      let messages = db.findMessages(user.following & user.username)
      resp renderMain(renderTimeline(user.username, messages))
    else:
      resp renderMain(renderLogin())

  get "/@name":
    cond '.' notin @"name"
    var user: User
    if not db.findUser(@"name", user):
      halt "User not found"
    let messages = db.findMessages(@[user.username])

    var currentUser: User
    if db.userLogin(request, currentUser):
      resp renderMain(renderUser(user, currentUser) & renderMessages(messages))
    else:
      resp renderMain(renderUser(user) & renderMessages(messages))
```

Now the Follow button should appear when you navigate to a user's page, but clicking it will again result in a 404 error.

7.5.6 Implementing the /follow route

Let's fix that error by implementing the /follow route. All that this route needs to do is call the `follow` procedure defined in the `database` module. The following listing shows how the /follow route can be implemented.

> #### Listing 7.32   The /follow route

```
post "/follow":
  var follower: User
  var target: User
  if not db.findUser(@"follower", follower):        ◁──  Retrieves the current user and the
    halt "Follower not found"                              target user to follow from the database
  if not db.findUser(@"target", target):            ◁──
    halt "Follow target not found"
  db.follow(follower, target)                       ◁──  Calls the follow procedure,
  redirect(uri("/" & @"target"))                    ◁──  which will store follower
                                                         information in the database
```

If either of the usernames isn't present in the database, responds with an error

The redirect procedure is used to redirect the user's browser back to the user page.

That's all there is to it. You can now log in to Tweeter, create messages, follow other users using a direct link to their timeline, and see on your own timeline the messages of users that you're following.

> **TESTING TWEETER**   Without the ability to log out, it's a bit difficult to test Tweeter. But you can log in using two different accounts by either using a different web browser or by creating a new private browsing window.

Currently, Tweeter may not be the most user-friendly or secure application. Demonstrating and explaining the implementation of features that would improve both of those aspects would take far too many pages here. But despite the limited functionality you've implemented in this chapter, you should now know enough to extend Tweeter with many more features.

As such, I challenge you to consider implementing the following features:

- The ability to unfollow users
- Authentication with passwords
- Better navigation, including a button that takes the user to the front page
- The ability to log out

7.6 *Deploying the web application*

Now that the web application is mostly complete, you may wish to deploy it to a server.

When you compile and run a Jester web application, Jester starts up a small HTTP server that can be used to test the web application locally. This HTTP server runs on port `5000` by default, but that can be easily changed. A typical web server's HTTP server runs on port `80`, and when you navigate to a website, your web browser defaults to that port.

You could simply run your web application on port `80`, but that's not recommended because Jester's HTTP server isn't yet mature enough. From a security point of view, it's also not a good idea to directly expose web applications like that.

A more secure approach is to run a reliable HTTP server such as NGINX, Apache, or lighttpd, and configure it to act as a *reverse proxy*.

7.6.1 *Configuring Jester*

The default Jester port is fine for most development work, but there will come a time when it needs to be changed. You may also wish to configure other aspects of Jester, such as the static directory.

Jester can be configured easily using a `settings` block. For example, to change the port to `80`, simply place the following code above your routes.

```
Listing 7.33   Configuring Jester
```

```
settings:
  port = Port(80)
```

Other Jester parameters that can be customized can be found in Jester's documentation: https://github.com/dom96/jester#readme.

7.6.2 *Setting up a reverse proxy*

A *reverse proxy* is a piece of software that retrieves resources on behalf of a client from one or more servers. In the case of Jester, a reverse proxy would accept HTTP requests from web browsers, ensure that they're valid, and pass them on to a Jester application. The Jester application would then send a response to the reverse proxy, and the

Figure 7.24   Reverse proxy in action

reverse proxy would pass it on to the client web browser as if it generated the response. Figure 7.24 shows a reverse proxy taking requests from a web browser and forwarding them to a Jester application.

When configuring such an architecture, you must first decide how you'll get a working binary of your web application onto the server itself. Keep in mind that binaries compiled on a specific OS aren't compatible with other OSs. For example, if you're developing on a MacBook running Mac OS, you won't be able to upload the binary to a server running Linux. You'll either have to cross-compile, which requires setting up a new C compiler, or you can compile your web application on the server itself.

The latter is much simpler. You just need to install the Nim compiler on your server, upload the source code, and compile it.

Once your web application is compiled, you'll need a way to execute it in the background while retaining its output. An application that runs in the background is referred to as a *daemon*. Thankfully, many Linux distributions support the management of daemons out of the box. You'll need to find out what init system your Linux distribution comes with and how it can be used to run custom daemons.

Once your web application is up and running, all that's left is to configure your HTTP server of choice. This should be fairly simple for most HTTP servers. The following listing shows a configuration suitable for Jester web applications that can be used for NGINX.

Listing 7.34   NGINX configuration for Jester

```
server {
        server_name tweeter.org;

        location / {
                proxy_pass http://localhost:5000;
                proxy_set_header Host $host;
                proxy_set_header X-Real_IP $remote_addr;
        }
}
```

All you need to do is save that configuration to /etc/nginx/sites-enabled/tweeter.org and reload NGINX's configuration, and you should see Tweeter at http://tweeter.org. That's assuming that you own tweeter.org, which you most likely don't, so be sure to modify the domain to suit your needs.

Other web servers should support similar configurations, including Apache and lighttpd. Unfortunately, showing how to do this for each web server is beyond the scope of this book. But there are many good guides online that show how to configure these web servers to act as reverse proxies.

7.7 Summary

- Web applications are typically modeled after the model-view-controller pattern.
- A route is a block of code that's executed whenever a certain HTTP path is requested.
- Jester is a Nim web microframework inspired by Sinatra.
- Nim's standard library offers connectivity to the MySQL, SQLite, and PostgreSQL databases.
- HTML can be generated in two ways: using the `htmlgen` module and using filters.
- Filters are expanded at compile time. They allow you to mix literal text and Nim code in the same file.
- A Jester web application should be deployed behind a reverse proxy.

Part 3

Advanced concepts

The concepts and examples become a bit more difficult in this last part, but they should also prove to be a lot more fun.

Chapter 8 looks at Nim's foreign function interface, which allows you to use libraries written in other programming languages. You'll learn how to interface with a C library called SDL and then use it to draw some 2D shapes on the screen. You'll also see the JavaScript backend in this chapter, and you'll learn how to recreate the same 2D shapes in the web browser using the Canvas API.

Chapter 9 is on metaprogramming. It will teach you about the three different metaprogramming constructs in Nim: generics, templates, and macros. It will also show you how to create a domain specific language for configuration parsing.

Interfacing with other languages

For many years, computer programmers have been writing software libraries in various programming languages. Many of these libraries have been in development for a very long time, accumulating features and maturing over the years. These libraries are not typically written in Nim; instead, they've been written in older programming languages such as C and C++.

When writing software, you might have required an external C library to perform a task. A good example of this is the OpenSSL library, which implements the SSL and TLS protocols. It's primarily used for securely transferring sensitive data over the internet, such as when navigating to a website using the HTTPS protocol.

Many of the HTTP client modules in the standard libraries of various programming languages, including Nim's, use the C library to transfer encrypted data to and from HTTP servers securely. It's easy to forget that this library is used, because it's usually invoked behind the scenes, reducing the amount of work the programmer needs to do.

The Nim standard library takes care of a lot of things for you, including interfacing with other languages, as is the case with the OpenSSL library. But there will be times when you'll need to interface with a library yourself.

This chapter will prepare you for those times. First, you'll learn how to call procedures implemented in the C programming language, passing data to those procedures and receiving data back from them. Then, you'll learn how to wrap an external library called SDL, and you'll use your wrapper to create a simple SDL application that draws on the screen. (A wrapper is a thin layer of code that acts as a bridge between Nim code and a library written in another programming language, such as C.) Last, you'll work with the JavaScript backend, wrapping the Canvas API and drawing shapes on the screen with it.

Nim makes the job of calling procedures implemented in the C programming language particularly easy. That's because Nim primarily compiles to C. Nim's other compilation backends, including C++, Objective-C, and JavaScript, make using libraries written in those languages easy as well.

8.1   Nim's foreign function interface

Nim's foreign function interface (FFI) is the mechanism by which Nim can call procedures written in another programming language. Most languages offer such a mechanism, but they don't all use the same terminology. For example, Java refers to its FFI as the Java Native Interface, whereas Common Language Runtime languages such as C# refer to it as P/Invoke.

In many cases, the FFI is used to employ services defined and implemented in a lower-level language. This lower-level language is typically C or C++, because many important OS services are defined using those languages. Nim's standard library makes extensive use of the FFI to take advantage of OS services; this is done to perform tasks such as reading files or communicating over a network.

In recent years, the web has become a platform of its own. Web browsers that retrieve and present web pages implement the JavaScript programming language, allowing complex and dynamic web applications to be run inside the browser easily. In order to run Nim applications in a web browser and make use of the services provided by the browser, like the DOM or WebGL, Nim source code can be compiled to JavaScript. Accessing those services and the plethora of JavaScript libraries is also done via the FFI. Figure 8.1 shows an overview of Nim's FFI.

It's important to note that the FFI allows you to interface with C, C++, and Objective-C libraries in the same application, but you can't interface with both C and JavaScript libraries at the same time. This is because C++ and Objective-C are both backward compatible with C, whereas JavaScript is a completely different language.

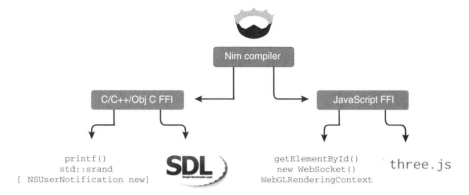

Figure 8.1   Using the Nim FFI, you can take advantage of services in other languages. Nim offers two versions of the FFI: one for C, C++, and Objective-C; and a second one for JavaScript. Both can't be used in the same application.

8.1.1   Static vs. dynamic linking

Before looking at the FFI in more detail, let's look at the two different ways that C, C++, and Objective-C libraries can be linked to your Nim applications.

When using an external library, your application must have a way to locate it. The library can either be embedded in your application's binary or it can reside somewhere on the user's computer. The former refers to a *statically linked library*, whereas the latter refers to a *dynamically linked library*.

Dynamic and static linking are both supported, but dynamic linking is favored by Nim. Each approach has its advantages and disadvantages, but dynamic linking is favored for several reasons:

- Libraries can be updated to fix bugs and security flaws without updating the applications that use the libraries.
- A development version of the linked library doesn't need to be installed in order to compile applications that use it.
- A single dynamic library can be shared between multiple applications.

The biggest advantage of static linking is that it avoids dependency problems. The libraries are all contained in a single executable file, which simplifies the distribution and installation of the application. Of course, this can also be seen as a disadvantage, because these executables can become very big.

Dynamically linked libraries are instead loaded when the application first starts. The application searches special paths for the required libraries, and if they can't be found, the application fails to start. Figure 8.2 shows how libraries are loaded in statically and dynamically linked applications.

It's important to be aware of the dynamically linked libraries that your application depends on, because without those libraries, it won't run.

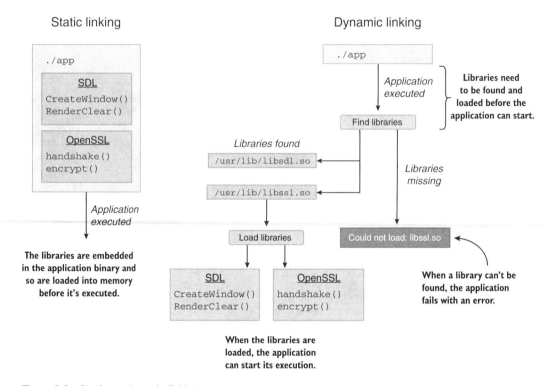

Figure 8.2   Static vs. dynamic linking

With these differences in mind, let's look at the process of creating wrappers in Nim.

8.1.2   *Wrapping C procedures*

In this section, we'll wrap a widely used and fairly simple C procedure: `printf`. In C, the `printf` procedure is declared as follows:

```
int printf(const char *format, ...);
```

What you see here is the procedure prototype of `printf`. A *prototype* specifies the procedure's name and type signature but omits its implementation. When wrapping procedures, the implementation isn't important; all that matters is the procedure prototype. If you're not familiar with this procedure, you'll find out what it does later in this section.

In order to wrap C procedures, you must have a good understanding of these procedure prototypes. Let's look at what the previous procedure prototype tells us about `printf`. Going from left to right, the first word specifies the procedure's return type, in this case an `int`. The second specifies the procedure name, which is `printf`. What follows is the list of parameters the procedure takes, in this case a `format` parameter of type `const char *` and a variable number of arguments signified by the ellipsis.

Table 8.1 summarizes the information defined by the `printf` prototype.

Table 8.1 Summary of the `printf` prototype

Return type	Name	First parameter type	First parameter name	Second parameter
`int`	`printf`	`const char *`	`format`	Variable number of arguments

This prototype has two special features:

- The `const char *` type represents a pointer to an immutable character.
- The function takes a variable number of arguments.

In many cases, the `const char *` type represents a `string`, as it does here. In C, there's no `string` type; instead, a pointer that points to the start of an array of characters is used.

When wrapping a procedure, you need to look at each type and find a Nim equivalent. The `printf` prototype has two argument types: `int` and `const char *`. Nim defines an equivalent type for both, `cint` and `cstring`, respectively. The c in those types doesn't represent the C programming language but instead stands for *compatible*; the `cstring` type is therefore a *compatible string* type. This is because C isn't the only language supported by Nim's FFI. The `cstring` type is used as a native JavaScript string as well.

These compatible types are defined in the implicitly imported `system` module, where you'll find a lot of other similar types. Here are some examples:

- `cstring`
- `cint`, `cuint`
- `pointer`
- `clong`, `clonglong`, `culong`, `culonglong`
- `cchar`, `cschar`, `cuchar`
- `cshort`, `cushort`
- `cint`
- `csize`
- `cfloat`
- `cdouble`, `clongdouble`
- `cstringArray`

Let's put all this together and create the wrapper procedure. Figure 8.3 shows a wrapped `printf` procedure.

The following code shows how the procedure can be invoked:

```
proc printf(format: cstring): cint {.importc, varargs, header: "stdio.h".}

discard printf("My name is %s and I am %d years old!\n", "Ben", 30)
```

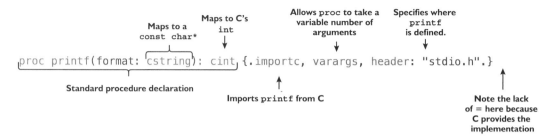

Figure 8.3 `printf` wrapped in Nim

Save the preceding code as ffi.nim. Then compile and run it with `nim c -r ffi.nim`. You should see the following output:

```
My name is Ben and I am 30 years old!
```

The `printf` procedure takes a string constant, `format`, that provides a description of the output. It specifies the relative location of the arguments to `printf` in the `format` string, as well as the type of output that this procedure should produce. The parameters that follow specify what each format specifier in the `format` string should be replaced with. The procedure then returns a count of the printed characters.

One thing you might immediately notice is the `discard` keyword. Nim requires return values that aren't used to be explicitly discarded with the `discard` keyword. This is useful when you're working with procedures that return error codes or other important pieces of information, where ignoring their values may lead to issues. In the case of `printf`, the value can be safely discarded implicitly. The `{.discardable.}` pragma can be used for this purpose:

```
proc printf(format: cstring): cint {.importc, varargs, header: "stdio.h",
                              discardable.}

printf("My name is %s and I am %d years old!\n", "Ben", 30)
```

What really makes this procedure work is the `importc` and `header` pragmas. The `header` pragma specifies the header file that contains the imported procedure. The `importc` pragma asks the Nim compiler to import the `printf` procedure from C. The name that's imported is taken from the procedure name, but it can be changed by specifying a different name as an argument to the `importc` pragma, like so:

```
proc displayFormatted(format: cstring): cint {.importc: "printf", varargs,
                              header: "stdio.h", discardable.}

displayFormatted("My name is %s and I am %d years old!\n", "Ben", 30)
```

That's pretty much all there is to it. The `printf` procedure now wraps the `printf` procedure defined in the C standard library. You can even export it and use it from other modules.

8.1.3 Type compatibility

You may wonder why the `cstring` and `cint` types need to be used in the `printf` procedure. Why can't you use `string` and `int`? Let's try it and see what happens.

Modify your ffi.nim file so that the `printf` procedure returns an `int` type and takes a `string` type as the first argument. Then, recompile and run the program.

The program will likely show no output. This underlines the unfortunate danger that comes with using the FFI. In this case, the procedure call does nothing, or at least it appears that way. In other cases, your program may crash. The compiler trusts you to specify the types correctly, because it has no way of inferring them.

Because the `cstring` type was changed to the `string` type, your program now passes a Nim string object to the C `printf` procedure. C expects to receive a `const char*` type, and it always assumes that it receives one. Receiving the wrong type can lead to all sorts of issues, one of the major ones being memory corruption.

Nim's string type isn't as simple as C's, but it is similar. A Nim string is an object that contains two fields: the length of the string and a pointer to an array of `char`s. This is why a Nim string can be easily converted to a `const char*`. In fact, because this conversion is so easy, it's done implicitly for you, which is why, even when you pass a `string` to `printf`, which expects a `cstring`, the example compiles.

> **CONVERSION FROM CSTRING TO STRING** A conversion in the other direction, from a `cstring` to a `string`, is not implicit because it has some overhead. That's why you must do it explicitly using a type conversion or the $ operator.

As for the `cint` type, it's very similar to the `int` type. As you'll see in the Nim documentation, it's actually just an alias for `int32`: http://nim-lang.org/docs/system .html#cint. The difference between the `int` type and the `int32` type is that the former's bit width depends on the current architecture, whereas the bit width of the latter type is always 32 bits.

The `system` module defines many more compatibility types, many of which are inspired by C. But there will come a time when you need to import types defined in C as well. The next section will show you how that can be done.

8.1.4 Wrapping C types

The vast majority of the work involved in interfacing with C libraries involves wrapping procedures. Second to that is wrapping types, which we'll look at now.

In the previous section, I showed you how to wrap the `printf` procedure. In this section, you'll see how to wrap the `time` and `localtime` procedures, which allow you to retrieve the current system time in seconds and to convert that time into calendar time, respectively. These procedures return two custom types that need to be wrapped first.

Let's start by looking at the `time` procedure, which returns the number of seconds since the UNIX epoch (Thursday, 1 January 1970). You can look up its prototype online. For example, C++ Reference (http://en.cppreference.com/w/c/chrono/time) specifies that its prototype looks like this:

```
time_t time( time_t *arg );
```

Further research into the type of `time_t` indicates that it's a *signed integer*.[1] That's all you need to know in order to declare this procedure in Nim. The following listing shows this declaration.

Listing 8.1   Wrapping `time`

The CTime type is the wrapped version of time_t, defined as a simple alias for a 64-bit signed integer.

The time C procedure is defined in the <time.h> header file. To import it, the header pragma is necessary.

```
type
  CTime = int64

proc time(arg: ptr CTime): CTime {.importc, header: "<time.h>".}
```

In this case, you wrap the `time_t` type yourself. The procedure declaration has an interesting new characteristic. It uses the `ptr` keyword to emulate the `time_t *` type, which is a pointer to a `time_t` type.

To convert the result of `time` into the current hour and minute, you'll need to wrap the `localtime` procedure and call it. Again, the specification of the prototype is available online. The C++ Reference (http://en.cppreference.com/w/c/chrono/localtime) specifies that the prototype looks like this:

```
struct tm *localtime( const time_t *time );
```

The `localtime` procedure takes a pointer to a `time_t` value and returns a pointer to a `struct tm` value. A `struct` in Nim is equivalent to an `object`. Unfortunately, there's no way to tell from the return type alone whether the `struct` that the `localtime` returns has been allocated on the stack or on the heap.

Whenever a C procedure returns a pointer to a data structure, it's important to investigate whether that pointer needs to be manually deallocated by your code. The documentation for this procedure states that the return value is a "pointer to a static internal tm object." This means that the object has a *static* storage duration and so doesn't need to be deallocated manually. Every good library will state the storage duration of an object in its documentation.

When wrapping code, you'll undoubtedly run into a procedure that returns an object with a *dynamic* storage duration. In that case, the procedure will allocate a new object every time it's called, and it's your job to deallocate it when you no longer need it.

> **DEALLOCATING C OBJECTS**   The way in which objects created by a C library can be deallocated depends entirely on the C library. A `free` function will usually be offered for this purpose, and all you'll need to do is wrap it and call it.

The `struct tm` type is much more complex than the `time_t` type. The documentation available in the C++ Reference (http://en.cppreference.com/w/c/chrono/tm) shows

---

[1] The type of `time_t` is described in this Stack Overflow answer: http://stackoverflow.com/a/471287/492186.

that it contains nine integer fields. The definition of this type in C would look something like this:

```c
struct tm {
    int tm_sec;
    int tm_min;
    int tm_hour;
    int tm_mday;
    int tm_mon;
    int tm_year;
    int tm_wday;
    int tm_yday;
    int tm_isdst;
};
```

Wrapping this type is fairly simple, although a bit mundane. Fortunately, you don't have to wrap the full type unless you need to access all the fields. For now, let's just wrap the tm_min and tm_hour fields. The following listing shows how you can wrap the tm type together with the two fields.

Listing 8.2 Wrapping `struct tm`

```nim
type
    TM {.importc: "struct tm", header: "<time.h>".} = object
        tm_min: cint
        tm_hour: cint
```

The two fields are defined as they would be for any Nim data type. The cint type is used because it's compatible with C.

The struct keyword can't be omitted in the argument to the pragma.

You can then wrap the `localtime` procedure and use it together with the `time` procedure as follows.

Listing 8.3 A complete `time` and `localtime` wrapper

```nim
type
    CTime = int64

proc time(arg: ptr CTime): CTime {.importc, header: "<time.h>".}

type
    TM {.importc: "struct tm", header: "<time.h>".} = object
        tm_min: cint
        tm_hour: cint

proc localtime(time: ptr CTime): ptr TM {.importc, header: "<time.h>".}

var seconds = time(nil)
let tm = localtime(addr seconds)
echo(tm.tm_hour, ":", tm.tm_min)
```

Passes the address of the seconds variable to the localtime procedure

Displays the current time

Assigns the result of the time call to a new seconds variable. The time procedure can also optionally store the return value in the specified argument; nil is passed here, as it's not needed.

The localtime procedure takes a "time_t *" and returns a "struct tm *", both of which are pointers. That is why the ptr keyword is used.

Save this code as ffi2.nim, and then compile and run it. You should see the current time displayed on your screen after execution, such as 18:57.

The main takeaway from the example in listing 8.3 is that wrapping a type essentially involves copying its structure into a Nim type definition. It's important to remember that the field names have to match those of the C type. You can specify the name of each field in an importc pragma if you wish to rename them. Figure 8.4 demonstrates this.

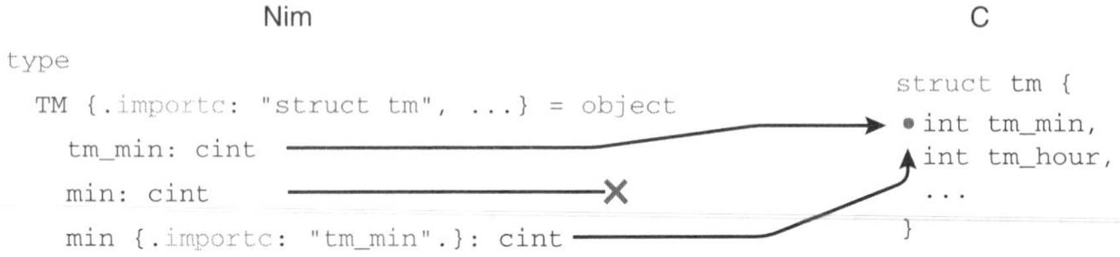

```
        Nim                                              C
type                                            struct tm {
  TM {.importc: "struct tm", ...} = object  ──────►• int tm_min,
    tm_min: cint  ──────────────────────────────▲ int tm_hour,
    min: cint  ───────────────────────────✕      ...
    min {.importc: "tm_min".}: cint  ──────────   }
```

Figure 8.4   **The mapping between fields in a wrapped type and a C struct**

Another interesting aspect of wrapping the localtime procedure is the need to pass a pointer to it. You need to account for this in your wrapper. The addr keyword returns a pointer to the value specified, and that value must be mutable, which is why the return value of time is assigned to a new seconds variable in listing 8.3. Writing localtime(addr time(nil)) wouldn't work because the return value isn't stored anywhere permanent yet.

You should now have a pretty good idea of how C types can be wrapped in Nim. It's time to wrap something a little more ambitious: an external library.

8.2   *Wrapping an external C library*

So far, I've shown you how to wrap some very simple procedures that are part of the C standard library. Most of these procedures have already been wrapped to some extent by the Nim standard library and are exposed via modules such as times.

Wrapping an external library is slightly different. In this section you'll learn about these differences as you wrap a small bit of the SDL library.

Simple DirectMedia Layer, or SDL, is a cross-platform multimedia library. It's one of the most widely used libraries for writing computer games and other multimedia applications. SDL manages video, audio, input devices, and much more. Some practical things that you can use it for are drawing 2D graphics on the screen or playing sound effects.

I'll show you how to draw 2D graphics. By the end of this section, you'll produce an application that displays the window shown in figure 8.5.

SDL WRAPPER   The wrapper shown here will be very basic. You'll find a full SDL wrapper that's already been created by the Nim community here: https://github.com/nim-lang/sdl2.

Figure 8.5   The application you'll produce in this section

8.2.1   Downloading the library

Before you begin writing the wrapper for the SDL library, you should download it. For this chapter's example, you'll only need SDL's runtime binaries, which you can download here: www.libsdl.org/download-2.0.php#source.

8.2.2   Creating a wrapper for the SDL library

A library, or package, wrapper consists of one or more modules that contain wrapped procedures and type definitions. The wrapper modules typically mirror the contents of C header files, which contain multiple declarations of procedure prototypes and types. But they may also mirror other things, such as the contents of JavaScript API reference documentation.

For large libraries like SDL, these header files are very large, containing thousands of procedure prototypes and hundreds of types. The good news is that you don't need to wrap it all completely in order to use the library. A couple of procedures and types will do. This means you can wrap libraries on demand instead of spending days wrapping the full library, including procedures that you're never going to use. You can just wrap the procedures that you need.

> **AUTOMATIC WRAPPING**   An alternative means of wrapping libraries is to use a tool such as c2nim. This tool takes a C or C++ header file as input and converts it into a wrapper. For more information about c2nim, take a look at its documentation: http://nim-lang.org/docs/c2nim.html.

As in the previous section, you can go online to look up the definition of the procedure prototypes that you're wrapping. Be sure to consult the project's official documentation and ensure that it has been written for the version of the library that you're using. Alternatively, you can look up the desired procedure or type inside the library's header files.

First, though, you need to figure out what needs to be wrapped. The easiest way to figure that out is to look for examples in C, showing how the library in question can be used to develop a program that performs your desired actions. In this section, your objective is to create an application that shows a window of a specified color with the letter N drawn in the middle, as shown in figure 8.5.

The SDL library can do a lot more than this, but in the interest of showing you how to wrap it, we'll focus on this simple example.

With that in mind, let's start. The wrapper itself will be a single module called `sdl`. Before moving on to the next section, create this module by creating a new file called sdl.nim.

8.2.3 *Dynamic linking*

Earlier in this chapter, I explained the differences between static and dynamic linking. The procedures you wrapped in the previous section are part of the C standard library, and as such, the linking process was automatically chosen for you. The process by which the C standard library is linked depends on your OS and C compiler.

When it comes to linking with external C libraries, dynamic linking is recommended. This process involves some trivial initial setup that we'll look at now.

Whenever you instruct the Nim compiler to dynamically link with a C library, you must supply it with the filename of that library. The filenames depend entirely on the library and the OS that the library has been built for. Table 8.2 shows the filenames of the SDL libraries for Windows, Linux, and Mac OS.

Table 8.2   The filenames of the SDL library

Windows	Linux	Mac OS
SDL2.dll	libSDL2.so	libSDL2.dylib

These files are called *shared library* files because in many cases, especially on UNIX-like OSs, they're shared among multiple applications.

The SDL wrapper needs to know these filenames, so let's define them in the `sdl` module you just created. The following listing shows how to define these for each OS. Add this code to your `sdl` module.

Listing 8.4   Defining the shared library filename conditionally

```
when defined(Windows):
  const libName* = "SDL2.dll"
elif defined(Linux):
```

```
    const libName* = "libSDL2.so"
elif defined(MacOsX):
    const libName* = "libSDL2.dylib"
```

This code is fairly simple. Only one constant, `libName`, is defined. Its name remains the same, but its value changes depending on the OS. This allows the wrapper to work on the three major OSs.

That's all the setup that's required. Strictly speaking, it's not absolutely necessary to create these constants, but they will enable you to easily change these filenames at a later time.

Now, recall the previous section, where I showed you the `header` and `importc` pragmas. These were used to import C procedures from a specific header in the C standard library. In order to instruct the compiler to dynamically link a procedure, you need to use a new pragma called `dynlib` to import C procedures from a shared library:

```
proc init*(flags: uint32): cint {.importc: "SDL_Init", dynlib: libName.}
```

The `dynlib` pragma takes one argument: the filename of the shared library where the imported procedure is defined. Every time your application starts, it will load a shared library for each unique filename specified by this pragma. If it can't find the shared library, or the wrapped procedure doesn't exist in the shared library, the application will display an error and terminate.

The `dynlib` pragma also supports a simple versioning scheme. For example, if you'd like to load either `libSDL2-2.0.1.so` or `libSDL2.so`, you can specify `"libSDL2(|-2.0.1).so"` as the argument to `dynlib`. More information about the `dynlib` pragma is available in the Nim manual: http://nim-lang.org/docs/manual .html#foreign-function-interface-dynlib-pragma-for-import.

Now, you're ready to start wrapping.

8.2.4 Wrapping the types

Before you can successfully wrap the required procedures, you first need to define four types. Thankfully, wrapping their internals isn't necessary. The types will simply act as stubs to identify some objects. The following listing shows how to define these types.

Listing 8.5 Wrapping the four necessary types

```
type
    SdlWindow = object
    SdlWindowPtr* = ptr SdlWindow
    SdlRenderer = object
    SdlRendererPtr* = ptr SdlRenderer
```

Defines an object stub. This object likely contains fields, but you don't need to access them in your application, so you can omit their definitions.

Many of the procedures in the SDL library work on pointers to objects, so it's convenient to give this type a name and export it instead of writing "ptr TheType" everywhere.

The type definitions are fairly simple. The `SdlWindow` type will represent a single on-screen SDL window, and the `SdlRenderer` will represent an object used for rendering onto the SDL window.

The pointer types are defined for convenience. They're exported because the SDL procedures that you'll wrap soon return them.

Let's look at these procedures now.

8.2.5 *Wrapping the procedures*

Only a handful of procedures need to be wrapped in order to show a colored window on the screen using SDL. The following listing shows the C prototypes that define those procedures.

> **Listing 8.6   The SDL C prototypes that will be wrapped in this section**

```
int SDL_Init(Uint32 flags)                        ⟵── Initializes the SDL library

int SDL_CreateWindowAndRenderer(int          width,              Creates an SDL
                                int          height,             window and
                                Uint32       window_flags,       rendering context
                                SDL_Window** window,             associated with
                                SDL_Renderer** renderer)  ⟵──┘   that window

int SDL_PollEvent(SDL_Event* event)               ⟵── Checks for input events

int SDL_SetRenderDrawColor(SDL_Renderer* renderer,
                           Uint8         r,
                           Uint8         g,
                           Uint8         b,              Sets the current draw color
                           Uint8         a)   ⟵──┘       on the specified renderer

void SDL_RenderPresent(SDL_Renderer* renderer)

int SDL_RenderClear(SDL_Renderer* renderer)   ⟵──┐      Clears the specified renderer
                                                         with the drawing color
int SDL_RenderDrawLines(SDL_Renderer*  renderer,
                        const SDL_Point* points,
                        int            count)  ⟵──┐      Draws a series of
                                                         connected lines
```

**Updates the screen with any
rendering that was performed**

You've already seen how to wrap the `SDL_Init` procedure:

```
proc init*(flags: uint32): cint {.importc: "SDL_Init", dynlib: libName.}
```

The wrapper for this procedure is fairly straightforward. The `Uint32` and `int` types in the prototype map to the `uint32` and `cint` Nim types, respectively. Notice how the procedure was renamed to `init`; this was done because the `SDL_` prefixes are redundant in Nim.

Now consider the rest of the procedures. Each wrapped procedure will need to specify the same `dynlib` pragma, but you can remove this repetition with another pragma called the `push` pragma. The `push` pragma allows you to apply a specified pragma to the procedures defined below it, until a corresponding `pop` pragma is used.

The following listing shows how the rest of the procedures can be wrapped with the help of the push pragma.

Listing 8.7 Wrapping the procedures in the `sdl` module

The pointer type in Nim is equivalent to a void *, which is a pointer of any type.

This ensures that each proc gets the dynlib pragma.

The var keyword is used in place of a ptr. In Nim, these end up generating equivalent C code.

```nim
{.push dynlib: libName.}
proc init*(flags: uint32): cint {.importc: "SDL_Init".}

proc createWindowAndRenderer*(width, height: cint, window_flags: cuint,
    window: var SdlWindowPtr, renderer: var SdlRendererPtr): cint
    {.importc: "SDL_CreateWindowAndRenderer".}

proc pollEvent*(event: pointer): cint {.importc: "SDL_PollEvent".}

proc setDrawColor*(renderer: SdlRendererPtr, r, g, b, a: uint8): cint
    {.importc: "SDL_SetRenderDrawColor", discardable.}

proc present*(renderer: SdlRendererPtr) {.importc: "SDL_RenderPresent".}

proc clear*(renderer: SdlRendererPtr) {.importc: "SDL_RenderClear".}

proc drawLines*(renderer: SdlRendererPtr, points: ptr tuple[x, y: cint],
    count: cint): cint {.importc: "SDL_RenderDrawLines", discardable.}
{.pop.}
```

The discardable pragma is used here to implicitly discard the return value.

This stops the propagation of the dynlib pragma.

The points parameter is a pointer to the beginning of an array of tuples.

Most of the code here is fairly standard. The createWindowAndRenderer procedure's arguments include one pointer to a pointer to an SdlWindow and another pointer to a pointer to an SdlRenderer, written as SdlWindow** and SdlRenderer**, respectively. Pointers to SdlWindow and SdlRenderer were already defined in the previous subsection under the names SdlWindowPtr and SdlRendererPtr, respectively, so you can define the types of those arguments as ptr SdlWindowPtr and ptr SdlRendererPtr. This will work well, but using var in place of ptr is also appropriate in this case.

You may recall var T being used in chapter 6, where it stored a result in a variable that was passed as a parameter to a procedure. The exact same thing is being done by the createWindowAndRenderer procedure. Nim implements these var parameters using pointers, so defining that argument's type using var is perfectly valid. The advantage of doing so is that you no longer need to use addr, and Nim also prevents you from passing nil for that argument.

For the pollEvent procedure, the argument type was defined as pointer. This type is equivalent to a void* type in C, essentially a pointer to any type. This was done because it avoids the need to wrap the SdlEvent type. You may run into C libraries that declare procedures accepting a void* type, in which case you can use the pointer type. In practice, however, it's better to use a `ptr T` type for improved type safety. But you can only do so if you know that the procedure you're wrapping will only ever accept a specific pointer type.

Lastly, the `drawLines` procedure is the most complicated, as it accepts an array of points to draw as lines. In C, an array of elements is represented by a pointer to the first element in the array and the number of variables in that array. In the case of the `drawLines` procedure, each element in the `points` array is an `SDL_Point` type, and it's defined as a simple C struct containing two integers that represent the x and y coordinates of the point. In Nim, this simple struct can be represented using a tuple.

Add the contents of listing 8.7 to your `sdl` module. It's time to use it to write the application.

8.2.6   *Using the SDL wrapper*

You can now use the wrapper you've just written. First, create an sdl_test.nim file beside your wrapper, and then import the wrapper by writing `import sdl` at the top of the file.

Before the library can be used, you'll have to initialize it using the `init` procedure. The `init` procedure expects to receive a `flags` argument that specifies which SDL subsystems should be initialized. For the purposes of this application, you only need to initialize the video subsystem. To do this, you'll need to define a constant for the `SDL_INIT_VIDEO` flag, like this:

```
const INIT_VIDEO* = 0x00000020
```

The value of this constant needs to be defined in the Nim source file because it's not available in the shared library. C header files typically define such constants using a `#define` that isn't compiled into any shared libraries.

Add this constant into your `sdl` module. Then, you'll finally be ready to use the `sdl` wrapper to implement a simple application. The following listing shows the code needed to do so.

> **Listing 8.8   An SDL application implemented using the `sdl` wrapper**

```
import os
import sdl

if sdl.init(INIT_VIDEO) == -1:
  quit("Couldn't initialise SDL")

var window: SdlWindowPtr
var renderer: SdlRendererPtr
if createWindowAndRenderer(640, 480, 0, window, renderer) == -1:
  quit("Couldn't create a window or renderer")
```

Initializes the SDL video subsystem

Quits with an error if the initialization fails

Quits with an error if the creation of the window or renderer fails

Creates a window and renderer to draw things on

This is where you'd handle any pending
input events. For this application, it's only
called so that the window initializes properly.

Sets the drawing color to
the specified red, green,
blue, and alpha values

```
discard pollEvent(nil)
renderer.setDrawColor 29, 64, 153, 255
renderer.clear

renderer.present
sleep(5000)
```

Clears the screen with the
specified drawing color

Shows the pixels drawn
on the renderer

Waits for 5 seconds before
terminating the application

Compile and run the sdl_test.nim file. You should see a window with a blue background, as shown in figure 8.6 (to see color versions of the figures, please refer to the electronic version of this book).

A blank SDL window is a great achievement, but it isn't a very exciting one. Let's use the drawLines procedure to draw the letter *N* in the middle of the screen. The following code shows how this can be done:

Figure 8.6   The result of running listing 8.8

```
renderer.setDrawColor 255, 255, 255, 255      Changes the draw color to white
var points = [
  (260'i32, 320'i32),
  (260'i32, 110'i32),
  (360'i32, 320'i32),
  (360'i32, 110'i32)
]
renderer.drawLines(addr points[0], points.len.cint)
```

Defines an array of points that define the
coordinates to draw an N. Each coordinate
must be an int32 because that's what a cint is.

Draws the lines defined
by the points array

Add this code just below the renderer.clear statement in the sdl_test.nim file. Then, compile and run the file. You should see a window with a blue background and the letter *N*, as shown in figure 8.7.

In the preceding code, the drawLines call is the important one. The address of the first element in the points array is passed to this procedure together with the length of the points array. The drawLines procedure then has all the information it needs to read all the points in the array. It's important to note that this call isn't memory safe; if the points count is too high, the drawLines procedure will attempt to read memory

Figure 8.7   The final sdl_test application with the letter N drawn

that's adjacent to the array. This is known as a *buffer overread* and can result in serious issues because there's no way of knowing what the adjacent memory contains.[2]

That's how you wrap an external library using Nim. Of course, there's plenty of room for improvement. Ideally, a module that provides a higher-level API should always be written on top of a wrapper; that way, a much more intuitive interface can be used for writing applications. Currently, the biggest improvement that could be made to the `sdl` module is to add exceptions. Both `init` and `createWindowAndRenderer` should raise an exception when an error occurs, instead of requiring the user to check the return value manually.

The last two sections have given you an overview of the C FFI. Nim also supports interfacing with other C-like languages, including C++ and Objective-C. Those two backends are beyond the scope of this book, but the concepts you've learned so far should give you a good starting point. For further information about these backends, take a look at the Nim manual: http://nim-lang.org/docs/manual.html#implementation-specific-pragmas-importcpp-pragma.

Next, we'll look at how to write JavaScript wrappers.

8.3   *The JavaScript backend*

JavaScript is increasingly becoming known as the "assembly language of the web" because of the many new languages that target it. Languages that can be translated to JavaScript are desirable for various reasons. For example, they make it possible to

---

[2] See the Wikipedia article for an explanation of buffer overreads: https://en.wikipedia.org/wiki/Buffer_over-read.

share code between client scripts that run in a web browser and applications that run on a server, reducing the need for code duplication.

As an example, consider a chat application. The server manages connections and messages from multiple clients, and a client script allows users to connect to the server and send messages to it from their web browser. These messages must be understood by all the clients and the server, so it's beneficial for the code that parses those messages to be shared between the server and the client. If both the client and the server are written in Nim, sharing this code is trivial. Figure 8.8 shows how such a chat application could take advantage of Nim's JavaScript backend.

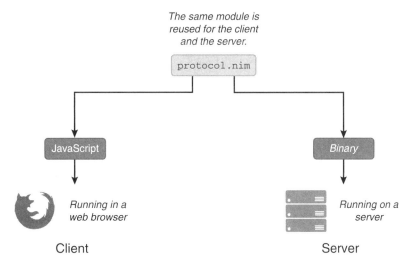

Figure 8.8   How the same code is shared between two platforms

Of course, when writing JavaScript applications, you'll eventually need to interface with the APIs exposed by the web browser as well as libraries that abstract those APIs. The process of wrapping JavaScript procedures and types is similar to what was described in the previous sections for the C backend, but there are some differences that are worth an explanation.

This section will show you how to wrap the JavaScript procedures required to achieve the same result as in the previous section with the SDL library: filling the drawable surface with a blue color and drawing a list of lines to form the letter N.

8.3.1   *Wrapping the canvas element*

The canvas element is part of HTML5, and it allows rendering of 2D shapes and bitmap images on an HTML web page. All major web browsers support it and expose it via a JavaScript API.

Let's look at an example of its usage. Assuming that an HTML page contains a <canvas> element with an ID of canvas, and its size is 600 x 600, the code in the following listing will fill the canvas with the color blue and draw the letter N in the middle of it.

Listing 8.9   Using the Canvas API in JavaScript

```
var canvas = document.getElementById("canvas");
canvas.width = 600;
canvas.height = 600;
var ctx = canvas.getContext("2d");

ctx.fillStyle = "#1d4099";
ctx.fillRect(0, 0, 600, 600);
ctx.strokeStyle = "#ffffff";
ctx.moveTo(250, 320);
ctx.lineTo(250, 110);
ctx.lineTo(350, 320);
ctx.lineTo(350, 110);
ctx.stroke();
```

The code is fairly self-explanatory. It starts by retrieving the canvas element from the DOM by ID. The canvas size is set, and a 2D drawing context is created. Lastly, the screen is filled with a blue color, the letter *N* is traced using the moveTo and lineTo procedures, and the letter is drawn using the stroke procedure. Wrapping the procedures used in this example shouldn't take too much effort, so let's begin.

Create a new file called canvas.nim. This file will contain the procedure wrappers needed to use the Canvas API. The getElementById procedure is already wrapped by Nim; it's a part of the DOM, so it's available via the dom module.

Unlike in C, in JavaScript there's no such thing as a header file. The easiest way to find out how a JavaScript procedure is defined is to look at the documentation. The following list contains the documentation for the types and procedures that will be wrapped in this section:

- CanvasRenderingContext2D type—https://developer.mozilla.org/en-US/docs/Web/API/CanvasRenderingContext2D
- canvas.getContext(contextType, contextAttributes); procedure—http://mng.bz/6kIp
- void ctx.fillRect(x, y, width, height); procedure—http://mng.bz/xN3Y
- void ctx.moveTo(x, y); procedure—http://mng.bz/A9Bk
- void ctx.lineTo(x, y); procedure—http://mng.bz/t355
- void ctx.stroke(); procedure—http://mng.bz/nv6C

Because JavaScript is a dynamically typed programming language, procedure definitions don't contain information about each argument's type. You must look at the documentation, which more often than not tells you enough to figure out the underlying type. The following listing shows how the CanvasRenderingContext2D type and the five procedures should be wrapped. Save the listing as canvas.nim.

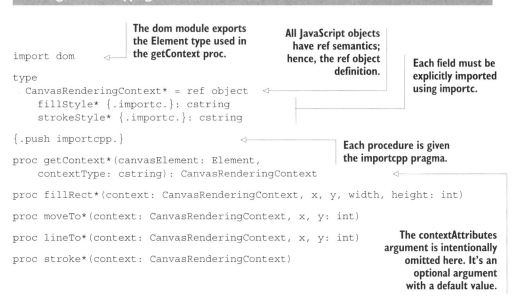

Listing 8.10   Wrapping the Canvas API

```
import dom
type
  CanvasRenderingContext* = ref object
    fillStyle* {.importc.}: cstring
    strokeStyle* {.importc.}: cstring

{.push importcpp.}
proc getContext*(canvasElement: Element,
    contextType: cstring): CanvasRenderingContext

proc fillRect*(context: CanvasRenderingContext, x, y, width, height: int)

proc moveTo*(context: CanvasRenderingContext, x, y: int)

proc lineTo*(context: CanvasRenderingContext, x, y: int)

proc stroke*(context: CanvasRenderingContext)
```

The dom module exports the Element type used in the getContext proc.

All JavaScript objects have ref semantics; hence, the ref object definition.

Each field must be explicitly imported using importc.

Each procedure is given the importcpp pragma.

The contextAttributes argument is intentionally omitted here. It's an optional argument with a default value.

This code is fairly short and to the point. You should be familiar with everything except the `importcpp` pragma. The name of this pragma is borrowed from the C++ backend. It instructs the compiler to generate JavaScript code that calls the specified procedure as if it were a member of the first argument's object. Figure 8.9 demonstrates the difference between `importc` and `importcpp` for the JavaScript backend.

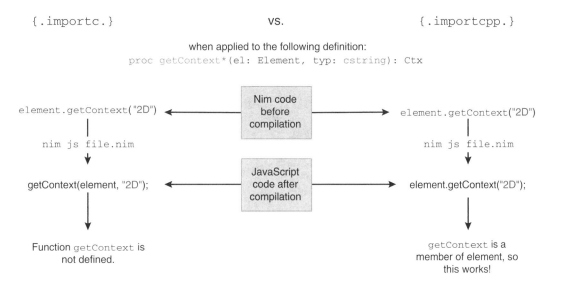

Figure 8.9   The differences in JavaScript code produced with the `importc` and `importcpp` pragmas

There aren't many other surprises, but one interesting aspect to note is that when you're wrapping a data type in JavaScript, the wrapped type should be declared as a `ref` object. JavaScript objects have reference semantics and so should be wrapped as such.

That's all there is to it! Time to put this wrapper to use.

8.3.2   *Using the Canvas wrapper*

Now that the wrapper is complete, you can write a little script that will make use of it, together with a small HTML page to execute it.

Save the following listing as index.html beside your canvas.nim file.

Listing 8.11   The index.html file

```html
<!DOCTYPE html>
<html>
  <head>
    <meta charset="utf-8"/>
    <title>Nim in Action - Chapter 8</title>
    <script type="text/javascript" src="canvas_test.js"></script>
    <style type="text/css">
      canvas { border: 1px solid black; }
    </style>
  </head>
  <body onload="onLoad();" style="margin: 0; overflow: hidden;">
    <canvas id="canvas"></canvas>
  </body>
</html>
```

The HTML is pretty bare bones. It's got some small style adjustments to make the canvas full screen, and it defines an `onLoad` procedure to be called when the `<body>` tag's `onLoad` event fires.

Save the next listing as canvas_test.nim beside your canvas.nim file.

Listing 8.12   The canvas_test.nim file

```nim
import canvas, dom

proc onLoad() {.exportc.} =
  var canvas = document.getElementById("canvas").EmbedElement
  canvas.width = window.innerWidth
  canvas.height = window.innerHeight
  var ctx = canvas.getContext("2d")

  ctx.fillStyle = "#1d4099"
  ctx.fillRect(0, 0, window.innerWidth, window.innerHeight)
```

Note how similar the code is to JavaScript. This code listing defines an `onLoad` procedure that's then exported, which allows the browser to use it as an event callback. The `exportc` procedure is used to do this. It simply ensures that the generated JavaScript code contains an `onLoad` procedure. This pragma also works for the other backends.

You may wonder what the purpose of the `.EmbedElement` type conversion is. The `getElementById` procedure returns an object of type `Element`, but this object doesn't have `width` or `height` properties, so it must be converted to a more concrete type. In this case, it's converted to the `EmbedElement` type, which allows the two `width` and `height` assignments.

Compile this `canvas_test` module by running `nim js -o:canvas_test.js canvas_test.nim`. You can then test it by opening the index.html file in your favorite browser. You should see something resembling figure 8.10.

Figure 8.10   The canvas_test.nim script showing a blue screen in the web browser

For now, this is just a blue screen. Let's extend it to draw the letter *N*. Add the following code at the bottom of the `onLoad` procedure:

Sets the stroke color to white

Creates a local letterWidth variable to store the desired letter width

Calculates the top-left position where the letter should be placed

```
ctx.strokeStyle = "#ffffff"
let letterWidth = 100
let letterLeftPos = (window.innerWidth div 2) - (letterWidth div 2)
ctx.moveTo(letterLeftPos, 320)
ctx.lineTo(letterLeftPos, 110)
ctx.lineTo(letterLeftPos + letterWidth, 320)
ctx.lineTo(letterLeftPos + letterWidth, 110)
ctx.stroke()
```

Begins tracing the lines of the letter

Draws the letter

In this case, the code calculates where the letter should be placed so that it's in the middle of the screen. This is necessary because the canvas size depends on the size of the web browser window. In the SDL example, the SDL window was always the same size, so this calculation wasn't needed.

Recompile the canvas_test.nim file by running the same command again, and then refresh your browser. You should see something resembling figure 8.11.

That's all there is to it. You should now have a good basic understanding of how to wrap JavaScript and how to make use of Nim's JavaScript backend.

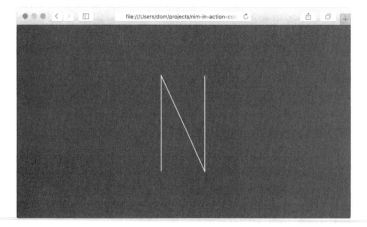

Figure 8.11   The canvas_test.nim script showing a blue screen with the letter N in the web browser

8.4   *Summary*

- The Nim foreign function interface supports interfacing with C, C++, Objective-C, and JavaScript.
- C libraries can be either statically or dynamically linked with Nim applications.
- C header files declare procedure prototypes and types that provide all the information necessary to wrap them.
- The `importc` pragma is used to wrap a foreign procedure, including C and JavaScript procedures.
- The `discardable` pragma can be used to override the need to explicitly discard values.
- The `cstring` type should be used to wrap procedures that accept a string argument.
- Using an external C library is best done via dynamic linking.
- The `dynlib` pragma is used to import a procedure from a shared library.
- The `importcpp` pragma is used to wrap C++ procedures and also member procedures in JavaScript.

Metaprogramming 9

This chapter covers

- Understanding metaprogramming and its uses
- Using generics to remove code duplication
- Constructing a Nim abstract syntax tree
- Executing code at compile time
- Using templates and macros

This chapter describes one of the most advanced and most powerful features in the Nim programming language: *metaprogramming*, composed of a number of components including *generics*, *templates*, and *macros*.

Metaprogramming is a feature of Nim that gives you the ability to treat your application's source code as data. This means you can write code that reads, generates, analyses, and modifies other code. Being able to perform such activities brings many advantages, including allowing you to minimize the number of lines of code needed to express a solution. In turn, this means that metaprogramming reduces development time.

Generating code is usually easy enough in most languages, but reading, analyzing, and modifying it isn't. Consider the following simple type definition:

```
type
  Person = object
    name: string
    age: int
```

Analyzing this code to retrieve information about the `Person` type isn't easy in a language without metaprogramming. For instance, in Java, you could do it via reflection at runtime. In other languages, you could attempt to treat the type definition as a string and parse it, but doing so would be very error prone. In Nim, there are facilities that allow you to analyze type definitions at compile time.

You may, for example, wish to iterate over each of the fields in a specified type:

```
import macros

type
  Person = object
    name: string
    age: int

static:
  for sym in getType(Person)[2]:
    echo(sym.symbol)
```

Compiling the preceding code will display the strings `name` and `age` among the compiler's output.

That's just one example of what metaprogramming allows you to accomplish. You might use this to serialize any data type, without having to write code specific to each data type, whether defined by you or someone else. You'll find that through this and many other features, metaprogramming opens up a vast number of possibilities.

Here are some other use cases for metaprogramming:

- Advanced control flow mechanisms, such as `async` procedures
- Lazy evaluation, used in the `logging` module to ensure that parameters are only evaluated if logging is enabled
- Lexer and parser generation

Metaprogramming adds a lot of flexibility to Nim, and because it's executed at compile time, it does so without causing any decrease in your program's execution time.

In this chapter, you'll learn about the three metaprogramming constructs, starting with *generics*, moving on to *templates*, and finishing up with *macros*. At the end of the chapter, you'll see how you can write a simple DSL for configuration files. DSLs are languages that are specialized to a particular application domain; they'll be discussed in more detail in section 9.4.

9.1 Generics

As you already know, Nim is a statically typed programming language. This means that each piece of data in Nim has a type associated with it. In some cases, these types are distinct but very similar. For example, the `int` and `float` types both represent numbers, but the former can't represent a fraction, whereas the latter can.

Generics are a feature that allows you to write your applications in a style called *generic programming*, in which you write algorithms in terms of types that aren't known until the algorithms are invoked. Generic programming is useful because it offers a reduction in code duplication.

Generics are related to the two other metaprogramming components in Nim—templates and macros—because they offer a way to generate repetitive code. This section covers generics in procedures and types, showing how to best utilize them in those contexts. It also briefly shows how generics can be constrained to make the definitions of algorithms more accurate.

Some languages refer to generics as *parametric polymorphism* or as *templates*. Many prominent statically typed programming languages include support for generics, including Java, C#, C++, Objective C, and Swift. There are also a few that consciously omit the feature; the Go programming language is infamous for doing so.

9.1.1 *Generic procedures*

To give you a better idea of how generics in Nim work, take a look at the following implementation of a generic myMax procedure:

```
proc myMax[T](a, b: T): T =
  if a < b:
    return b
  else:
    return a

doAssert myMax(5, 10) == 10
doAssert myMax(31.3, 1.23124) == 31.3
```

The key part of this example is the first line. There, a generic type, T, is defined in square brackets after the procedure name, and it's then used as the type for the parameters a and b as well as the procedure's return type.

Occasionally, the compiler may not be able to infer generic types. In those cases, you can specify them explicitly using square brackets, as shown in the following code:

```
doAssert myMax[float](5, 10.5) == 10.5
```

This code tells the compiler explicitly that the generic type T should be instantiated to float for this myMax procedure call.

You can define as many generic types in a procedure definition as you want. Currently, the myMax procedure only accepts two arguments of the same type. This means that the following procedure call will fail with a type mismatch error:

```
doAssert myMax(5'i32, 10.5) == 10.5
```

The preceding code fails to compile because the type of argument a is int32, whereas the type of b is float. The myMax procedure defined previously can only be called with arguments of the same type.

9.1.2   *Generics in type definitions*

When writing Nim code, you may run into cases where you'd like to specify the types of one or more fields in an object during initialization. That way, you can have a single generic type definition, and you can specialize it by specifying a particular type on a case-by-case basis.

This is useful for container types, such as lists and hash maps. A simple single-item generic container can be defined as follows:

```
type
  Container[T] = object
    empty: bool
    value: T
```

This code defines a `Container` type that accepts a generic type `T`. The type of the `value` that the `Container` type stores is then determined by the generic type `T` specified when a `Container` variable is defined.

A constructor for the `Container` type can be defined like this:

```
proc initContainer[T](): Container[T] =
  result.empty = true
```

You can then call this constructor as follows:

```
var myBox = initContainer[string]()
```

Specifying the generic type in between the square brackets is currently mandatory. This means that the following code will not work:

```
var myBox = initContainer()
```

Compiling this code will result in an "Error: cannot instantiate: 'T'" message. As mentioned previously, the compiler can't always infer the generic type, and this is one case where it can't.

9.1.3   *Constraining generics*

Occasionally, you may wish to limit the types accepted by a generic procedure or type definition. This is useful for making the definition stronger and therefore more clear to yourself and other users of your code. Consider the `myMax` procedure defined previously and what happens when it's called with two strings:[1]

```
proc myMax[T](a, b: T): T =
  if a < b:
    return b
  else:
    return a

echo myMax("Hello", "World")
```

---

[1]   There's a reason why I named this procedure `myMax` and not `max`. I wanted to avoid a conflict with the `max` procedure defined in the `system` module.

If you save this code, compile, and run it, you'll see the string `World` displayed.

Let's assume that you don't want your algorithm to be used with a pair of strings, but only with integers and floats. You can constrain the `myMax` procedure's generic type like so:

```
proc myMax[T: int | float](a, b: T): T =
  if a < b:
    return b
  else:
    return a

echo myMax("Hello", "World")
```

Compiling this code will fail with the following error:

```
/tmp/file.nim(7, 11) Error: type mismatch: got (string, string)
but expected one of:
proc myMax[T: int | float](a, b: T): T
```

To make the constraint process more flexible, Nim offers a small number of *type classes*. A type class is a special pseudo-type that can be used to match against multiple types in a constraint context. You can define custom type classes like so:

```
type
  Number = int | float | uint

proc isPositive(x: Number): bool =
  return x > 0
```

Many are already defined for you in the `system` module. There are also a number of built-in type classes that match whole groups of types. You can find a list of them in the Nim Manual: http://nim-lang.org/docs/manual.html#generics-type-classes.

9.1.4 Concepts

Concepts, sometimes known as *user-defined type classes* in other programming languages, are a construct that can be used to specify arbitrary requirements that a matched type must satisfy. They're useful for defining a kind of interface for procedures, but they're still an experimental Nim feature. This section will give you a quick overview of concepts without going into too much detail, because their semantics may still change.

The `myMax` procedure defined earlier includes a constraint that limits it to accepting only `int` and `float` types as parameters. For the purposes of the `myMax` procedure, though, it makes more sense to accept any type that has the `<` operator defined for it. A concept can be used to specify this requirement in the form of code:

```
type
  Comparable = concept a
    (a < a) is bool
```

A concept definition is introduced with the concept keyword. What follows are the type identifiers.

For this concept to match the type, a `<` procedure that returns a bool value must be defined for the type.

```
proc myMax(a, b: Comparable): Comparable =
  if a < b:
    return b
  else:
    return a
```

A concept is composed of one or more expressions. These expressions usually utilize the instances that are defined after the concept keyword. When a type is checked against a concept, the type is said to implement the concept as long as both of these are true:

- All the expressions in the concept body compile
- All the expressions that evaluate to a Boolean value are true

The is operator determines whether the specified expression returns a value of type bool by returning true if it does and false if it doesn't.

You can check whether the Comparable concept works as expected by writing some quick tests. The following is from a previous example:

```
doAssert myMax(5, 10) == 10
doAssert myMax(31.3, 1.23124) == 31.3
```

You'd expect both lines to work, and they do. The first line specifies two int arguments; a proc `<`(a, b: int): bool exists, so int satisfies the Comparable concept. The second line specifies two float arguments, and a similar proc `<`(a, b: float): bool also exists.

But attempting to pass two arrays into the myMax procedure by writing echo myMax([5, 3], [1, 6]) fails as follows:

```
/tmp/file.nim(11, 9) Error: type mismatch: got (Array constructor[0..1, int],
 ➥Array constructor[0..1, int])
but expected one of:
proc myMax[Comparable](a, b: Comparable): Comparable
...
```

Concepts are powerful, but they're also a very new Nim feature, and as such are considered experimental. As a result, this chapter doesn't go into detail about them, but you're more than welcome to read about them in the Nim manual: http://nim-lang .org/docs/manual.html#generics-concepts.

Now let's move on to templates.

9.2   Templates

A *template* in Nim is a procedure that generates code. Templates offer one of the easiest ways to generate code directly, the other being *macros*, which you'll learn about in the next section. Unlike generics, templates offer a substitution mechanism that allows you to substitute arguments passed to them in the body of the template. Just like with all metaprogramming features, their code-generation ability helps you deal with boilerplate code.

In general, templates offer a simple way to reduce code duplication. Some features, like their ability to inject variables into the calling scope, are easiest to achieve in Nim by defining a template.

Templates are invoked in the same way as procedures. When the Nim compiler compiles your source code, any template invocations are substituted with the contents of the template. As an example, take a look at the following template from the standard library:

```
template `!=` (a, b: untyped) =
  not (a == b)
```

◁— **Don't worry about the "untyped" type right now. It will be explained later.**

It would be possible to define the != operator as a procedure, but that would require a separate implementation for each type. You could use generics to get around this, but doing so would result in a lot more call overhead.

This template definition of != means that this line

```
doAssert(5 != 4)
```

gets rewritten as follows:

```
doAssert(not (5 == 4))
```

This is done during compilation, as shown in figure 9.1.

The primary purpose of templates is to offer a simple substitution mechanism that reduces the need for code duplication. In addition, templates offer one feature that procedures don't: a template can accept blocks of code.

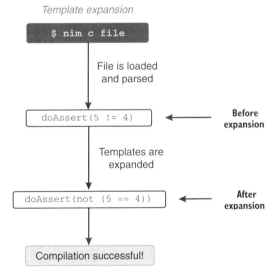

Figure 9.1 Templates are expanded during the compilation of Nim source code

9.2.1   *Passing a code block to a template*

Code blocks are composed of one or more statements, and in an ordinary procedure call, passing multiple statements into the procedure can only be done using an anonymous procedure. With templates, you can pass a code block much more directly. Nim supports a special syntax for templates that allows one or more code statements to be passed to them.

The following code shows a template definition that accepts a code block as one of its parameters:

```
import os              ◁——┐  Needed for the        The template accepts a
                           │  sleep procedure.      statements parameter that
template repeat(statements: untyped) =   ◁——┘      corresponds to the code block.
  while true:
    statements          ◁——   The code block is substituted into here.

repeat:                 ◁——   Templates that accept code blocks are used like this.
  echo("Hello Templates!")
  sleep(1000)
```

> **CODE BLOCKS IN MACROS**   Macros, which you'll learn about in the next section, also support code blocks as parameters.

The statements identifier in the body of the template is replaced with whatever code block is passed into the template. After the compiler expands the template, the remaining code looks like this:

```
import os

while true:
  echo("Hello Templates!")
  sleep(1000)
```

Figure 9.2 shows the code that's generated by the repeat template, which accepts a code block as an argument. This shows some of the amazing substitution capabilities of templates.

Of course, template parameters don't always have to accept a code block. The next section describes how template parameters are substituted into the body of a template and how the parameter's type affects this.

> **MULTIPLE CODE BLOCKS**   There are also ways to pass multiple code blocks to a template or macro via do notation, but this is beyond the scope of this chapter. See the Nim manual's discussion of do notation for more information: http://nim-lang.org/docs/manual.html#procedures-do-notation.

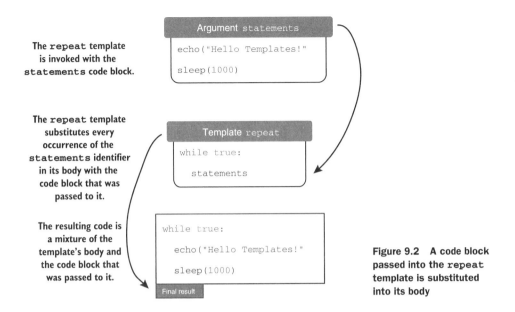

The **repeat** template is invoked with the **statements** code block.

The **repeat** template substitutes every occurrence of the **statements** identifier in its body with the code block that was passed to it.

The resulting code is a mixture of the template's body and the code block that was passed to it.

Figure 9.2 A code block passed into the repeat template is substituted into its body

It's important to know how code blocks and other parameters interact. The rule is that when a code block is passed into a template, the last parameter always contains it. Here's an example:

```
import os
template repeat(count: int, statements: untyped) =
  for i in 0 .. <count:
    statements

repeat 5:
  echo("Hello Templates!")
  sleep(1000)
```

The last parameter named "statements" contains the code block.

9.2.2 *Parameter substitution in templates*

Templates can accept multiple parameters, and these parameters are often simple identifiers, such as variable or type names. In this section, I'll explain the different template-specific parameter types and how they modify the parameter-substitution behavior in templates.

Arguments can be passed into templates in the same manner as with procedures:

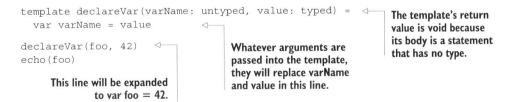

```
template declareVar(varName: untyped, value: typed) =
  var varName = value

declareVar(foo, 42)
echo(foo)
```

The template's return value is void because its body is a statement that has no type.

Whatever arguments are passed into the template, they will replace varName and value in this line.

This line will be expanded to var foo = 42.

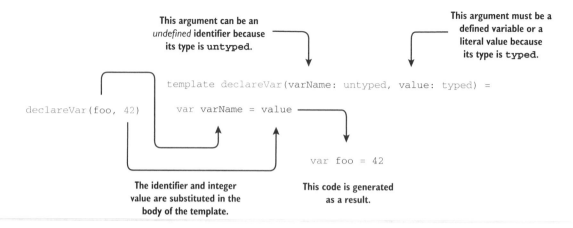

Figure 9.3   Arguments are substituted as-is in templates. Their types determine whether an undefined identifier is accepted.

When the declareVar template is called, it expands into a simple variable declaration. The name and value of the variable is specified in the template using two arguments that differ in type, the first being u.typed and the second typed. Figure 9.3 shows how the declareVar template produces code that defines a new variable.

The difference between the untyped and typed argument types is simple:

- *Untyped*—An untyped template argument allows identifiers that haven't been declared yet to be specified. The reason this type is named untyped is because undeclared identifiers have no type yet. The foo identifier in the preceding example isn't declared anywhere and is thus untyped.
- *Typed*—A typed template argument allows an identifier that has been declared, or a value that has a type, to be specified. In the preceding example, the value 42 has the type int. The typed type allows any type to be specified, but templates also allow you to specify concrete types like int, float, and string.

To see the difference in more detail, take a look at the following declareVar calls:

```
var myInt = 42                  This will compile because
declareVar(foo, myInt)          myInt is declared above.

declareVar(foo, myUndeclaredVar)
```
This won't compile because
myUndeclaredVar is not
declared anywhere.

Remember that the second parameter of declareVar is typed, so undeclared variables can't be passed to it. Only if a variable has the specified identifier defined can it be passed into declareVar.

Compiling the preceding code listing will result in an "undeclared identifier" error.

9.2.3 *Template hygiene*

As shown with the preceding `declareVar` template, templates can define variables that are accessible after the template is instantiated, but this feature may not always be desirable. There may be cases when you wish to declare a variable inside a template without exposing it to the outside scope, a practice referred to as *template hygiene*.

Consider the previous template example again:

```
template declareVar(varName: untyped, value: typed) =
  var varName = value

declareVar(foo, 42)
echo(foo)
```

Calling the `declareVar` template declares a new variable because the `varName` variable is *injected* into the calling scope. The injection occurs automatically because the name of the variable is taken from the template's arguments.

Normally, variables aren't injected into templates unless they're marked explicitly with the `{.inject.}` pragma. The following code shows a comparison of the different cases where variables are injected and where they aren't:

```
template hygiene(varName: untyped) =
  var varName = 42                              ◁——— Injected implicitly because
  var notInjected = 128              ◁———————            its name is taken from the
  var injected {.inject.} = notInjected + 2   ◁———         varName parameter

hygiene(injectedImplicitly)                             Only accessible in
                                                        this template
doAssert(injectedImplicitly == 42)
doAssert(injected == 130)                       Injected because of the {.inject.}
                                                pragma. Note how the notInjected
                                                variable can still be used.
```

Attempting to access the `notInjected` variable outside the template will result in an "Error: undeclared identifier: 'notInjected'" message. The other variables are accessible because they're injected by the template into the calling scope.

When writing templates, make sure that you document precisely the variables that are injected by the template, and be careful that only those variables are exposed. Keep in mind that, in general, injecting variables is considered bad style. The standard library only injects variables in rare cases, such as in the `mapIt` procedure or the `=~` operator defined in the `re` module.

For reference, the following definitions are all hygienic by default:

- `type`
- `var`
- `let`
- `const`

In contrast, the following definitions aren't hygienic by default:

- `proc`
- `iterator`
- `converter`
- `template`
- `macro`
- `method`

The decision to make certain identifiers hygienic and others not was made to capture the most common use cases without annotations.

The next section explains *macros*, a component of Nim related to templates that's a lot more flexible and many times more powerful than templates.

9.3   *Macros*

A macro in Nim is a special kind of procedure that's executed at compile time and that returns a Nim expression or statement. Macros are the ultimate way to read, generate, analyze, and modify Nim code.

In the world of computer science, macros exist in many different forms. Templates are indeed a form of macro, albeit a very simple form that mostly consists of simple substitutions. Templates are said to be *declarative*, because in their body they show what the code that should be produced looks like, instead of describing the steps needed to produce that code.

A Nim macro, on the other hand, is said to be *procedural* because it contains steps that describe how the code should be produced. When macros are invoked, their body is executed at compile time, which means a related feature of the Nim programming language, *compile-time function execution*, is also relevant to the study of macros. This feature allows procedures to be executed by the compiler during compilation, and you'll learn more about it in the next section.

Macros operate on Nim code, but not in the same way that you operate on code. You, as a programmer, are used to dealing with the textual representation of code. You write, read, and modify code as text. But macros don't work that way. They operate on a different representation known as an *abstract syntax tree* (AST). The abstract syntax tree is a special tree structure that represents code; you'll learn more about it in section 9.3.2.

Figure 9.4 shows the primary difference between templates and macros.

We'll go through each of these concepts to teach you the ins and outs of macros. At the end, you'll also get to use your new macro skills to write a simple configuration library.

First, to understand how macros work, you'll need to learn about the concept of compile-time function execution.

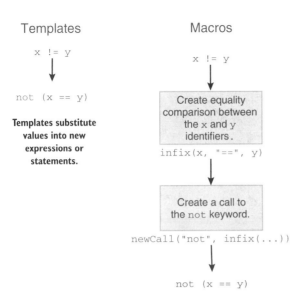

Templates

```
x != y
  |
  v
not (x == y)
```

Templates substitute values into new expressions or statements.

Macros

```
x != y
  |
  v
```

Create equality comparison between the x and y identifiers.

```
infix(x, "==", y)
      |
      v
```

Create a call to the not keyword.

```
newCall("not", infix(...))
             |
             v
      not (x == y)
```

Macros generate new code procedurally.

Figure 9.4 Templates are declarative, whereas macros are procedural.

9.3.1 *Compile-time function execution*

Compile-time function execution (CTFE) is a feature of Nim that allows procedures to be executed at compile time. This is a powerful feature that's relatively uncommon among programming languages.

CTFE was introduced briefly in chapter 2, where you were shown that the value of a constant in Nim must be computable at compile time.

```
proc fillString(): string =
  result = ""
  echo("Generating string")
  for i in 0 .. 4:
    result.add($i)

const count = fillString()
```

When the preceding code is compiled, the message "Generating string" will be shown among the compilation messages. This is because the `fillString` procedure is executed at compile time.

Compile-time execution has some limits, including the following:

- There's no access to the foreign function interface (FFI), which means that some modules or procedures can't be used. For example, you can't generate random numbers at compile time unless you do so indirectly using `staticExec`.

- Global variables that aren't annotated with the {.compileTime.} pragma can't be accessed at compile time.

Despite these limitations, Nim includes workarounds to permit common operations like reading files and executing external processes at compile time. These operations can be performed using the staticRead and staticExec procedures, respectively.

Because macros are used to generate, analyze, and modify code, they must also be executed at compile time. This means that the same limits apply to them as well.

9.3.2   Abstract syntax trees

An AST is a data structure that represents source code. Many compilers use it internally after the source code is initially parsed. Some, like the Nim compiler, expose it to the user.

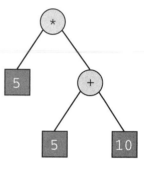

The AST is a tree with each node representing a single construct in the code. Let's look at an example. Consider a simple arithmetic expression such as 5 * (5 + 10). The simplest AST for this might look something like the one shown in figure 9.5.

I'll refer to this AST as the *Simple AST* for the rest of this chapter. Let's look at how the Simple AST can be represented as a Nim data type. The following listing shows the definition for a Node type that's then used to model the Simple AST shown in figure 9.5.

Figure 9.5   A simple AST for 5 * (5 + 10)

Listing 9.1   Modeling the Simple AST shown in figure 9.5

```
type
  NodeKind = enum
    Literal, Operator

  Node = ref object
    case kind: NodeKind
    of Literal:
      value: int
    of Operator:
      left, right: Node
      operator: char

proc newLiteralNode(value: int): Node =
  result = Node(
    kind: Literal,
    value: value
  )

var root = Node(
  kind: Operator,
  operator: '*',
```

In the Simple AST, there are only two node kinds: literals, which include any number, and operators, which specify the type of arithmetic operation to perform.

When the node is a literal, an int can be stored in its value field.

Each operator node may have up to two child nodes. This recursive definition allows a tree to be formed.

When the node is an operator, a char can be stored in its operator field.

A convenience proc to create a new literal node

The "root" variable holds a reference to the *root* node in the AST.

```
  left: newLiteralNode(5),
  right: Node(
    kind: Operator,
    operator: '+',
    left: newLiteralNode(5),
    right: newLiteralNode(10),
  )
)
```

The root node holds the full representation of 5 * (5 + 10) in the form of an AST. Figure 9.6 shows how the Simple AST diagram maps to the Node data structure defined in listing 9.1.

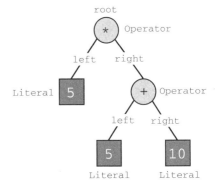

Figure 9.6   An annotated version of figure 9.5 showing how it maps onto root in listing 9.1

You could write a procedure to convert any Node instance into its textual representation, or to display it as a tree using an indentation-based format as follows.

Listing 9.2   A simplified AST for 5 * (5 + 10) displayed using an indentation-based format

```
Operator '*'
  Literal 5
  Operator '+'
    Literal 5
    Literal 10
```

Nim's AST isn't as simple as this because it models a language that's far more complex than simple arithmetic expressions. However, the arithmetic expression modeled by the Simple AST is valid Nim code, so we can compare Nim's AST to it. The dumpTree macro defined in the macros module takes a block of code as input and outputs the code block's AST in the same indentation-based format as shown in listing 9.2.

To display the AST of 5 * (5 + 10) in Nim, compile the following code:

```
import macros

dumpTree:
  5 * (5 + 10)
```

Among the messages from the compiler, you should see the following.

Listing 9.3   The Nim AST for 5 * (5 + 10) displayed using an indentation-based format

```
StmtList
  Infix
    Ident !"*"
    IntLit 5
    Par
      Infix
        Ident !"+"
        IntLit 5
        IntLit 10
```

You'll note that the Nim AST differs from the Simple AST of the arithmetic expression in two important ways:

- It includes many more node kinds, such as StmtList, Infix, and Ident.
- The AST is no longer a binary tree: some nodes contain more than two children.

The structure is the same, but this AST contains more information about the expression. For example, it indicates that infix notation was used to invoke the * and + operators, and that a part of the expression is enclosed in parentheses.

The AST can represent any valid Nim code, so there are many node kinds. To get a feel for the different node kinds, try displaying the AST of some common constructs, such as procedures, for loops, procedure calls, variable declarations, and anything else you can think of.

The Nim AST is described in the documentation for the macros module (http://nim-lang.org/docs/macros.html). The documentation includes the definition of a NimNode type that's very similar to the Node type defined in listing 9.1. The macros module also contains many procedures that can be used for building, modifying, and reading the AST.

Before moving on, let's look at some of these node kinds. Table 9.1 describes each of the node kinds in the Nim AST that you've seen so far.

Table 9.1   Various Nim node kinds and what they mean

Node kind	Description	Children
StmtList	A list of statements.	Arbitrary number of other Nim nodes that represent a statement.
Infix	An infix expression, such as 5 * 5.	Infix operator, the infix operator's two arguments.
Ident	An identifier, such as the name of a procedure or variable. The node's ident field contains the identifier.	*Cannot contain children.*
Par	Parentheses	The code inside the parentheses.
IntLit	An integer literal. The node's intVal field contains the integer value.	*Cannot contain children.*

Let's try to build the Nim AST of 5 * (5 + 10) in a way that's similar to the definition of root in listing 9.1, using the procedures defined in the macros module. The following listing shows the code needed to create this AST.

Listing 9.4 Creating the Nim AST of 5 * (5 + 10)

```
import macros                          ◁        The macros module defines all
                                                the necessary procedures for
static:                               ◁         constructing the AST.
  var root = newStmtList(
    infix(
      newIntLitNode(5),                         The static keyword runs its body at
      "*",                                      compile time. It's used because the
      newPar(                                   AST procedures are only available at
        infix(                                  compile time.
          newIntLitNode(5),
          "+",
          newIntLitNode(10)
        )
      )
    )                                           The repr call converts the root
  )                                             node to a textual representation
  echo(root.repr)                    ◁          of the Nim code.
```

Compile listing 9.4, and you'll see that the output is 5 * (5 + 10). You've successfully constructed your first Nim AST!

9.3.3 Macro definition

So far, you've learned what an AST is, including how it can be constructed and the different ways of displaying it during compilation. But you're still missing an important piece of knowledge: how to add the Nim code that the AST represents into the final executable.

A *macro* is used for precisely that purpose. In the previous section, you constructed a simple arithmetic expression that produces a numeric value. Let's write a macro that emits this expression's AST so its result can be calculated.

Listing 9.5 A macro that emits 5 * (5 + 10)

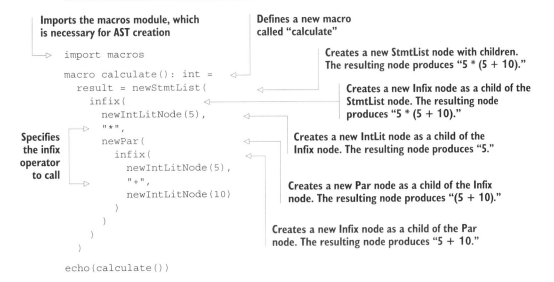

```
                    import macros

                    macro calculate(): int =
                      result = newStmtList(
                        infix(
                          newIntLitNode(5),
                          "*",
                          newPar(
                            infix(
                              newIntLitNode(5),
                              "+",
                              newIntLitNode(10)
                            )
                          )
                        )
                      )

                    echo(calculate())
```

Imports the macros module, which is necessary for AST creation

Defines a new macro called "calculate"

Creates a new StmtList node with children. The resulting node produces "5 * (5 + 10)."

Creates a new Infix node as a child of the StmtList node. The resulting node produces "5 * (5 + 10)."

Creates a new IntLit node as a child of the Infix node. The resulting node produces "5."

Specifies the infix operator to call

Creates a new Par node as a child of the Infix node. The resulting node produces "(5 + 10)."

Creates a new Infix node as a child of the Par node. The resulting node produces "5 + 10."

There are two important things to note about listing 9.5:

- Macros can be invoked in the same way as procedures and templates.
- The AST tree structure constructed in the body of the macro is very similar to the Nim AST shown in listing 9.3.

The `calculate` macro currently generates only a single expression, so the `StmtList` node can be safely removed from the `calculate` macro. Once you remove it, the macro will generate functionally equivalent code with no extraneous AST nodes.

That was a very simple macro, designed to show you how macros use the AST to emit Nim code. The equivalent template is much simpler and achieves the same thing:

```
template calculate(): int = 5 * (5 + 10)
```

```
echo(calculate())
```

The `calculate` macro produces a static AST, but the true power of macros is their ability to produce ASTs dynamically. The next section will show you how to best make use of this power.

9.3.4   *Arguments in macros*

As with procedures and templates, when macros are called, you may pass one or more arguments to them. Doing so allows you to alter the behavior of your macro, changing the code that it produces. You may, for example, wish to pass the name of a variable that the macro should use in the code that it generates.

You should think about arguments passed to macros a little bit differently from those passed to procedures and templates. For example, a macro parameter's type may be `int`, but in the body of the macro, it's a `NimNode`. The following code demonstrates this:

```
import macros

macro arguments(number: int, unknown: untyped): untyped =
  result = newStmtList()
  echo number.treeRepr()
  echo unknown.treeRepr()

arguments(71, ["12", "89"])
```

Every macro must have a return type.

Every macro must generate a valid AST; an empty StmtList node is created here to satisfy this rule.

The treeRepr procedure is similar to the dumpTree macro; it returns a textual representation of a NimNode.

Compiling this listing will result in the following output:

```
IntLit 71
Bracket
  StrLit 12
  StrLit 89
```

The AST of the first argument passed to the macro: 71

The AST of the second argument passed to the macro: ["12", "89"]

There are two things that you need to take away from this example:

- A macro must always have a return type, and it must always return a valid AST, even if that AST is essentially empty.
- All macro parameters are Nim AST nodes (with the exception of static[T] and typedesc parameters; you can find information about such special types in the Nim manual: http://nim-lang.org/docs/manual.html#special-types).

The latter point makes perfect sense because macros already manipulate the AST. Representing each macro argument as an AST node allows for constructs that ordinarily wouldn't be possible in Nim. One example of this is the following:

```
arguments(71, ["12", 876, 0.5, -0.9])
```

This example displays the following AST for the second argument:

```
Bracket
  StrLit 12
  IntLit 876
  Float64Lit 0.5
  Prefix
    Ident !"-"
    Float64Lit 0.9
```

Arrays in Nim are *homogeneous*, so each value that they contain must be of the same type. Attempting to declare an array with the values "12", 876, 0.5, -0.9 wouldn't be possible because the value's types include string, int, and float. In this case, macros give greater flexibility, allowing the possibility to use a heterogeneous array constructor when calling macros.

That should give you a good idea of the basic macro concepts. In the next section, I'll show you how to build a configuration DSL.

9.4 Creating a configuration DSL

Perhaps most usefully, metaprogramming allows you to create a DSL: a language that's specialized to a particular application domain. Within the bounds of Nim's syntax, you can define very flexible and intuitive languages that make writing software easier.

For example, you might write a DSL for defining the structure of HTML. Instead of writing a long, error-prone string literal, you could write something like the following:

```
html:
  head: title("My page")
  body: h1("Hello!")
```

That's just one example. In this section, I'll show you how to create a configuration DSL that will allow you to more easily define the structure of a configuration file and to read and write configuration files easily. You'll first see how a typical DSL is represented in Nim's AST, and then we'll look at the AST representation of the desired generated code. Finally, we'll look at how to build that AST based on information specified by the user when they use the DSL.

The DSL that you'll create as part of this chapter will allow the following code to be written:

```
import configurator

config MyAppConfig:
  address: string
  port: int

var config = newMyAppConfig()
config.load("myapp.cfg")
echo("Configuration address: ", config.address)
echo("Configuration port: ", config.port)
```

This code defines a simple configuration file named MyAppConfig that stores two pieces of information: an address that's a string, and a port that's an integer. The definition is initialized using a constructor, and it's then loaded from a local myapp.cfg file. The address and port are then accessible as fields and their values are displayed on the screen.

Specifying a configuration like this is useful because it streamlines the process of reading and writing configuration files. There's only a single place where the configuration file is defined, and that file is very easy to read and understand.

This DSL will be written as a library named *configurator*. Let's get started!

9.4.1   *Starting the configurator project*

Begin by creating a new configurator directory somewhere on your filesystem. As with any project, set up a project directory structure containing a src directory and a Nimble file. Remember that you can use the `nimble init` command to help with this. Finally, create a configurator.nim file inside the src directory, and open it in your favorite code editor.

Macros will be used to implement the configurator DSL, so import the `macros` module at the top of your newly created configurator.nim file.

When working on a DSL, it's a good idea to start by writing down what you'd like the language to look like. Chances are that the code you have in mind may not be possible due to syntax restrictions,[2] so it's a good idea to test your language's syntax first. The easiest way to do so is to use the `dumpTree` macro defined in the `macros` module. For example, to test whether the configuration DSL can be used, you can compile the following:

```
import macros

dumpTree:
  config MyAppConfig:
    address: string
    port: int
```

---

[2]   These syntax restrictions are often a good thing because they ensure that Nim programmers can always parse Nim DSLs.

The dumpTree macro doesn't need the code inside it to be defined; the code only needs to be syntactically valid. If the syntax is correct, you'll see the compiler output its AST, and you can be sure that it can be used as a DSL.

After testing the validity of your DSL, you can write a macro for that DSL and display the various arguments' ASTs, as in the following listing.

Listing 9.6 A simple `config` macro

```
import macros

macro config(typeName: untyped, fields: untyped): untyped =
  result = newStmtList()
  echo treeRepr(typeName)
  echo treeRepr(fields)

config MyAppConfig:
  address: string
  port: int
```

The config macro takes a type name and a list of fields.

Each macro must return a valid AST, so create a basic one here.

For now, display the AST of the typeName and fields arguments.

Save this code into configurator.nim and compile the file. You'll see the following among the output:

```
Ident !"MyAppConfig"
StmtList
  Call
    Ident !"address"
    StmtList
      Ident !"string"
  Call
    Ident !"port"
    StmtList
      Ident !"int"
```

This gives you an idea of the AST structure that you'll be working with. Next, it's time to decide what code needs to be emitted in order to implement the desired code logic. To implement the example shown at the start of this section, the macro will need to create three separate constructs:

- A MyAppConfig object type, to store the configuration data
- A newMyAppConfig constructor procedure that initializes a new MyAppConfig type
- A load procedure that parses the specified file and then populates the specified instance of the MyAppConfig object with the information stored in the parsed file

The name of the generated type and constructor procedure depends on the name specified in the config construction. For the example in listing 9.6, the name specified in the config construction is MyAppConfig. This name will be used by the macro for the generated type and for the constructor, which derives its name from the generated type.

The fields included in the generated type will also depend on those specified in the `config` construction body. This includes the `address string` field and the `port int` field in listing 9.6.

The next three sections focus on implementing functionality in the macro to create the three constructs: an object type, a constructor procedure, and a `load` procedure.

9.4.2   *Generating the object type*

Before you begin to write AST-generation code in the macro, you'll first need to figure out what AST you want to generate, which means you need to know the Nim code that you want the macro to emit.

Let's start by writing down the type definition that should be generated by the `config` construct. You saw this construct earlier:

```
config MyAppConfig:
  address: string
  port: int
```

The type definition that needs to be generated from this is very simple:

```
type
  MyAppConfig = ref object
    address: string
    port: int
```

Two pieces of information specified in the `config` construct have been used to create this type definition: the type name `MyAppConfig`, and the two fields named `address` and `port`.

Like any code, this code can be represented as an AST, and you need to find out what that AST looks like in order to generate it. Let's take a look at the information that `dumpTree` shows us about this type definition:

```
import macros

dumpTree:
  type
    MyAppConfig = ref object
      address: string
    , port: int
```

Compiling this code should show the following AST.

Listing 9.7   The AST of the `MyAppConfig` type definition

```
StmtList
  TypeSection
    TypeDef
      Ident !"MyAppConfig"          Empty nodes reserve
      Empty                ◁──────  space for extra features
      RefTy                         like generics in the AST.
        ObjectTy
```

```
Empty
Empty
RecList
  IdentDefs
    Ident !"address"
    Ident !"string"
    Empty
  IdentDefs
    Ident !"port"
    Ident !"int"
    Empty
```

Empty nodes reserve space for extra features like generics in the AST.

The AST in listing 9.7 contains a large number of `Empty` nodes. These exist for optional constructs like generics, in order to ensure that the index position of each node remains the same. This is important, because navigating an AST is done using the `[]` operator and an index, which you'll see in action later in this chapter.

Now that you know what the AST that needs to be generated looks like, you can begin to write code to generate it. In some cases, the `macros` module contains procedures that make the process of generating an AST for a specific construct easier. Unfortunately, in this case you'll need to generate the AST in listing 9.7 manually using certain primitive procedures because there currently is no type section constructor in the `macros` module. The following listing shows a procedure that generates a large chunk of the AST shown in listing 9.7.

Listing 9.8 Generating the AST for a type definition

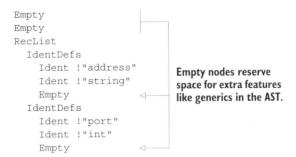

This procedure takes two arguments: an identifier that specifies the name of the type to define and a list of identifier definitions, which includes information about the type's fields. It returns a new NimNode.

Each node is created using the newTree procedure, which allows children to be easily added during its creation.

```
proc createRefType(ident: NimIdent, identDefs: seq[NimNode]): NimNode =
  result = newTree(nnkTypeSection,
    newTree(nnkTypeDef,
      newIdentNode(ident),
      newEmptyNode(),
      newTree(nnkRefTy,
        newTree(nnkObjectTy,
          newEmptyNode(),
          newEmptyNode(),
          newTree(nnkRecList,
            identDefs
          )
        )
      )
    )
  )
```

Each child node is given as an argument to the outer newTree call.

Certain specialized procedures make the process of creating nodes easier.

The code in listing 9.8 creates each node, one by one, manually using the `newTree` procedure. It takes a node kind as an argument, together with zero or more child nodes. These child nodes are added automatically to the resulting new Nim AST node returned by newTree.

Each node kind begins with the nnk prefix. For example, in the procedure's body, the first line shows the creation of a nnkTypeSection node. This matches the output of dumpTree shown in listing 9.7, except that the output doesn't contain the nnk prefixes.

Note the striking similarities between the dumpTree output shown in listing 9.7 and the code in listing 9.8. The way in which the nodes are nested is even the same. The differences lie in the procedure calls: most of them involve newTree, but there are also a couple of specialized procedures:

- newIdentNode—This procedure takes either a string or a NimIdent argument and creates an appropriate nnkIdent node out of it. A nnkIdent node can also be created via newTree, but doing so would be more verbose because the ident would also need to be assigned. An ident node can refer to any identifier, such as a variable or procedure name, but, as in this case, it may contain an identifier that hasn't been defined yet.
- newEmptyNode—This procedure creates a new nnkEmpty node. It's simply an alias for newTree(nnkEmpty).

Now let's look at the createRefType procedure implemented in listing 9.8. It doesn't generate the full AST shown in listing 9.7—it misses out on a key part, the identDefs. Instead, it accepts the identDefs as an argument and assumes that they were generated somewhere else. A single nnkIdentDefs node represents a field definition, including the name and type of the field. In order to generate these, let's define a new procedure. The next listing shows the toIdentDefs procedure, which converts a list of call statements to a list of nnkIdentDefs nodes.

Listing 9.9 Converting a list of call statements to a list of nnkIdentDefs nodes

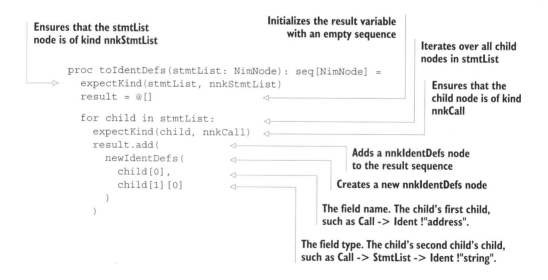

```
proc toIdentDefs(stmtList: NimNode): seq[NimNode] =
  expectKind(stmtList, nnkStmtList)
  result = @[]

  for child in stmtList:
    expectKind(child, nnkCall)
    result.add(
      newIdentDefs(
        child[0],
        child[1][0]
      )
    )
```

Ensures that the stmtList node is of kind nnkStmtList

Initializes the result variable with an empty sequence

Iterates over all child nodes in stmtList

Ensures that the child node is of kind nnkCall

Adds a nnkIdentDefs node to the result sequence

Creates a new nnkIdentDefs node

The field name. The child's first child, such as Call -> Ident !"address".

The field type. The child's second child's child, such as Call -> StmtList -> Ident !"string".

The `stmtList` argument that will be passed to the `toIdentDefs` procedure is the second argument in the `config` macro. More to the point, as you saw previously, the AST of `stmtList` will look like this:

```
StmtList
  Call
    Ident !"address"
    StmtList
      Ident !"string"
  Call
    Ident !"port"
    StmtList
      Ident !"int"
```

It's the job of the `toIdentDefs` procedure to take this AST and convert it to a list of `nnkIdentDefs` nodes that matches the ones in listing 9.7. The code is fairly short, but it could be shortened further at the cost of some error checking.

The `expectKind` procedure is used to ensure that the input AST doesn't contain any unexpected node kinds. It's a good idea to use this when writing macros because sometimes your macro may get an unusual AST. Adding such checks makes debugging easier and is akin to using the `doAssert` procedure.

The conversion process is fairly simple:

1. The statement list node's children are iterated over.
2. Each child's children and grandchildren are accessed using the [] operator to retrieve the two identifiers corresponding to the name and type of the fields.
3. The `newIdentDefs` procedure is used to create a new `nnkIdentDefs` node.
4. The new `nnkIdentDefs` node is added to the `result` sequence.

Both the conversion and the indexing depend on the structure of the AST. The structure shouldn't change unless the user of the `configurator` library passes something unexpected in the `config` macro's body. Later in this section, you'll see how this code reacts to different inputs and how to make the failures more informative.

You have now defined enough to generate the correct type definition in the `config` macro. All you need to do is add a call to `createRefType` and `toIdentDefs`:

```
let identDefs = toIdentDefs(fields)
result.add createRefType(typeName.ident, identDefs)
```

Add these two lines after the `result` variable is defined in your macro. Then, at the end of the macro, add `echo treeRepr(result)` to display the produced AST. Compile the code, and your AST should match the one shown in listing 9.7.

Another way to confirm that the generated AST is correct is to convert it to code and display that. You can do so by writing `echo repr(result)` at the end of your file. After compiling, you should see the following:

```
type
  MyAppConfig = ref object
    address: string
    port: int
```

That's the first and most lengthy part of this macro finished! The two remaining parts shouldn't take as long.

9.4.3   *Generating the constructor procedure*

The `config` macro can now generate a single type definition, but this type definition needs a constructor to be usable. This section will show you how to create this very simple constructor.

The constructor doesn't need to do much—it only needs to initialize the reference object. Because of this, the code that needs to be generated is simple:

```
proc newMyAppConfig(): MyAppConfig =
  new result
```

> The new call initializes the reference object in memory.

You could generate this code much like the type definition in the previous section, but there's an easier way. Instead of manually creating the AST for the procedure and its body, you can use a template. The following code shows the required template. Add this template just above your `config` macro in the configurator.nim file:

```
template constructor(ident: untyped): untyped =
  proc `new ident`(): `ident` =
    new result
```

> For the procedure name, the compiler concatenates the text "new" with whatever the ident parameter holds. This is a simple way by which templates allow you to construct identifiers.

This template creates a new procedure, naming it `newIdent`, where `Ident` is the `ident` argument passed to the template. The `ident` argument is also used for the return type of the created procedure. If you were to call this template via `constructor(MyApp-Config)`, you'd essentially define the following procedure:

```
proc newMyAppConfig(): MyAppConfig =
  new result
```

But how can this template be used in the `config` macro? The answer lies in the `getAst` procedure defined in the `macros` module. This procedure converts the code returned by a template or a macro into one or more AST nodes.

Thanks to `getAst` and the power of templates, you can add `result.add getAst(constructor(typeName.ident))` right after the `createRefType` call. Your `config` macro should now look like the following code listing.

Listing 9.10   The `config` macro

```
macro config*(typeName: untyped, fields: untyped): untyped =
  result = newStmtList()

  let identDefs = toIdentDefs(fields)
  result.add createRefType(typeName.ident, identDefs)
  result.add getAst(constructor(typeName.ident))
```

```
echo treeRepr(typeName)
echo treeRepr(fields)

echo treeRepr(result)
echo repr(result)
```

You should be able to compile the code again and see that the constructor procedure is now generated.

9.4.4 Generating the load procedure

Last but not least is the `load` procedure. It will load the configuration file for you, parse it, and populate an instance of the configuration type with its contents.

For the `config` definition shown in the previous sections, which contains an `address` string field and a `port` integer field, the `load` procedure should be defined as follows:

```
proc load*(cfg: MyAppConfig, filename: string) =      Loads the JSON file from filename
    var obj = parseFile(filename)                     and saves it into the obj variable
    cfg.address = obj["address"].getStr
    cfg.port = obj["port"].getNum.int
```

Gets the address field from the parsed JSON object, retrieves its string value, and assigns it to the configuration instance's address field

Gets the port field from the parsed JSON object, retrieves its integer value, and assigns it to the configuration instance's port field. The type conversion is needed because the getNum procedure returns a BiggestInt type.

For simplicity, the underlying configuration format used in this example is JSON. The `load` procedure starts by parsing the JSON file, and it then accesses the `address` and `port` fields in the parsed JSON object and assigns them to the configuration instance.

The `address` field is a string, so the `load` procedure uses `getStr` to get a string for that field. The `port` field is similarly filled, although in this case the field is an integer, so the `getNum` procedure is used. The type of the field will need to be determined by the macro when the procedure is generated.

In order to generate these statements, you'll need information about the config fields, including their names and types. Thankfully, the code already deals with this information in the form of `IdentDefs`. You can reuse the `IdentDefs` that have already been created to generate the `load` procedure. Let's take a look at these `IdentDefs` for the `MyAppConfig` definition again:

```
IdentDefs
  Ident !"address"
  Ident !"string"
  Empty
IdentDefs
  Ident !"port"
  Ident !"int"
  Empty
```

The structure is pretty simple. There are two nodes, and they each contain the field name and type. Let's use these to generate the load procedure. I'll show you how to write it in steps.

First, define a new createLoadProc procedure and add it just above the config macro in your configurator.nim file:

```
proc createLoadProc(typeName: NimIdent, identDefs: seq[NimNode]): NimNode =
```

Just like the createRefType procedure defined previously, createLoadProc takes two parameters: a type name and a list of IdentDefs nodes. This procedure will use a semi-automatic approach to generating the necessary AST.

The load procedure takes two parameters—a cfg and a filename—and you need to create an Ident node for each of them. In addition to that, you should create an Ident node for the obj variable used in the procedure:

| The cfg parameter that will store an instance of the configuration object | The filename parameter that will store the filename of the configuration file | The obj variable that will store the parsed JSON object |

```
var cfgIdent = newIdentNode("cfg")
var filenameIdent = newIdentNode("filename")
var objIdent = newIdentNode("obj")
```

Add this code to the body of the createLoadProc procedure.

The preceding code is pretty straightforward. It creates three different identifier nodes that store the names of the two parameters and one of the variables. Let's use these to generate the first line in the load procedure:

| Defines a variable that stores the body of the load procedure | The quote procedure returns an expression's AST. It allows for nodes to be quoted inside the expression. | The expression whose AST is generated is the first line of the load procedure, essentially: var obj = parseFile(filename) |

```
var body = newStmtList()
body.add quote do:
  var `objIdent` = parseFile(`filenameIdent`)
```

Append this code to the end of the createLoadProc body.

This code starts off by creating a new StmtList node to hold the statements in the load procedure's body. The first statement is then generated using the quote procedure defined in the macros module. The quote procedure returns a NimNode in a manner similar to the getAst procedure, but instead of needing to declare a separate template, it allows you to pass statements to it. Code inside the body of quote can be substituted by surrounding it with backticks.

In the preceding code, the name that the objIdent node holds is substituted into the var definition. A similar substitution happens for the filenameIdent node. This results in var obj = parseFile(filename) being generated.

The next step is to iterate through the IdentDefs and generate the correct field assignments based on them.

Iterates through the IdentDefs nodes

Retrieves the field name from the IdentDefs node

Converts the Ident into a string

```
for identDef in identDefs:
    let fieldNameIdent = identDef[0]
    let fieldName = $fieldNameIdent.ident
    case $identDef[1].ident
    of "string":
      body.add quote do:
        `cfgIdent`.`fieldNameIdent` = `objIdent`[`fieldName`].getStr
    of "int":
      body.add quote do:
        `cfgIdent`.`fieldNameIdent` = `objIdent`[`fieldName`].getNum().int
    else:
      doAssert(false, "Not Implemented")
```

Generates different code depending on the field's type

For a string field, generates the getStr call

For an int field, generates the getNum call and a type conversion

Append this code to the end of the `createLoadProc` body.

This is a rather large chunk of code, but it generates very simple statements that depend on the fields specified in the `config` body. For the `config` definition shown in the previous sections, it will generate the following two statements:

```
cfg.address = obj["address"].getStr

cfg.port = obj["port"].getNum.int
```

With that code, the procedure body is fully generated. All that's left is to create the AST for the procedure, and this can be done easily using the `newProc` procedure defined in the `macros` module.

```
return newProc(newIdentNode("load"),
    [newEmptyNode(),
     newIdentDefs(cfgIdent, newIdentNode(typeName)),
     newIdentDefs(filenameIdent, newIdentNode("string"))],
    body)
```

The name of the procedure

A StmtList node containing statements to be included in the body of the procedure

The second procedure parameter, in this case filename

The first procedure parameter, in this case cfg

The return type of the procedure; an empty node is used to signify a void return type

The `newProc` procedure generates the necessary AST nodes that model a procedure. You get to customize the procedure by specifying the name, the parameters, the return type, and the procedure body.

All that's left to do is add a call to generate the `load` proc in the `config` macro. Just add `result.add createLoadProc(typeName.ident, identDefs)` below the `getAst` call.

That's all there is to it! Let's make sure that it all works now.

9.4.5 *Testing the configurator*

Before testing the code, you should create a JSON file that can be read. Create a new file called myappconfig.json beside your configurator.nim file,[3] and add the following code to it:

```
{
  "address": "http://google.com",
  "port": 80
}
```

This will be read by the configurator in your test. The following listing shows how to test it.

Listing 9.11 Testing the `config` macro

```
import json

config MyAppConfig:
  address: string
  port: int

var myConf = newMyAppConfig()
myConf.load("myappconfig.json")
echo("Address: ", myConf.address)
echo("Port: ", myConf.port)
```

Add the code in listing 9.11 to the bottom of the configurator.nim file. Then compile and run the file. You should see the following output:

```
Address: http://google.com
Port: 80
```

> **WARNING: WORKING DIRECTORY** Be sure to run the program from the src directory; otherwise, your `myappconfig.json` file will not be found.

The DSL is finished! Based on this example, you should have a good idea of how DSLs can be written in Nim and how macros work. Feel free to play around with the resulting DSL. For an extra challenge, you might wish to add support for more field types or to export the generated types and procedures to make them usable from other modules.

9.5   *Summary*

- Metaprogramming consists of three separate constructs: generics, templates, and macros.
- Generic procedures reduce code duplication.
- Concepts are an experimental feature related to generics that allows you to specify requirements that a matched type must satisfy.
- You can define generic procedures to reduce code duplication.

---

[3] This was done for simplicity; ideally, you'd create a new tests directory and place the JSON file there.

- Templates are an advanced substitution mechanism; they're expanded at compile time.
- Templates support hygiene, which is a way to control access to variables defined in them.
- Templates and macros are the only constructs that can take a code block as an argument.
- Macros work by reading, generating, and modifying code in the form of an abstract syntax tree.
- You can get an AST representation of any piece of Nim code.
- You can generate code by constructing an AST using macros.

appendix A
Getting help

While reading this book, you may run into cases where some concepts might be tough to understand, one of the examples doesn't work, or you have trouble installing something like the Nim compiler on your machine.

The Nim community, which includes me, is available to help with such issues. This appendix describes different ways that you can get in touch with people who will be happy to help.

A.1 Real-time communication

The fastest way to get help is via one of the two real-time communication applications used by Nim programmers: IRC and Gitter. At the time of writing, there are more than 100 users in both Nim's IRC channel and Gitter room.

The messages are relayed between IRC and Gitter, so speaking in one will send an equivalent message to the other. This means you can speak with the same set of people regardless of whether you're using IRC or Gitter.

Gitter is far more approachable, so I suggest using it, especially if you're not already familiar with IRC. You can find it here: https://gitter.im/nim-lang/Nim.

IRC can also be accessed via the web, or you can use one of the many available IRC clients, such as HexChat. The #nim IRC channel is hosted on freenode and can be accessed using the web chat client available here: http://webchat.freenode.net/?channels=nim.

Feel free to join and ask whatever questions you might have. In some cases, you might not hear from anyone for a while, so please be patient. If you need to leave but want to come back later to see if your question was answered, you can look at the messages written in the channel in Gitter and also in our IRC logs, located here: http://irclogs.nim-lang.org/.

A.2 Forum

There are two forums that you can use to get help. The first is the Nim forum, available at http://forum.nim-lang.org/. The second is the Manning forum for this book, available at https://forums.manning.com/forums/nim-in-action.

For questions relating to this book, feel free to use either forum. For more-general Nim questions, please use the Nim forum.

A.3 Other communication methods

For other ways to get in touch with the Nim community, take a look at the community page on the Nim website: http://nim-lang.org/community.html.

appendix B
Installing Nim

Before you begin writing Nim code, you need to install and set up the Nim compiler. The Nim compiler is the tool that will transform your Nim source code into a binary format that your computer can then execute. It's only used during development, so users of your application won't need it.

You have the option of installing Aporia, the Nim IDE, as well. Aporia is a useful tool for beginning Nim programmers: it allows you to compile and run Nim code easily, and it can also be used as a Nim-centric alternative to popular source-code editors such as gedit, Sublime Text, or Atom. Visual Studio Code is another editor that offers functionality similar to Aporia (through a plugin) and can be installed relatively easily.

In this appendix, you'll learn how to install both the Nim compiler and an appropriate text editor. You'll then test this Nim development environment by compiling and executing a Hello World example.

Let's get started. Grab any computer—even a Raspberry Pi will work—and follow along![1]

B.1   Installing the Nim compiler

It's difficult to write installation instructions that will remain accurate for years to come.[2] This is especially true for a compiler that's still evolving. In this appendix, I can't provide a step-by-step installation guide for Nim, but I can discuss some potential troubleshooting steps and let you know where to look for installation instructions.

B.1.1   Getting up-to-date installation info

It's best to consult the Nim website for up-to-date installation information. In particular, see the install page: https://nim-lang.org/install.html.

---

[1] Seriously, though, please don't use a Raspberry Pi for development.
[2] During the development of this book, the installation instructions changed at least once.

That page should be your first stop when installing Nim because it also contains the downloads for Nim. There will be different downloads for each OS and each will have different installation instructions. You may need to build the compiler yourself or simply execute an installer.

Depending on your OS, the installation might be easy or difficult. As Nim evolves, installation should become easier for all OSs, but as of the time of writing that's not yet the case. Follow whatever instructions the Nim website offers, and if they fail, you can get in touch with me or somebody else in the Nim community (as discussed in appendix A).

For completeness, I'll describe the installation process offered by Nim since its inception—building from source. This installation method should work more or less the same way for the foreseeable future, but remember that there are likely simpler ways to install Nim.

> **POSSIBLE PROBLEMS** There's nothing more annoying than not being able to install something. Please remember that the Nim community is happy to help out. Consult appendix A for ways to get in touch with us so that we can help you solve your issue.

B.1.2 *Building from source*

This installation method will work on all platforms. It relies on a compressed archive that contains the C source code, which has been generated for a specific version of the Nim compiler. What you'll be doing here is compiling the Nim compiler yourself.

To compile the C source code, you need to have a C compiler installed on your system. If you don't already have one, you'll need to install one first.

Installing a C compiler

The installation of a C compiler is fairly straightforward. The recommended C compiler and the process for installing it differs depending on your OS.

Windows

You can install GCC by installing the MinGW package available here: www.mingw.org/.

Mac OS

The recommended C compiler on Mac OS is Clang. Clang can be installed in two ways.

If you have Homebrew, simply execute `brew install clang` to install Clang.

Otherwise, follow these steps:

- Open a terminal window.
- Execute `clang` or `gcc`.

A dialog box asking whether you'd like to install the Command Line Developer Tools should appear. Alternatively, you can execute `xcode-select --install`.

(continued)
Click the Install button. Wait for the installation to finish, and then verify that the installation was successful by executing `clang --version`.

Linux
In all likelihood, you already have a C compiler installed. Before attempting to install, you can verify this by running `gcc --version` or `clang --version`.

The recommended C compiler for Linux is GCC. The installation instructions depend on your distribution's package manager.

On Yum-based distributions, you should be able to execute `sudo yum install gcc` to install GCC.

On Debian-based distributions, you can execute `apt-get` like so: `sudo apt-get`

DOWNLOAD THE NIM COMPILER ARCHIVE

Once you have a working C compiler installed, it's time to download the C sources for the latest version of the Nim compiler.

Navigate to the Nim download page and find the download links for the generated C sources for Windows, Mac OS, or Linux.

You may see two download links, one of them a zip archive and another a tar.xz archive. If you're unsure which one to pick, download the zip archive.

EXTRACT THE ARCHIVE AND MOVE IT TO A SAFE LOCATION

Once the download completes, extract the archive. You should be able to simply double-click the zip archive in your OS's file manager to extract it.

You should now see a folder containing files belonging to the Nim compiler (see figure B.1). The folder's name will likely be nim-<ver>, where <ver> is the version of the Nim compiler that you downloaded (for example, nim-0.12.0).

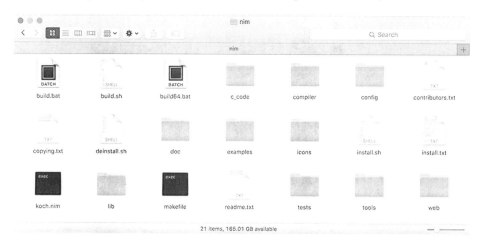

Figure B.1   The nim directory after it's been extracted from the archive

Move the Nim folder to a safe place where you'd like to install it, such as ~/programs/ nim.

COMPILE THE NIM COMPILER

Now open a terminal. Navigate into the nim directory using the `cd` command; for example, `cd ~/programs/nim`. Your terminal should look similar to figure B.2.

Figure B.2 Terminal after navigating to /home/dom/programs/nim

You can now build the Nim compiler by executing one of the `build` scripts. The build.bat and build64.bat scripts are for Windows, and the build.sh script is for all other OSs. To execute the build.sh script, type `sh build.sh` into the terminal.

Depending on the CPU power of your computer, this may take some time. But unless you're compiling Nim on a 1995 IBM NetVista, it shouldn't take more than a minute.

When the compilation is successful, you should see "SUCCESS" at the bottom of your terminal, as in figure B.3.

```
● ● ●          nim — dom@Dominiks-MacBook-Pro — ~/programs/nim — -zsh — 80×10
erns.o c_code/3_2/compiler_semmacrosanity.o c_code/3_2/compiler_semparallel.o c_
code/3_2/compiler_plugins.o c_code/3_2/compiler_active.o c_code/3_2/compiler_loc
als.o c_code/3_2/compiler_cgen.o c_code/3_2/compiler_ccgutils.o c_code/3_2/compi
ler_cgendata.o c_code/3_2/compiler_ccgmerge.o c_code/3_2/compiler_jsgen.o c_code
/3_2/compiler_passaux.o c_code/3_2/compiler_depends.o c_code/3_2/compiler_docgen
2.o c_code/3_2/compiler_service.o c_code/3_2/stdlib_net.o c_code/3_2/stdlib_nati
vesockets.o c_code/3_2/compiler_modules.o c_code/3_2/compiler_nodejs.o c_code/3_
2/compiler_scriptconfig.o  -ldl -lm
SUCCESS
~/programs/nim »
```

Figure B.3 The compilation succeeded

> **GETTING HELP** Did the compilation fail? Are you having other issues? There are many ways to get help, and one of the easiest is to ask on the Nim forum or on IRC. For more information, see appendix A.

The bin directory should now contain a `nim` binary, but the installation is not finished yet.

ADD NIM TO YOUR PATH

In order for the nim binary to be visible to other applications, such as the terminal, you need to add the bin directory to your PATH. In the previous example, the path you'd need to add would be /Users/dom/programs/nim/bin because the username in that example was dom and the ~ was expanded.

> **EXPANDING THE TILDE**   Keep in mind that the ~ expands to /home/<your_ username> on Linux. The preceding examples are for Mac OS. In certain cases, adding a file path that includes the ~ to PATH may not work, so it's usually best to just add an absolute path.

How to add Nim to your PATH

Windows
To add Nim to your PATH, you need to access the advanced system settings, which you can do by opening Control Panel > System and Security > System. You should then see Advanced System Settings in the left sidebar. Click on it and a dialog box should appear. It will include an Environment Variables button that will display another dialog box allowing you to edit the environment variables. Edit the Path variable either under System Variables or User Variables. Make sure the path you add is separated from the other paths by a semicolon (;).

Mac OS
There are multiple ways to edit your PATH on Mac OS. You can open the /etc/paths file (as root using sudo nano /etc/paths or via your favorite editor) and append the Nim bin path to the bottom. Alternatively, you can edit the ~/.profile file and add export PATH=$PATH:/home/user/path/to/Nim/bin to the bottom.

Linux
If you want the change to be system-wide, you can edit the /etc/profile file. To make Nim available only for your user, you can edit the ~/.profile file. In both cases you should add export PATH=$PATH:/home/user/path/to/Nim/bin to the bottom of those files.

VERIFY THAT THE INSTALLATION WAS SUCCESSFUL

Ensure that you've completed these steps successfully by opening a new terminal window and executing nim -v. The output should look similar to the following:

```
Nim Compiler Version 0.14.2 (2016-08-09) [MacOSX: amd64]
Copyright (c) 2006-2016 by Andreas Rumpf

git hash: e56da28bcf66f2ce68446b4422f887799d7b6c61
active boot switches: -d:release
```

Assuming you were successful in installing Nim, you're now ready to begin developing Nim software! Before testing your new development environment, you have the option of installing the Aporia IDE, discussed in the next section. You can skip this if you'd like to use another IDE or text editor for writing Nim code. Section B.3 will show you how to compile your first Nim application.

B.2   *Installing the Aporia IDE*

The installation of Aporia is entirely optional. Aporia integrates with the Nim compiler, so it makes experimenting with Nim easier. With Aporia, you'll be able to compile and run Nim source code by pressing the F5 key on your keyboard. Later in this section, you'll also learn how to compile Nim source code using the command line, so you won't miss out by using a different source code editor.

Releases of Aporia can be downloaded from GitHub, and you'll find detailed instructions on how to install it on your OS here: https://github.com/nim-lang/Aporia#readme.

There are also other editors that can be used instead of Aporia. For example, Visual Studio code with the Nim plugin is another good choice, especially for Mac OS users. For a full list, see the following Nim FAQ answer: https://nim-lang.org/faq .html#what-about-editor-support.

B.3   *Testing your new development environment*

You should now have a basic Nim development environment set up. This setup should include the Nim compiler and may also include Aporia or a different source code editor that supports Nim syntax highlighting.

You can test your new environment with a simple Nim Hello World program.

Open your source code editor and type in the following short piece of code.

Listing B.1   Hello World

```
echo "Hello World!"
```

Save the file as hello.nim. Then, open a new terminal in the directory that contains the file you just saved, and execute `nim c -r hello.nim`. This command will compile the hello.nim file you've written, generating as output a brand-new binary file (the `c` subcommand stands for *compile*). Once the compilation finishes, the binary will be executed, as specified by the `-r` option (which stands for *run*).

Nim command syntax

The Nim command syntax takes the form of `nim command [options] projectFile .nim`, where the `options` are optional. The following table shows some common Nim commands.

Command	Description
`c, compile`	Compiles the projectFile.nim file and all its dependencies into an executable using the default backend (C).
`cpp`	Compiles the projectFile.nim file and all its dependencies using the C++ backend. The result is an executable.
`js`	Compiles the projectFile.nim file and all its dependencies using the JavaScript backend. The result is a JavaScript file.
`check`	Parses the projectFile.nim file and checks it for errors, displaying all the errors found.

(continued)

For a full list of commands, execute `nim --help` and `nim --advanced`. When you're compiling with the C/C++ backends, passing in the `-r` flag will run the resulting executable after compilation. Arguments to this executable can be passed after the projectFile.nim param: `nim c -r projectFile.nim arg1 arg2`.

APORIA   In Aporia, you can simply press F5 to compile and run your program. You don't even have to save it manually!

At this point, if you've followed along and performed these steps yourself (I strongly encourage you to do this!), you may be wondering what to make of all the messages being output to your screen. These messages come from the Nim compiler. By default, the Nim compiler displays information about which modules it's currently processing to notify you of its progress. Other information includes warnings, errors, and other messages triggered by your source code. The following listing shows a sample of output from the Nim compiler.

Listing B.2   Compiler output

Added Nimble packages to its module search path

Used a config file located in ~/nim/config/nim.cfg

```
config/nim.cfg(54, 3) Hint: added path: '~/.nimble/pkgs/' [Path]
Hint: used config file '~/nim/config/nim.cfg' [Conf]
Hint: system [Processing]
Hint: hello [Processing]
CC: hello
CC: stdlib_system
[Linking]
Hint: operation successful (9407 lines compiled; 1.434 sec total;
   14.143MB; Debug Build) [SuccessX]
/Users/dominikp/nim-in-action/examples/hello
Hello World!
```

Parsing and compiling the system module to C

Using a C compiler to compile the hello module to a binary format

Executing the resulting binary located at that file path

Output from the resulting binary's execution

You're probably surprised at just how short the Hello World example is. In comparison to other programming languages like C, Nim doesn't require a `main` function, which drastically reduces the amount of code needed for this example. In Nim, top-level statements are executed from the top of the file to the bottom, one by one.

WARNING: PERFORMANCE   Top-level statements are generally harder to optimize for the compiler. To get maximum performance, use a `main` procedure and compile with the `-d:release` flag.

Congratulations! You've successfully written your first Nim application. More importantly, you have successfully set up a Nim development environment and are now ready to begin learning the basics of the Nim programming language.

B.4 Troubleshooting

This section identifies some problems that you may run into during the installation of Nim, and provides solutions. This is certainly not a complete list, and I invite you to consult the following website, which I'll be keeping up to date, with solutions to other problems that various users run into: https://github.com/dom96/nim-in-action-code/wiki/Installation-troubleshooting.

Please get in touch if you run into a problem that isn't described in this section or on the website. Instructions for getting in touch are available in appendix A.

B.4.1 Nim command not found

If you attempt to execute `nim -v` (or similar), and you see a message such as this,

```
command not found: nim
```

the likely problem is that you haven't successfully added Nim to your PATH. Ensure that the directory you added to your PATH contains the `nim` binary. You may need to restart your terminal for the PATH changes to take effect.

Another diagnosis tool you can use is displaying the contents of the PATH environment variable using `echo $PATH` on Unix or `echo %PATH%` on Windows.

B.4.2 Nim and C compiler disagree on target architecture

This problem manifests in an error that looks something like this:

```
error: 'Nim_and_C_compiler_disagree_on_target_architecture'
    declared as an array with a negative size
```

Usually the problem is that your Nim compiler's architecture isn't the same as your C compiler's. For example, this can mean that the C compiler targets 32-bit CPUs, whereas Nim targets 64-bit CPUs, or vice versa.

To solve this issue, you can either ensure that a C compiler that targets the correct architecture is in your PATH, or you can build a Nim compiler that targets the other architecture. This is usually a problem on Windows, and you just need to use `build32.bat` instead of `build64.bat`, or vice versa.

B.4.3 Could not load DLL

This issue usually presents itself when you're executing a Nim application, either your own or one of the Nim tools like the Nimble package manager.

You might see a variation of the following error when executing the application:

```
could not load: (ssleay64|libssl64).dll
```

This error means that the application can't find a DLL that it depends on to execute. In the preceding case, the missing DLL is used for secure socket connections via the TLS or SSL protocols, such as HTTPS.

This is usually an issue only on Windows. Mac OS and Linux typically already have these dependencies installed.

The solution is to download or install the missing DLLs. Unfortunately, on Windows it's not easy to find them online, and the Nim distribution might not include them. That said, the Nim website does usually have a link to download them. Look for them here: https://nim-lang.org/install.html. After downloading them, place them somewhere in your `PATH` or beside your executable file.

For Linux and Mac OS, you should be able to use a package manager to install them if they're missing.

index